KV-638-039

NOVELL'S

NDS® Basics

PETER KUO

Novell.

Novell Press, Provo, UT

Novell's NDS® Basics
Published by
Novell Press
1800 S. Novell Place
Provo, UT 84606
Copyright © 2000 Novell, Inc. All rights reserved. No part of this book, including interior design, cover design, and icons, may be reproduced or transmitted in any form, by any means (electronic, photocopying, recording, or otherwise) without the prior written permission of the publisher.
ISBN: 0-7645-4726-7
Printed in the United States of America
10 9 8 7 6 5 4 3 2 1
1O/SZ/QY/QQ/FC
Distributed in the United States by IDG Books Worldwide, Inc.
Distributed by CDG Books Canada Inc. for Canada; by Transworld Publishers Limited in the United Kingdom; by IDG Norge Books for Norway; by IDG Sweden Books for Sweden; by IDG Books Australia Publishing Corporation Pty. Ltd. for Australia and New Zealand; by TransQuest Publishers Pte Ltd. for Singapore, Malaysia, Thailand, Indonesia, and Hong Kong; by Gotop Information Inc. for Taiwan; by ICG Muse, Inc. for Japan; by Intersoft for South Africa; by Eyrolles for France; by International Thomson Publishing for Germany, Austria, and Switzerland; by Distribuidora Cuspide for Argentina; by LR International for Brazil; by Galileo Libros for Chile; by Ediciones ZETA S.C.R. Ltda. for Peru; by WS Computer Publishing Corporation, Inc., for the Philippines; by Contemporanea de Ediciones for Venezuela; by Express Computer Distributors for the Caribbean and West Indies; by Micronesia Media Distributor, Inc. for Micronesia; by Chips Computadoras S.A. de C.V. for Mexico; by Editorial Norma de Panama S.A. for Panama; by American Bookshops for Finland. For general information on IDG Books Worldwide's books in the U.S., please call our Consumer Customer Service department at 800-762-2974. For reseller information, including discounts and premium sales, please call our Reseller Customer Service department at 800-434-3422.

For information on where to purchase IDG Books Worldwide's books outside the U.S., please contact our International Sales department at 317-572-3993 or fax 317-572-4002.
For consumer information on foreign language translations, please contact our Customer Service department at 800-434-3422, fax 317-572-4002, or e-mail rights@idgbooks.com.
For information on licensing foreign or domestic rights, please phone +1-650-653-7098.
For sales inquiries and special prices for bulk quantities, please contact our Order Services department at 800-434-3422 or write to IDG Books Worldwide, 919 E. Hillsdale Blvd., Suite 400, Foster City, CA 94404.
For information on using IDG Books Worldwide's books in the classroom or for ordering examination copies, please contact our Educational Sales department at 800-434-2086 or fax 317-572-4005.
For press review copies, author interviews, or other publicity information, please contact our Public Relations department at 650-653-7000 or fax 650-653-7500.
For authorization to photocopy items for corporate, personal, or educational use, please contact Novell, Inc., Copyright Permission, 1800 S. Novell Place, Mail Stop PRV-A231, Provo, UT 84606 or fax 801-228-7077.
For general information on Novell Press books in the U.S., including information on discounts and premiums, contact IDG Books Worldwide at 800-434-3422 or 650-655-3200. For information on where to purchase Novell Press books outside the U.S., contact IDG Books International at 317-572-3993 or fax 317-572-4002.
Library of Congress Cataloging-in-Publication Data
Kuo, Peter, 1959-
   Novell's NDS basics / Peter Kuo.
       p. cm.
   ISBN 0-7645-4726-7 (alk. paper)
   1. Directory services (Computer network technology)
I. Title.
   TK5105.595 .K86   2000
   005.7'1369--dc21   00-058214

John Kilcullen, *CEO, IDG Books Worldwide, Inc.*
Richard K. Swadley, *Senior Vice President, Technology Publishing*
The IDG Books Worldwide logo is a registered trademark or trademark under exclusive license to IDG Books Worldwide, Inc. from International Data Group, Inc. in the United States and/or other countries.

Phil Richardson, *Publisher,*
Novell Press, Novell, Inc.
Novell Press is a trademark and the Novell Press logo is a registered trademarks of Novell, Inc.

Welcome to Novell Press

Novell Press, the world's leading provider of networking books, is the premier source for the most timely and useful information in the networking industry. Novell Press books cover fundamental networking issues as they emerge — from today's Novell and third-party products to the concepts and strategies that will guide the industry's future. The result is a broad spectrum of titles for the benefit of those involved in networking at any level: end user, department administrator, developer, systems manager, or network architect.

Novell Press books are written by experts with the full participation of Novell's technical, managerial, and marketing staff. The books are exhaustively reviewed by Novell's own technicians and are published only on the basis of final released software, never on prereleased versions.

Novell Press at IDG Books Worldwide is an exciting partnership between two companies at the forefront of the knowledge and communications revolution. The Press is implementing an ambitious publishing program to develop new networking titles centered on the current versions of NetWare, GroupWise, BorderManager, ManageWise, and networking integration products.

Novell Press books are translated into several languages and sold throughout the world.

Phil Richardson
Publisher
Novell Press, Novell, Inc.

Novell Press

Publisher
Phil Richardson

IDG Books Worldwide

Acquisitions Editor *Ed Adams*	**Graphics and Production Specialists** *Bob Bihlmayer* *Jude Levinson* *Michael Lewis* *Ramses Ramirez*
Project Editor *Julie M. Smith*	
Technical Editor *Ken Neff*	**Illustrators** *Clint Lahnen* *Gabriele McCann* *Rashell Smith*
Copy Editors *Julie Campbell Moss* *Michael D. Welch*	
Proof Editor *Patsy Owens*	**Quality Control Technician** *Dina F Quan*
Project Coordinators *Danette Nurse* *Marcos Vergara*	**Proofreading and Indexing** *York Production Services*

About the Author

Peter Kuo, Ph.D., president of DreamLAN Network Consulting Ltd. (www.DreamLAN.com), is a Master CNI, Master CNE, NCIP, CNX, and one of the first CDEs. He coauthored *Novell's Guide to Troubleshooting NDS* and has authored and coauthored over a dozen NetWare and networking titles. Peter has been working with NetWare since the early 1980s, and has been working with NDS since NetWare 4.0 was still in beta. He has assisted many companies in implementing NDS trees of various sizes and has been developing NDS-aware applications since 1995. Peter is also a volunteer SysOp for the Novell Support Connection and Novell DeveloperNet forums.

To Ted & Kate — this one's for Abby

Preface

In 1993, Novell ventured into the arena of directory services by introducing Novell Directory Services (NDS) with NetWare 4. Since then, NDS has been ported to various major enterprise server platforms, such as Sun Solaris servers and even IBM S/390 mainframes. Today NDS is by far the most widely developed directory service in the world; more than 80 million users a day access the services on their networks.

NDS is a multiple-platform, distributed, and replicated database that stores information about the hardware and software resources available on your network. It provides network users, administrators, and application developers with seamless, global access to all network resources. NDS also provides a flexible directory database schema, unmatched network security, and a consistent cross-platform development environment.

No matter the size of your NDS tree, this book helps prepare you by providing a solid foundation in the basics of setting up and managing Novell Directory Services.

▶ . . . . ◀

Why Start with the Basics?

Novell Directory Services is an incredibly powerful tool. It can be extremely complex, if you design it to be, but it doesn't have to be that way. NDS is a full-service, platform-independent directory that serves as the foundation for a myriad of directory-enabled services. These services enable you to provide a wide range of networking and business needs. For example, you can give your users access to network resources with a single logon, regardless of their location on the network; these services can also enable you to provide a secure foundation for e-commerce over the Internet.

If you're new to NDS, or to networking in general, starting with a "baby step" is probably a good idea. Even if you are a veteran NetWare administrator coming from a NetWare 3 background, you'll find NDS takes a little getting use to. Therefore, take a small step into the NDS world before jumping in with both feet. Even for experienced NDS users, "getting back to the basics" provides a refresher of some of the fundamentals that you may have forgotten or have missed the first time around. Because NDS has evolved in the past couple of years, and because of the introduction of NDS eDirectory (also referred to as NDS v8) in late 1999, some new elements that you're not already aware of are bound to appear.

Novell's NDS Basics introduces you to the following concepts, management procedures, and knowledge that helps you install and set up your NDS tree:

▶ Explanations of the basic terms and concepts used in Novell Directory Services so that you're fluent in the lingo.

▶ Step-by-step instructions on creating Users and various types of objects for your tree using different tools.

▶ Detailed instructions on creating and managing NDS partitions and replicas.

▶ In depth discussion about time synchronization configuration strategies.

▶ Understanding and implementing NDS security.

▶ Troubleshooting tips for commonly encountered NDS problems.

▶ . . . . ◀

What You Need to Know

Novell's NDS Basics is designed to provide the fundamental concepts and procedures you need to understand, install, create, and manage an NDS tree, regardless of the size of the tree.

This book assumes that you're familiar with the operating systems that run on the workstations and servers you use for NDS, such as DOS, Windows 9*x*, Windows NT/2000, NetWare 4, NetWare 5, Sun Solaris, and Linux. I also provide Internet URLs and references to other resources for finding more information about certain topics.

TIP

In case you need more detailed instructions or description of the advanced topics and procedures that are not covered in this book, you should have access to the online documentation that came with your NetWare or NDS eDirectory software. Should you not have the online documentation handy, you can access them on the Internet at www.novell.com/documentation.

If you are interested in the details of NDS and troubleshooting techniques and issues, an excellent source is the book, "Novell's Guide to Troubleshooting NDS," from Novell Press.

What this Book Contains

The basic components of NDS are explained throughout the chapters of this book.

- **Chapter 1** describes what Novell Directory Services is all about, including an introduction to the features of NDS eDirectory. Also discussed are the basic building blocks of NDS — objects, object classes, schema, partitions and replicas, and time synchronization — everything that makes up NDS, is a feature of NDS, or is required for NDS to function correctly.

- **Chapter 2** explains how to upgrade a NetWare 5 server running a previous version of NDS to NDS eDirectory *and* how to install NDS eDirectory on non-NetWare servers, such as Windows NT/2000, Sun Solaris, and Red Hat Linux. An introduction to tree design concepts is given.

- **Chapter 3** describes how your network infrastructure, such as WAN links, and placement of different network resources affects your NDS tree design. Some guidelines and recommendations are provided.

- **Chapter 4** covers some special-purpose NDS objects, such as Aliases and Template objects, and how you can make use of them to make NDS management easier.

- **Chapter 5** provides instructions for creating and managing users, groups, and other object types. It also explains the different types of login scripts.

- **Chapter 6** covers the ins-and-outs of NDS security and includes several examples of setting up security for different tasks.

- **Chapter 7** deals with the management of NDS partitions and replicas.

- **Chapter 8** explains time synchronization strategies and how to configure time synchronization using IPX and IP protocols.

- **Chapter 9** provides troubleshooting tips for commonly encountered NDS problems, such as user login and NDS database inconsistency problems.

This book also includes a glossary and, of course, a detailed index that helps you easily find the information you need.

Acknowledgments

Writing a book about Novell Directory Services requires not only knowledge of the current information that needs to be put into print, but knowing the people who can provide me with or nudge me in the direction of the correct information. Without the DS Support team at Novell, some of the information in this book would not have come to light.

I appreciate the backing received from the various groups at Novell. I'm grateful that Kim Groneman (*Chief Grasshopper Herder*) tolerated my disappearance from the Novell Support Connection (NSC) Forums for weeks at a time while I was busy meeting the book schedule. In particular, I can't say thank you enough to Kim for bringing Pam Robello and Dave Williams into the Novell Support Connection team for the NSC SysOps; and thanks to Pam and Dave for agreeing to put up with us SysOps as a group, especially Pam who had a *lot* of patience in answering many of my stupid queries. Furthermore, my sincere thanks goes to Andrew Taubman (Novell Technical Support, Australia) and Maurice Smulders (Novell World Wide Support) for answering many of my "what if I do this" and "why does it happen" DS questions. Last, but not least, I must express my deep appreciation to my fellow SysOps for putting up with my lack of appearance in the forums during this project.

The folks at IDG Books/Novell Press who were involved with this project provided much-needed guidance and prodding throughout the project. Julie Smith, my development editor, did an outstanding job in performing the important task of shaping and formatting the book. Ken Neff, my technical editor, worked very hard to ensure this book was as technically accurate as possible. Copy editor Julie Moss did a fine job of fine-tuning my words. This book would never have been written if not for my acquisitions editors, Jim Sumser and Ed Adams, who recognized the need for this book and prodded me to finish it.

As usual, thanks to Dad and Mom for stocking the fridge with food and Classic Coke for my midnight writing marathons.

And finally, Tasha, my one-year old golden retriever, thank you for being such a good girl and for understanding during the times that I had to say "No" when you wanted to play.

Contents at a Glance

Contents

What is Novell's NDS and How Does Novell's NDS Work?

In 1993, Novell introduced the concept of using directory services in the corporate networking world, with X.500 as a starting model. In this chapter, you find out what a directory service is and why you need one, and why Novell Directory Services (NDS) is the directory of choice. You also learn some terms used when working with NDS.

What is a Directory Service?

Everyone *needs* directories. Why? Imagine having a telephone in your house, but not having a telephone directory, or recourse to the "directory assistance" service. The phone suddenly becomes a lot less useful than it was. How can you telephone your Auntie Bonnie in Scotland to wish her a happy birthday when you don't recall her exact telephone number? You may not remember all the several hundred different country codes and the thousands of city codes. What if Auntie Bonnie has recently moved and you don't yet have her new address? Or what if you want to call up several stores in town to see which one of them has the latest Robin Cook novel in stock, and which one has the most competitive price? These examples might seem inconsequential, but they make the point. While it may be possible to keep your own address book of the friends, colleagues, and relatives whom you call most frequently, it certainly is not possible to keep an address book of *everyone* whom you have ever called, or whom you are likely to want to call in the future. Who is going to update your personal directory when people change addresses, or get a new job, or install a new line for a fax machine? So you can see that everyone needs access to address books and (telephone) directories at some point in their lives.

Ideally, we would all like access to more than the conventional telephone directory. As it stands, a paper directory, or directory assistance service, is very limited in the service and information that it offers. To start with, the paper one is always months out of date and you only get an update perhaps once a year. Furthermore, the directory assistance service can be expensive to use for some countries. Not only that, but the national and international ones are accessed differently — and not all telephone numbers are listed, because in some countries you can get unlisted numbers. Computer access to a conventional database gives you many more features, such as the ability to do the following:

- Scan thousands of entries rapidly
- Retrieve all entries with similarly spelled names
- Find the name of a person with a given telephone number or address

This list just names a few. If only we could computerize the entire set of global telephone directories, and interconnect them, and give people access to them all via a standard interface, then we would have a real directory service.

Computers have similar directory access requirements too. In order to make a connection (such as for an FTP session), or send a message (such as an e-mail), or whatever the driving application requires, the software (and hardware) needs an address to process. While it is possible to provide the application directly with the address of the remote entity, in practice it is found to be better to provide a level of indirection. This is achieved by giving a (symbolic) name to the remote service, or computer, or application, and providing the local application with that name. The remote name-to-address "look up" is then provided via a table, a database, or a directory. This shields the local application from changes of address of the remote entity caused by such things as reconfiguration, replacement of hardware, or migration of a service between different nodes in a distributed system. The service that maps the name into an address, which is, in essence, identical to the white pages telephone directory service, has been given various titles such as name server, white pages, WHOIS, and so forth.

NOTE

Domain Name Service (DNS) that we use daily to access the Internet is an example of name-to-address look up "directory service."

What is X.500?

The X.500 standard of International Telecommunication Union-Telecommunication Standardisation Bureau, commonly called the ITU-T (and formerly known as the CCITT), is designed to provide this type of white pages service to computer systems. First published in 1988, both human and computer targeted information is to be held in the same global database.

Another requirement, and from the perspective of ITU-T perhaps the most important requirement, is that demanded by electronic mail users. E-mail users need to know the electronic mail addresses of other e-mail users. The requirement is identical to that of the telephone or fax user, but the need is more urgent, because an existing paper based service does not already exist. Proprietary e-mail systems such as GroupWise, Lotus Notes, and Profs have built-in directories containing the e-mail addresses of all their local users; but inter-system mail is not usually included in such a directory. In order to send the first e-mail message to a colleague in another organization, it is often necessary to telephone them first to get their e-mail address. Once the first message exchange has taken place, we can usually store the e-mail address in our local directory, where it stays useful until it changes, but it is not automatically updated when it does.

X.500 is designed to solve these problems by allowing all local e-mail addresses to be entered and stored locally. Both local and remote users are allowed to have equal (subject to local security policy) access to them, and the local users may have access to remotely stored e-mail addresses. If organizations or divisions want to store local copies of remote e-mail addresses held on remote systems, then automatic copying and updating of the data is possible. However, keep in mind that X.500 is not just for storing and looking up e-mail addresses — it's a specification for storing *any* type of directory information.

The X.500 model specifies the following:

▶ **How the data is organized in the Directory.** This determines how the entries (or objects) are related to each other, how the values of each attribute associated with the objects are stored, and how the objects are named. (X.500 organizes the objects in a hierarchical — inverted tree — manner.) The database is generally referred to as the *Directory Information Base* (DIB).

▶ **A schema for the database.** All good databases have a schema. This is the set of rules that controls all aspects of what can be put into the database.

▶ **The various components of the Directory.** X.500 breaks the Directory into three levels of abstraction (see Figure 1.1). At the First Level it regards the Directory system as a black box (an object, to use object-oriented terminology) with a defined interface, called the *Directory Abstract Service*, to components that act on behalf of users of the Directory. The components that act on behalf of the users are called *Directory User Agents*, or DUAs for short. What happens inside the Directory black box is of no direct concern to the users, as long as the correct answers are returned to their queries. At a more detailed level of abstraction, one can look inside the Directory black box, to see what is happening in there. One sees that the Directory system is made up of individual components — called *Directory System Agents*, or DSAs for short — that co-operate to provide the service that the user has requested. The service that DSAs provide to each other, is called the DSA Abstract Service. A third even more detailed abstract view looks inside a DSA to see how it functions. The Standard says nothing about the actual software components that make up a real DSA. The building and design of a DSA are left entirely up to individual implementers, and this is how competition is introduced into standard conformant products. DUAs communicate with DSAs through the *Directory Access Protocol* (DAP).

F I G U R E   I.I   *The components of the Directory*

DUA = Directory User Agent
DSA = Directory System Agent

Directory
Access
Protocol

Directory
User

DUA

DSA

BSA

The
Directory

Directory
Access
Point

NOTE

The Standard calls the service the Directory Abstract Service, because the service interface is defined in abstract terms, using ASN.1 (Abstract Syntax Notation One). Real-world implementations may provide a service to the user using programming language constructs, such as C procedures and data structures (or APIs).

▶ **The Directory service and associated protocols.** The service is the functionality offered by the standard to users of the standard. In the case of X.500, the service is the functionality that is provided to a DUA by the Directory. The service provides a simple capability to modify and retrieve information stored in the Directory. The protocol is the mechanism that is used to relay a user's service request between OSI entities. In X.500 the protocol used by a DUA to relay a request to a DSA is the Directory Access Protocol (DAP).

NOTE

The Internet community has defined a Lightweight Directory Access Protocol (LDAP), for the communication between DUAs and DSAs, that is now widely supported by implementations.

▶ **Replication of Directory information.** Replication of data improves performance during retrieval, because copies of the data can be located nearer to the end users where fewer users need to access each copy; and offers reliability, because if one copy is temporarily unavailable another one may be used in its place. X.500 adopts a "master copy" replication scheme where one copy is designated as the master and all updates are sent to it. It then schedules the update of the nonmaster, or "shadow copies," at a later time. X.500 does not specify the wait time between the master receiving the update and when it must update all shadow copies. It is simply specified that it is a time that is convenient to both the supplier and the receiver of the copy. Furthermore, X.500 does not insist that all the copies are updated at the same time. Some could be updated within milliseconds of the master being updated, others a few days later. This scheme is referred to as providing weak consistency or transient inconsistency of the data.

NOTE

Novell uses a similar approach and thus refers to NDS being a "loosely consistent" database — however, the term "loosely synchronized" is perhaps more fitting.

▶ **User authentication and controlling access to the Directory data.** X.500 defines two mechanisms for providing security of the information that is held in the Directory. Firstly, the Directory needs to know that the person or application accessing the Directory is who they say they are. This process is termed *authentication*. This is generally done through password verification. Secondly, the Directory needs to know which information this person (or application) is allowed to access, and also what type of access has been granted to them. This second process is termed *access control*. The access control scheme is based on access control lists — lists of users' names against the information that they can access and the type of access that they are being given.

It is interesting to note that the replication (shadowing) and access control features were not included in the original 1988 edition of X.500. They were later introduced in the 1993 edition.

Why Novell Directory Services?

The X.500 standard, published by ITU-T in 1988 had a great deal of promise as a global standard for a computer version of the white pages telephone directory service. However, due to its complexity, there has been little actual practical application developed to be truly X.500-compliant. Novell envisioned what directory services could do and delivered Novell Directory Services (NDS) in 1993, a solution — based on X.500 specifications — that has since become the standard for managing enterprise networks.

When you start working with NDS, you find that its implementation follows very closely that of X.500, including the naming conventions, need for authentication in order to access data, access control, partitioning and replication of data, and so forth. Once you become more familiar with the inner workings of NDS, you notice that Novell has taken the best features from X.500, enhanced them with up-to-date technologies (such as the use of RSA public-private key pairs for password authentication), and replaced the not-so-good features (such as the use of master/shadow copies in data replication) with a scheme that any writeable copy of the database may be used to update the information; the changes are then sent from that copy to all others at a convenient time. The only time the "master" and "secondary" copies come into play is during any partitioning operations that must be performed against the master (so that concurrency control is greatly simplified).

NDS allows the entire network to be viewed as a single logical entity. With NDS, network administrators can perform their jobs from a single point on the network, even administrating nodes scattered around the world. Within NDS, users and various network resources are defined globally throughout the system, so a network administrator only needs to establish a user's account one time in order for that user to be eligible to have access to all resources on the network. For example, Tasha is defined as a user, *once*, on the network, and she can be granted privileges to use any network resources she may require. It is easier than ever before for administrators to manage large internetworks — without directory service, where a common database is shared among all servers, you have to define an account for Tasha on every single server that she needs access to.

The users benefit from NDS also. Tasha can now log into the "network" rather than logging in specifically to one or more servers. Users can search globally — throughout the network — for available resources, such as printers and modems. To search for a printer compatible with her software, Tasha can use the workstation software and find any such printer located on the entire internetwork. Tasha doesn't need to worry about having to attach to servers before searching for resources attached to that server. Instead, the search is performed transparently in the background by NDS.

If Tasha decides she wants information about specific network resources, NDS can provide her with that information. In fact, NDS maintains more information about network resources than was available under previous versions of NetWare (and other operating systems). Information is stored about printers, servers, users, and other resources located on the servers throughout the entire network. Should there be a piece of information you need (such as the Employee ID) that is not provided by the default NDS configuration, you can easily extend the NDS database schema to include that attribute.

NOTE

Extensions made to the base NDS schema are not readily viewable with the shipped tools, such as the NetWare Administrator utility. However, you can download ScheMax, free from Novell (see `www.novell.com/download` for details), to easily create NetWare Administrator snap-ins that display the NDS extensions without programming.

A typical use of ScheMax is to add some new attributes to the user object, create a NetWare Administrator snap-in to edit these attributes, and allow users to view the data. A snap-in is created that enables the helpdesk to add this data to each user from NetWare Administrator. Users are then given a program that enables them to search for a particular user, display their security clearance, employee id number, and a photograph.

The logical view of the network provided by NDS is intuitive to both administrators and users because NDS can be designed to resemble the operational structure of your organization. Much like a common hierarchical organizational chart, the resources on your network are organized into a tree-like structure.

To date, NDS is the only enterprise-wide directory service that has a *proven and documented* track record of supporting networks of all sizes, ranging from a simple 5-user setup to networks consisting of hundreds of users, or even tens of thousands of users. For example, CNN Interactive uses NDS (eDirectory) to serve over 25,000,000 HTML page views per day—the correlation of pages viewed to NDS searches is one to one, because each page is customized to the visitor's preferences, which is stored in NDS.

NOTE

For details about CNN Interactive's NDS eDirectory implementation, visit `www.novell.com/corp/collateral/docs/4621088.01/4621088.html` and `www.novell.com/corp/collateral/docs/4680507.01/4680507.html`.

The following are some of the *unique* features available in NDS (most of these features and terms are discussed later in this chapter):

▸ **Multi-master replication.** Allows data synchronizing in multiple directions, which enables *no* single point of failure unlike master/slave directory implementations. Through replication, one can achieve traffic reduction by having "writeable" copy of the data at any WAN boundary (so one doesn't have to cross a slow WAN link to read or update data).

▸ **Hierarchical datastore.** Offers logical view of data organization and facilitates ease of management delegation (through application of NDS security).

▸ **Partitionable database.** Offers high scalability by enabling database to be divided into manageable "pieces." Allows fault in one "branch" of NDS tree without affecting other "branches" of the tree. Partitioning also improves network response time and reduces network traffic by placing only the required information near the users who need it most.

▸ **Data integrity enforcement.** Each object change is time-stamped to ensure data integrity through both forward and reverse reference links across partitions.

▸ **Low traffic overhead.** NDS only replicates necessary changes, at the attribute value level and not the whole object itself. In the case where the change is to a multi-valued attribute, only the affect value is sent.

▸ **Transitive synchronization.** Enables for "route around" capability with regard to network and server outages. Enables server-to-server communication (read/write) via a "proxy" if the source and target server speak different protocols.

▸ **Self-healing/repairing and maintaining database.** NDS provides internal capabilities to self-correct minor inconsistencies automatically. It also uses roll forward/back transaction logging to guarantee data consistency.

▸ **Cross platform support.** NDS is currently available for NetWare 4 and 5, Windows NT/2000, Sun Solaris, and Linux; support for Compaq Tru64 UNIX is being planned.

▸ **Dynamically extensible replicated schema.** Schema definitions and changes are automatically replicated to all servers and can be performed with no server downtime or protracted performance impact.

What is NDS eDirectory?

NDS eDirectory is the latest evolution of NDS. Based on NDS v8, NDS eDirectory provides a full service directory that provides for flexible and extensible discovery, rich security tools, an extremely scalable storage engine, and the ability to manage relationships—whether internal or external to your organization.

A full service directory *as defined by Novell* is a general-purpose database that manages and provides the following features:

- **Discovery.** Discovery enables you to browse, search, and retrieve specific information from the directory. For example, you should be able to search for specific object types, such as users, groups, and printers, or search for their specific properties such as a user name, group membership, phone number, address, network number and so on. Discovery must support the industry standard access methods, for example, the Lightweight Directory Access Protocol (LDAP) protocol.

- **Security.** Security controls access to the all the information that is stored in the directory. This means that you should be able to establish rules and grant rights to the users for the information in the directory. In addition, you would be able to control the flow of information within your company, across networks of partners, and even to your customers.

- **Storage.** Storage is the database structure for the directory. It should give you the basic ability to save information in the database for future reference, as a minimum. The database should be indexed, cached, and guarded from data corruption by a transaction system. Besides merely storing data, the database should enable you to automatically control the type of data by applying classifications to the data structures. The classifications should be flexible and extensible to provide future representations in the database. The database should be capable of being split into physical pieces and distributed or placed on multiple servers. These features would enable you keep a portion of the data close to the users and resources that need them and make multiple copies of the data for redundancy.

- **Relationships.** Relationship provides you with the ability to build associations between the people, network devices, network applications, and information on the network. For example, instead of storing the user's desktop configuration profile information on the local machine, it should be to be stored in the directory.

This would result in the profile information becoming global within the scope of the directory and the user being able to access the profile information from anywhere. This means that the user receives the same desktop configuration profile of where he or she attaches and logs in to the network. In addition, the access to the profile information is tightly controlled. The only user that can gain access is the one with the proper credentials. Thus, the integrity of profile information is protected and secure, and the user can access it globally, and easily.

Visit www.novell.com/products/nds/fsd/index.html for more information about the full service directory.

NDS is the foundation for all of Novell's solutions. For example, Novell's management solutions such as ZENworks for Desktops, ZENworks for Servers, ZENworks for Networks, and many other Novell products, such as GroupWise and BorderManager, all leverage NDS to provide for integrated end-to-end management and configuration storage. In large networks, especially in the areas of Internet e-business where Novell delivers solutions that address both business-to-business (B2B) and business-to-consumer (B2C) e-commerce, the high performance of NDS eDirectory addresses the needs of organizations of all sizes.

For example, Novell's iChain solution leverages NDS eDirectory to create portal and e-commerce sites that provide for proven secure and scalable identity, content, and billing transaction management. Many other uses exist such as automated provisioning, enhanced security, customer profiling, electronic wallets, automated notification systems, customized Web interfaces, and virtual private networks (VPNs). These uses are of importance to Internet Service Providers (ISPs), Application Service Providers (ASPs), and e-businesses alike.

Of particular importance are the NetWare independence and native LDAP support of NDS eDirectory:

> **NetWare independence.** Originally built for NetWare servers only, this latest version of NDS is a truly cross-platform global directory that operates *natively* on NetWare, Windows 2000, Windows NT, Solaris UNIX, and Linux, thus ensuring compatibility with your customers' and partners' current systems. In the very near future, NDS eDirectory is expected to also run on Compaq Tru64 UNIX.

At the time of this writing, the following platforms are supported by NDS eDirectory:

> NetWare 5.0 with Service Pack 2 or later; NetWare 5.1

> Windows NT server 4.0 with Service Pack 3 or higher

> Windows 2000

- ▶ Sun Solaris 7 (SPARC platform edition) or Solaris 2.6
- ▶ Red Hat Linux 5.2, 6.0, or 6.1
- ▶ LDAP Support

NDS eDirectory features a native implementation of LDAP v3, which provides fast searches, auxiliary classes, referrals, and controls. Such native LDAP implementation provides an open structure for applications and developers and simple integration with applications that are written to this Internet standard. To this end, Novell has released an OpenLDAP Software Developer Kit (SDK) that makes developing to LDAP and NDS eDirectory easy and practical.

If you're familiar with pre-NDS eDirectory (as in NDS v6 shipped with NetWare 4 or NDS v7 shipped with NetWare 5) as a user, you should find no difference in terms of how to access NDS information, except for the improved performance. As an administrator, however, you are going to find NDS eDirectory to be a lot more flexible and easier to manage. As a developer, you are going to find developing to NDS eDirectory and making existing applications, especially those that are LDAP-based, NDS eDirectory-aware to be a much simpler task than before.

At first glance, NDS eDirectory seems to be geared towards large sites or sites that need e-commerce. But small- to medium networks can also benefit from the flexibility and ease of management of the NDS database when running NDS eDirectory. Therefore, regardless of the size of your network and whether you support e-commerce or not, you should not overlook using NDS eDirectory in your environment. Furthermore, given the NetWare-independence of NDS eDirectory, you don't need a single NetWare server on your network in order to take full advantage of the features and benefits of NDS eDirectory.

NOTE

In order for a directory to become ubiquitous and interoperable enough to make a real difference, it needs to run *natively* on every OS that's important to the Internet — not just one like many of the other directories. NDS eDirectory is robust, scalable, and LDAP-aware — which is exactly the kind of directory needed by businesses of any size.

It is worth noting that two varieties of eDirectory exist — NDS eDirectory and NDS Corporate Edition (also known as NDS eDirectory, Corporate Edition). In essence, NDS eDirectory offers you the ability to implement NDS on non-NetWare platforms, such as Windows NT/2000 and various UNIX servers. This is so that you can use a non-NetWare server to host your NDS database. With NDS Corporate Edition, however, you get all the scalability, utility, and extensibility of NDS eDirectory *as well as* the ability to manage user information on these non-NetWare platforms via the use of redirectors.

The redirection technology included with NDS Corporate Edition makes it possible to manage a mixed network as if it were one platform. For example, with the redirector for Windows NT you can represent NT objects as NDS objects and then manipulate them according to NDS conventions. Because NDS presents a simple, intuitive interface, object management becomes easy: redundant tasks are eliminated, a unified interface replaces many disparate ones, and conversion between network operating systems is effortless.

Imagine you have a network consisting of NetWare, Windows NT, and Sun Solaris servers. Using NDS Corporate Edition as the global directory, you as a network supervisor can eliminate a number of redundant tasks. For example, to give a user access rights to all servers on a heterogeneous network, you would normally have to create that user on each platform individually and assign separate rights to each server. With NDS Corporate Edition, however, you only need to create one user object. That one object assigns the user the same user ID for every platform and server on the network.

Basic NDS Concepts

As discussed earlier, Novell's NDS is a "hierarchically organized, global, distributed, loosely synchronized database" whose implementation follows closely that of X.500 specification. Therefore, you find much of the terminology used to discuss NDS mirrors that used for X.500. To be able to understand and create a good NDS design, you need to understand the following basic NDS terms and concepts, especially those related to naming. The following topics are covered in this chapter:

- ▶ Objects and attributes
- ▶ Common name
- ▶ Context
- ▶ Distinguished name
- ▶ Current context
- ▶ Relative distinguished name
- ▶ Trailing periods
- ▶ Typeful naming
- ▶ Typeless naming
- ▶ Time synchronization
- ▶ Partitions and replicas
- ▶ Object Ids
- ▶ NDS-related traffic

Objects and Attributes   The entire NDS logical framework is based on the tree analogy — an upside-down tree, that is. Imagine a tree turned upside-down, with its tap-root at the top. Below the root is the main trunk. Branches extend directly off the main trunk and grow downwards; branches may split once or several times. Finally, at the bottom of the upside-down tree, leaves sprout. Leaves are the terminal objects of the tree (see Figure 1.2).

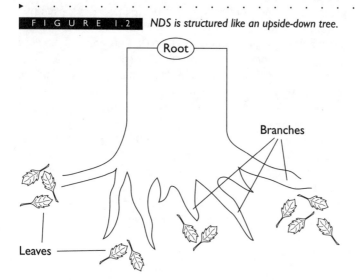

FIGURE 1.2 *NDS is structured like an upside-down tree.*

The items that make up a network are represented as objects in NDS. Objects are building blocks of the NDS tree. An object is a *structure* where information about a particular network resource is stored; it is not the actual resource itself. An object holds types of information, called *attributes* (or *properties*), about itself and its relationship to other objects. At the top of the tree is a [Root] object (note that the square brackets are part of the name) and under it are container objects and leaf objects organized in a hierarchical manner, as shown in Figure 1.3.

FIGURE 1.3 *Possible configurations of the NDS objects*

```
                                    [ROOT]
       ┌──────────┬───────────────┬──────────┬──────────┬──────────┐
    Country       Country       Country   Organization  Organization
       │        ┌────┴────┐        │          │             │
  Organization  Organization Organization  Locality      Leaf    Organizational Unit
       │           │          │             │                        │
Organizational Unit Leaf  Organizational Unit Organization           Leaf
       │                      │             │
     Leaf                   Leaf           Leaf
```

NOTE

Novell documentation uses the terms *attribute* and *property* interchangeably. This book uses the term *attribute* whenever possible.

The NDS object naming conventions, borrowed from x.500, include terms such as "root," "container" objects or branches (which may in turn contain or hold other objects), and "leaf" or terminal objects, which are end points on a tree and represent actual network resources. A leaf object cannot contain other objects. *Container* objects contain other objects and are used to logically organize the objects in an NDS tree. Container objects that have other container objects or leaf objects in them are called *parent container objects.*

Leaf objects are located at the end of the branch. The population of the NDS tree by leaf objects, combined with the containment of these leaf objects, forms the entire logical framework of NDS. Leaf objects are considered *terminal objects* and as such, cannot contain other objects. Rather, they represent the actual network resources, such as users, printers, computers, and so on. NDS provides many other types of leaf objects that you can define and place in the NDS according to your organization's requirements. You can even create new types of objects as needed.

NOTE

In addition to information useful to humans, such as telephone numbers and addresses, NDS leaf objects contain information required by the NetWare operating system such as network addresses, node addresses, security information, and more.

An analogy to NDS container and leaf objects is your computer's file system. NDS containers can be compared to directories where leaf objects are the files within each directory. You can have subcontainers just like you can have subdirectories within a given directory; but you *can't* have a file within a file (that is, a leaf object cannot contain other objects).

Common Name   Common Name or CN is the abbreviation for referencing all leaf objects. A leaf object's CN is the name shown next to the leaf object in the NDS tree. A common name is a *relative distinguished name* (covered in a later section of this chapter). For example, the common name for both User objects found in Figure 1.4 is Shirley.

As is discussed in the next section, NDS uses periods as a delimiter in its naming, therefore, you can't use a period as part of your common name.

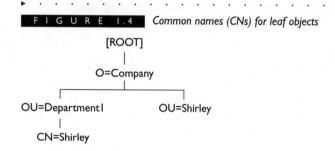

FIGURE 1.4   *Common names (CNs) for leaf objects*

[ROOT]
|
O=Company
|
OU=Department1   OU=Shirley
|
CN=Shirley

TIP

If you must create an object with a period as part of the common name, you can precede the period with a backslash; for example, Test\.User, and ConsoleOne displays this object as Test.User, without the backslash. However, other utilities, such as NetWare Administrator, show the backslash as part of the name; and when you reference this object, the backslash is required.

Note that NDS does not distinguish between uppercase and lowercase in object names. Therefore, User object "Tasha" can be referenced as Tasha, TASHA, tasha, tAsha, or any combinations thereof. Following is a commonly-encountered naming convention:

- All uppercase letters for container-type objects
- Initial-cap, all lowercase, or all uppercase for leaf objects

It is also of interest to note that you can create NDS objects with embedded blanks in the name, such as "Richmond Hill." It is more customary to use underscores instead of blanks as it reduces confusion for some utilities. However, because NDS treats underscores the same as embedded blanks, you can safely create objects with embedded blanks and when a specific utility doesn't support embedded blanks in an object name, enter the name using underscores instead.

Context   *Context* is an object's position in the NDS tree. It is a list of *all* the container objects leading from the object to the [Root]. Using the file system analogy: locating an object through context is similar to locating a file using the directory path. In Figure 1.4, the difference between the two Shirley User objects is their context. The User object on the left is in OU=Department1.O =Company, thus her context is OU=Department1.O=Company; while the User object on the right is in O=Company, so her context is simply O=Company.

Notice that each intermediate container name is separated by a period. This is the delimiter used by NDS to separate object names (just like DOS uses backslashes in its file path). Those familiar with LDAP naming know that it used a comma as a delimiter.

Distinguished Name   An object's *distinguished name* (DN) is a combination of its common name and its context. For example, in Figure 1.4, the distinguished name for the User object Shirley in the Organizational Unit Department1 in the Organization Company is as follows:

`.CN=Shirley.OU=Department1.O=Company`

The distinguished name for the User object Shirley in the Organization Company is as follows:

`.CN=Shirley.O=Company`

Notice a distinguished name starts with a leading period. The following sections have more information about the "period rules."

An object is exactly, and uniquely, identified with a distinguished name. No two objects can have the same distinguished name.

Current Context   Your *current context* can be thought of as your current (logical) position in the NDS tree — it is a pointer to tell NDS where in the tree to look for the object if a complete name is not given. This is analogous to working with DOS drive letters. For example, a simple DIR command returns a list of files and directories in the current working directory, your current *context*. If you need information from elsewhere, you need to specify the directory path, such as \DOS.

Current context is also referred to as the *name context*.

Your current context can affect how much of an object's distinguished name you must provide with a command to access the resource. When you use Novell Client, the current context setting (name context) identifies the default NDS container for your workstation. If your current context and the object's context are the same, you can then refer to an object in your current context by its common name. In other words, name context specifies the portion of the complete name that is automatically supplied. That way a user only needs to perform a minimum amount of typing. For instance, by setting the name context to OU=Department1.O=Company, any object names you reference are assumed to be in this container unless a full, complete name is given (refer to Figure 1.4).

TIP

For those of you familiar with Internet domain name conventions, name context works in exactly the same way. When you simply specify a host name (object name), a default domain (context) is appended to construct a full name.

Relative Distinguished Name   A *relative distinguished name* (RDN) lists the path of objects leading from the object being named to the current context. A relative distinguished name does *not* start with a leading period, but the objects in the name are separated by periods. Trailing periods (explained in the next section) can also be used.

When you use a relative distinguished name, NDS — actually the NDS APIs — must construct a distinguished name from it. NDS accomplishes this by appending the current context information to the relative distinguished name you supplied:

```
Relative Distinguished Name + Current Context =
Distinguished Name
```

Table 1.1 shows how a different current context creates a different distinguished name when the same relative distinguished name is submitted.

T A B L E 1.1	*Different Relative Distinguished Names Depending on the Current Context*	
OBJECT NAME SPECIFIED	**CURRENT CONTEXT**	**RESULTING DISTINGUISHED NAME**
CN=Shirley	O=Company	CN=Shirley.O=Company
CN=Shirley	OU=Department 1.O=Company	CN=Shirley.OU= Department1.O=Company

TIP

From a DOS prompt, you can find out what your current context is using CX.EXE (found in the SYS:PUBLIC directory). By default, your current context is most likely set to where your User object is located.

Trailing Periods   Each *trailing period* tells NDS to remove one object name from the left side of the current context. For example, your current context is OU=Department1.O=Company You enter the following relative distinguished name:

```
CN=Admin.
```

NDS removes *one* name (OU=Department1) from the left side of the current context and appends the relative distinguished name (CN=Admin) to the remaining name. This produces the following distinguished name:

```
.CN=Admin.O=Company
```

Multiple periods can be used to move up multiple levels in the tree; some utilities (such as CX.EXE) return an error if you specify too many trailing periods that take you past the [Root] level in the tree.

Typeful Naming   All the naming examples discussed so far use *typeful names*. A typeful name uses attribute type abbreviations—better known as "object name types"—to distinguish between the different container types and leaf objects in an object's distinguished or relative distinguished name. Table 1.2 lists the attribute type abbreviations. Note that all leaf objects use the common name (CN) attribute type abbreviation.

TABLE 1.2	Attribute Type Abbreviations
OBJECT	**ATTRIBUTE TYPE ABBREVIATION**
Country	C
Locality	L
Organization	O
Organizational Unit	OU
All leaf objects	CN

For example, .CN=Shirley.OU=Department1.O=Company is a typeful distinguished name. Although not mandatory, attribute types help avoid the confusion that can occur with *typeless* naming.

Typeless Naming   A *typeless name* does not include any of the object name type. For example, the typeless distinguished name for .CN=Shirley.OU=Department1.O=Company is

```
.Shirley.Department1.Company
```

If you do not provide a typeful object name, NDS uses the following defaults for the attribute types for each object:

▸ The leftmost object is assumed to be CN=

▸ The rightmost object is assumed to be O=

▸ All intermediate objects are assumed to be OU=

NDS, however, is smart enough to automatically determine if the leftmost object is a leaf or container object and derive a proper type for it.

NOTE

Because the rightmost object is always assumed to be an Organization (O=) in a typeless name, using Country (C=) or Locality (L=) in your tree, poses a problem.

The Need for Time Synchronization   In a distributed environment in which asynchronous events occur, time synchronization is an important factor in ensuring these events take place in the proper sequence. If accurate time were not kept, events could happen out of sequence, which could result in inconsistent information about *what* took place *when*. The server process that maintains synchronization of the information in the NDS database requires this type of time synchronization.

NDS is referred to as a *transactional database*. Whenever a change is made to the local database, the change is set up and then a function is called to make the change actually occur. When an NDS server receives the request for a change, a few things happen internally:

▸ The server checks to make sure the user requesting the change has sufficient rights to make the requested change.

▸ The change is stamped with the current time, represented as *Universal Time Coordinated* (UTC).

▸ If the user has sufficient rights, the information is changed in the local database.

▸ The change enters a queue to be sent out to servers containing replicas of the information in the partition where the change took place. Delivery of these changes, however, is not necessarily guaranteed.

In a simple network, the changed information is updated fairly rapidly. In a more complex network, though, those changes might take some time to propagate from server to server. Without providing a reliable sequence of events, changes in the database might occur in the wrong order. This could be problematic if, for example, an administrator deleted an object and then recreated it. If a replica thought that the attempt to create the object happened before the object was deleted, it might delete the object the administrator had just recreated. This ultimately would result in an inconsistent NDS database and would lead to problems using those objects. One server might think that an object exists, but another server that contains information on that same object might believe it doesn't exist. Another possible instance is changing a user's password and then having the user log in to the network from another server prior to the propagation of the password to the other servers in the network. The loosely consistent nature of the NDS database can result in this type of situation, and underlines the need for good NDS design.

The possibility remains that the sequence of events could become confused unless some method is used to ensure that events occur in the sequence in which they really occurred. Given the distributive nature of NDS, the logical answer to determining the sequence is to use the timestamp, because the design of NDS is such that no single point exists at which all the changes are tracked.

To use a timestamp, though, the servers must maintain accurate time, and that time must be synchronized between the servers. The distributive nature of NDS and lack of the necessity of a centralized point for information exchange to occur between the servers means that the implementation of such time synchronization should provide some measure of fault tolerance, in the event that a server becomes unavailable.

NDS Partitions   NDS can divide its database — the Directory Information Base (DIB) — into units, and can store the database across multiple servers in multiple locations. These NDS database units are known as *partitions*. NDS partitions are logical divisions of the directory database. Each partition forms a major subtree of the NDS tree; the name of the top-most level container is used for naming the partition. If the top-most container in that subtree, for example, is OU=Markham, then the partition is called Markham (see Figure 1.5).

You can consider partitions in NDS to be pieces of a puzzle. One or more pieces (partitions) make up the complete NDS database. Because the [Root] object is located at the top of the tree, a [Root] partition is always present. The [Root] partition is the first partition created and it is created automatically during installation of NDS. Any other partitions are managed by you, the network administrator.

Each NDS tree partition is named by its top-most container.

```
Partition Root              [ROOT]              Partition Vancouver
                               |
   D=Systems           O=Toronto            O=Vancouver
       |                    |                    |
   OU=Test                  |                OU=Sales

Partition Markham  OU=Markham  OU=Richmond_Hill  OU=Scarborough
                      |             |                 |
                   OU=Testing   OU=Development     OU=Sales
                                                      |
              Partition Testing                   CN=NETWARE_51

                                              Partition Scarborough
```

NOTE

Do not confuse NDS partitions with file system partitions. NDS partitions do not contain any file system information, such as logical disk partitions. They only contain information about NDS objects and the associated attributes of those objects.

Partitions are the logical divisions of NDS that enable you to divide the database among servers. An NDS server can contain one or more partitions or no partitions at all. The partitions stored on a server can contain data from *any* part of the tree—they don't have to hold the partition in which they themselves are located. The partitions do *not* have to be contiguous, or adjacent to each other. Server NETWARE_51, for example, can hold both the Markham and Vancouver partitions, but not the [Root] nor Scarborough partition (refer to Figure 1.5).

Partitioning occurs along the boundaries of container objects. That means a partition can include more than one container but cannot overlap another partition. An NDS object only exists in one partition, and all leaf objects in a container are in the same partition as the container. In other words, you cannot partition out a leaf object from its container.

The top-most level container of a partition is called the *partition root object*—the container object that defines where the partition begins. Each partition can only have a single partition root object. You cannot have two containers on the same top-most level in the same partition. As mentioned previously, partitions are named using the name of the partition root object. Each partition root object has an attribute that contains a list of server names and their network addresses. This list is known as the *replica attribute* (or *replica list*). All the servers that contain a copy of the same replica form a *replica ring*.

A partition is classified as either a parent partition or a child partition, depending on its point of reference. A *child partition* (sometimes called a subordinate partition) is a partition that starts with a container at a point lower than the partition root of a partition. Referring back to Figure 1.5, partitions Markham and Scarborough are child partitions to partition [Root] as they start with containers lower than the [Root] object. A *parent partition* (sometimes called a superior partition) is a partition located at a higher point in the NDS tree with respect to the child partition. Partition [Root], for example, is parent to partition Markham; and partition Markham is parent to partition Testing.

No special NDS attribute denotes a parent or child partition. The terms merely describe the relationship between two adjacent partitions in the same branch of an NDS tree. A partition can be both a parent and child partition, depending on the particular partition it is being referenced against. Partition Markham (refer to Figure 1.5) offers such an example. It is a child partition when referencing the [Root] partition; it is a parent partition when referencing the Testing partition.

NOTE

You must grasp the relationship between a parent and a child partition before you can gain an understanding of a Subordinate Reference replica (discussed later in this chapter).

Also, note the difference between the NDS tree root and a partition root. The NDS tree root, an object called [Root], is the top-most object in the entire NDS tree. A partition root is the top-most container in an NDS subtree or partition.

In addition to the logical partitions you can create within NDS, the following types of NDS partitions exist on every NDS server:

▶ **System partition.** Contains system-and server-specific NDS data. This partition is not synchronized with the NDS system partitions on other NDS servers.

▶ **Dynamic Bindery partition.** Contains *Service Advertising Protocol* (SAP) and *Service Location Protocol* (SLP) data received by the server. This information is server centric and is not synchronized with the Dynamic Bindery partitions on other servers.

▶ **Schema partition.** Contains the schema for the NDS tree. It is synchronized with other schema partitions on the network. NDS schema is discussed later in this chapter.

▶ **External reference partition.** Contains externally referenced objects on the server. It is server centric, and is not synchronized with other servers.

Of these four partition types, external reference warrants more explanation because it relates to file system security and is used by servers that do not have NDS data partition information.

When a user logs in to the network, NDS looks up the user information by performing what is called a name resolution process commonly known as *tree walking* (discussed in the following section "Tree Walking"). The client software navigates the different partitions in the NDS tree until it finds the User object. If the data is not found on the local server (the server the client is sending the request to), the server asks another server for the data. If this process is repeated, however, every time the user logs in or the object is referenced, efficiency suffers. To avoid having to repeat the process, NDS builds an *external reference* (as the desired information is not on the local server) to that object and stores it in a partition on the server from which the User object is making the request. The next time this user authenticates to the network, the external reference is used to locate quickly the object within NDS. Such external references are deleted if not used for an extended period of time.

You can create permanent external references in the case of file system rights. Figure 1.6 offers an example: the [Root] partition exists on server FS1, and a different partition (partition Testing) exists on server FS2. User DemoUser needs Read and File Scan file system rights to the FS1_DATA volume. Because the Testing partition where the User object DemoUser exists does not exist on server FS1, the server creates external references to OU=Testing (the partition root object of the partition containing the User object) and CN=DemoUser. OU=Testing.OU=Markham.O=Toronto (the User object).

In order to associate the real object with its external reference, a pointer called a *backlink* is created. The backlink enables the User object to track its external reference, which is stored on a different server. A backlink from CN=DemoUser.OU=Testing.OU=Markham.O=Toronto to FS1 is created to keep track of the external reference. Once you examine the tree-walking process, you better understand the importance of external references and backlinks in assigning file system rights.

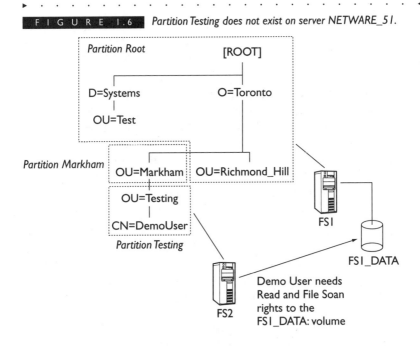

FIGURE 1.6 *Partition Testing does not exist on server NETWARE_51.*

Partition Root — [ROOT]

D=Systems — O=Toronto

OU=Test

Partition Markham — OU=Markham — OU=Richmond_Hill

OU=Testing

CN=DemoUser

Partition Testing

FS1

FS1_DATA

FS2

Demo User needs
Read and File Soan
rights to the
FS1_DATA: volume

NDS Replicas   A copy of a partition is called a *replica*. You can create as many replicas as you want for each partition; no physical limit exists. Experience shows, however, that you should generally not have more than six to eight copies of replica for any given partition. You should, however, have at least three copies for fault tolerance considerations.

NOTE   Although the terms often are used interchangeably, partition and replica are not synonymous. A partition is the same as a replica only when referring to the Master replica (and when no other types of replicas exist). If you have only one huge partition ([Root]) with no replicas — that is, you have only the one copy, the Master — then a partition is the same as a replica.

Replicas are used for two key reasons:

▸ They provide fault tolerance for the NDS database to minimize the risk of any single point of failure.

▸ They provide faster access to NDS information for users operating across WAN links.

If the NDS database is stored on only one server, a disk or server crash prevents new users from logging in to the network, and prevents logged-in users from accessing NDS information. By placing replicas on several servers, users can authenticate to the network and access NDS information even when one of the servers is unavailable.

NOTE

Replicating NDS partitions does not provide fault tolerance for the file systems. Replicas only duplicate NDS information. To duplicate file system information, you must mirror or duplex your hard disks. For the best option in server hardware fault tolerance, consider System Fault Tolerant Level III (SFT III), where servers are mirrored, or NetWare Cluster Services where a common set of disks are shared among multiple servers (see www.novell.com/products/clusters).

If users frequently access NDS information across a WAN link, you can decrease their look-up time substantially by placing a replica of the partition that is most often referenced on one of their local servers. If users in Vancouver, for example, are frequently looking up NDS-related information — such as telephone numbers — on servers in Toronto, placing replicas with this information on a server in Vancouver would definitely increase efficiency. In addition to decreasing look-up time, these replicas provide fault tolerance. If the Toronto server or the WAN link between Toronto and Vancouver is down, for example, Vancouver users can still look up information using the replicas.

NDS uses four types of replicas. These replicas, listed following, have different functions in the NDS:

- Master (replica type 0)
- Secondary or Read/Write (replica type 1)
- Read-Only (replica type 2)
- Subordinate Reference (replica type 3)

The *Master* replica is the copy of the partition that is generally considered to be most correct. There can be many replicas, but you have only one Master. Through the use of partition management tools, such as NDS Manager, you can create replicas and change replicas from one type to another. You can change, for example, a Master replica to Read-Only, and vice versa. NDS Manager and other partition management tools are discussed in Chapter 7, "Managing Partitions and Replication."

NDS information can be accessed and updated using either the Master replica or a Read/Write (or Secondary) replica. You must have access to the

Master, however, to perform certain specific operations. To change the tree structure — such as creating a new partition (a *split*) or moving a partition — you must work with the Master replica. To protect the integrity of NDS, only one partition operation is valid at any given time for that partition. Having to use the Master replica enforces that requirement.

A *Read/Write* (sometimes called *Secondary* and often simply referred to as RW) replica is a copy of the Master replica. It is the most common type of replica. A Read/Write replica functions in the same manner as the Master. You can use it to read and update NDS information. Any changes made to a Read/Write replica are replicated to the Master and to other Read/Write replicas of the same partition. The Read/Write replica's inability to create or move a partition provides its only limitation. You must use the Master replica for such operations.

As the name implies, you can only retrieve NDS information from a *Read-Only* replica. It is relatively static. The replica changes only when update traffic is received from the Master or a Read/Write replica. Because you cannot write to a Read-Only replica, you cannot use it to support user login. You can use it, however, to look up NDS information, such as User object attributes.

When a user logs in, three User object attributes are updated: the Network Address, the Last Login Date, and the Last Login Time. Upon logout, the Network Address attribute is updated again.

NOTE

The term Subordinate Reference replica — or Subordinate Reference (SubRef), as these replicas often are called — is little known or understood to users of versions prior to NetWare 4.10. The older utilities, such as PARTMGR, do not show Subordinate Reference replicas. Starting with NetWare 4.10, you can see them, and therefore, you need to understand how they work.

In simplest terms, a *Subordinate Reference* is a (downward) pointer to the child partitions. It links a parent partition to a child partition. A Subordinate Reference contains a complete copy of the partition root object of the child partition. It does not contain, however, any other data for the child partition. Because it is a complete copy of the partition root object, it has a Replica attribute that contains a list of servers where replicas of the child partition are stored, their network addresses, and replica types, as well as other NDS partition information, such as an Access Control List (ACL) with a summary of all rights to this point in the tree. In essence, Subordinate Reference can be considered the glue that binds parts of the NDS tree together.

NOTE

SubRefs are managed by NDS and as such, they cannot be manually created or deleted. You can neither directly create nor directly delete Subordinate Reference replicas. You can add or remove one indirectly, however, by removing or adding the parent replica from that server.

Each server that contains a replica of the parent partition also contains a Subordinate Reference of every child partition that is not located physically on that server. Consider the sample NDS tree shown in Figure 1.7. This tree contains four partitions: [Root], A, B, and C. Three file servers — FS1, FS2, and FS3 — are installed in this tree, one server in each of the O= containers. Each server holds the only copy of the partition (Master replica) in which the server is contained; the [Root] partition is stored on FS1.

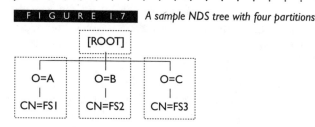

F I G U R E 1.7 *A sample NDS tree with four partitions*

Table 1.3 shows the replicas types and servers on which they are located.

T A B L E 1.3 *Replica Structure of Sample NDS Tree*

SERVER	PARTITION [ROOT]	PARTITION A	PARTITION B	PARTITION C
FS1	Master	Master	SubRef	SubRef
FS2			Master	
FS3				Master

Without the knowledge of Subordinate Reference replica, you would expect only four replicas for the tree. In fact, though, six replicas are present — a Master replica for each partition plus two Subordinate References. FS1 contains Subordinate References because the parent of partitions B and C, partition [Root], resides on the server but partitions B and C do not. Neither FS2 nor FS3 needs a Subordinate Reference because neither partition B nor partition C has a child partition. If the Master partition of [Root] were placed on FS2 rather than FS1, FS2 would contain Subordinate References to partitions A and C.

NOTE

In summary, a Subordinate Reference replica exists everywhere the parent partition is and the child partition is not.

As the number of servers containing replicas of the [Root] partition increases, the number of Subordinate References most likely increases as well. Using the preceding example, adding a Read/Write replica of [Root] to servers FS2 and FS3 results in the information found in Table 1.4.

TABLE 1.4 *Replica Table of Sample NDS Tree with Additional* [Root] *Partition Replicas*

SERVER	PARTITION [ROOT]	PARTITION A	PARTITION B	PARTITION C
FS1	Master	Master	SubRef	SubRef
FS2	Read/Write	SubRef	Master	SubRef
FS3	Read/Write	SubRef	SubRef	Master

Again, without the knowledge of Subordinate Reference replicas, you would expect only two additional replicas. But in fact, you have doubled the number of replicas from six to twelve.

Subordinate References also can be created when you remove a replica. Consider the sample NDS tree shown in Figure 1.8. Imagine that server FS1 contains the Master replica of partitions [Root], OU=Regional, and OU=Remote. Imagine that server FS2 holds a Read/Write replica of the same partitions. If you remove the OU=Remote replica from FS2, a Subordinate Reference is automatically created. You might have thought you reduced the replica count on server FS2 by removing OU=Remote, but in fact, a (smaller) Subordinate Reference replica of OU=Remote is created (because it has a copy of the parent partition, OU=Regional but not of the child partition, OU=Remote), resulting in the same number of replicas.

Although replicas are necessary for fault tolerance, creating unnecessary replicas of [Root] can needlessly increase the number of Subordinate References in your tree, generating additional NDS traffic. Fortunately, a Subordinate Reference does not contain all child partition data; it need not be updated regularly. A Subordinate Reference is updated only when a change in its parent partitions occurs, such as addition or removal of object rights. This type of change causes less NDS traffic than would be created if the Subordinate Reference were another type of replica.

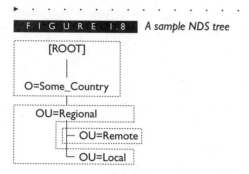

FIGURE 1.8 *A sample NDS tree*

On the other hand, because Subordinate References contain only pointers, they are essentially useless if a Master, Read/Write, or Read-Only replica of the child partition is not available.

Table 1.5 summarizes the characteristics of the four types of NDS replicas.

TABLE 1.5 *Characteristics of the Four NDS Replica Types*

CHARACTERISTIC	MASTER	READ/WRITE	READ-ONLY	SUBREF
Maintains list of all other replicas	✓	✓	✓	✓
Contains a complete copy of all object information of the partition	✓	✓	✓	
Controls partition boundary changes (merging, splitting, moving, creating, deleting, and repairing)	✓			
Controls object changes (creating, moving, deleting, and modifying objects and object property values)	✓	✓		
Supports authentication	✓	✓		
Supports viewing of objects and their information	✓	✓	✓	
Can have multiple replicas per partition		✓	✓	✓
Can be changed into a master replica		✓	✓	(see note)
Can be changed into a Read/Write replica	✓			✓

CHARACTERISTIC	MASTER	READ/WRITE	READ ONLY	SUBREF
Can be used on a server where bindery services is required	✓	✓		
Only contains the partition root object				✓
Is automatically removed if you add a replica of that child partition to the server				✓
Can be created by the network administrator	✓	✓	✓	
Cannot be created by the network administrator (created automatically by the system)				✓
Controls background processes	✓			

NOTE Subordinate reference replicas can be changed to master replicas, but should only be changed during a disaster recovery or when no other options are available. If you change a subordinate reference replica to a master replica, your objects are lost in the process. You would then need to restore the objects from a physical backup of the NDS data.

Tree Walking   *Tree walking* is the process of a NetWare client walking through the NDS tree of partitions to obtain information about a particular object. The NetWare client can either be a workstation or an NDS server — each NDS server has a built-in client agent to facilitate NDS name resolution and tree walking.

Name resolution is the process of NDS navigating through the different partitions in the tree — using tree walking — until it finds the requested object. All NDS information requests can be broken down into one or more names identifying the objects. In pursuing each name component in a request, NDS searches for a partition that contains some part of the name path associated with the request. Once a partition is found, the search moves from that partition to the partition that actually contains the object. Until a relevant partition is found, the search proceeds *upwards* toward the [Root], because any request can be pursued successfully by beginning at the [Root] and working downwards.

The tree-walking process relies on Subordinate References to connect the tree. If a server can provide no other information, the least it can offer is another server that has a partition with information about objects that is higher in the tree than itself. When walking the tree, a server is given the object name of interest. Based on the name, the server decides if it needs to move upward toward [Root] or downward away from [Root] in order to access the next partition in an effort to locate the object.

The name-resolution and tree-walking processes are best illustrated by the following login example. Three different partitions in the NDS tree are located on three separate servers (see Figure 1.9). Server FS1 holds the Testing partition, server FS2 holds the Markham partition, and server FS3 holds the Toronto partition.

FIGURE 1.9 *Tree-walking an NDS tree with three partitions*

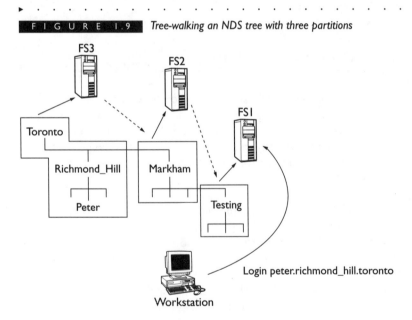

Suppose the workstation is initially attached to FS1. The user logs in as Peter.Richmond_Hill.Toronto. Server FS1 does not contain information for this User object, nor does it have information about Richmond_Hill or Toronto. Rather than immediately returning an error message to the workstation, however, FS1 passes the query up the tree — using its internal NDS client agent — to FS2. (It knows FS2 is closer to [Root] because of the Subordinate Reference pointer.)

If FS2 does not contain information for the object, it passes the name of the server containing a parent partition to it—in this case, FS3—back to FS1. Then FS1 queries FS3 for the desired information; FS1 has walked up the NDS tree structure, toward [Root]. In this instance, FS3 holds the partition that contains the User object. FS1, therefore, asks the workstation to query FS3 directly.

Tree walking can go up *or* down an NDS tree, depending on the location of the partition that holds the desired information.

NOTE

The act of the workstation locating the server that holds the partition with the desired object constitutes half the name-resolution process. Up to this half-way point, the tree-walking process is solely carried out by the server on behalf of the workstation. The second half of name resolution is complete when the workstation retrieves the object ID from the server containing the partition.

Tree walking gives an NDS client the ability to log in or authenticate without having to attach to the specific server holding the partition (or replica of the partition) that contains the User object. Tree walking is also used to locate services—such as servers and print queues—anywhere within an NDS tree.

In an NDS environment, once a client is authenticated to an NDS tree, that client can locate any (NDS-aware) service within the tree without the use of a SAP or SLP packet. NetWare 2 and NetWare 3 services, such as print servers and database servers, must broadcast the availability of the services (over IPX) on a regular basis (default is 60 seconds), so clients can locate these services.

NOTE

This feature is especially beneficial for networks with many services. The use of NDS to locate services significantly reduces the amount of network broadcast or multicast traffic due to SAP or SLP. This reduction in network traffic is also of importance to companies that have WAN links.

Replicas and Object IDs   To maintain backward compatibility, rather than using NDS object names, NDS uses the corresponding object ID (hex-adecimal) numbers when assigning file system trustee rights. If, for example, the object ID for CN=Peter.OU=Richmond_Hill.O=Toronto is 0505330B, then this ID number is used in the file system trustee assignment. Because object IDs are server centric, however, any given NDS object's object ID varies from server to server.

NOTE

In eDirectory, a Global User ID (GUID) is associated with each object. However, in order to provide backwards compatability, server-centric object IDs are still used.

Refer back to a previous example about external references in this chapter. User DemoUser needs Read and File Scan file system rights to FS1_DATA. Because the Testing partition holding the User object DemoUser does not exist on server FS1, the server creates an external reference to OU=Testing and CN=DemoUser.OU=Testing. This external reference is simply a placeholder for the object outside a server's replica. The external reference has an object ID but does not contain any object attribute information, and it is not synchronized with the actual object.

On the other hand, the actual object's backlink is a pointer to the external reference. It contains the name of the server where the external reference resides and the object ID of the external reference. This backlink enables the external reference to be updated in case the actual object is moved or deleted.

NDS backs objects up by name. Object IDs are not backed up in an NDS environment as they are server-centric. NetWare 2 and 3, in contrast, back up object IDs rather than names. When NDS is restored, new object IDs are assigned on a server-by-server basis. Because of the lack of uniqueness of object IDs when NDS is reinstalled or restored from backup, some caveats arise in terms of file system trustee information when external references and backlinks are involved.

Bindery Services   Those of you familiar with NetWare 2 and NetWare 3 know that each server has a *bindery*—a set of data files that contain information such as users, groups, and so on for that server. Bindery information is server-centric. NDS replaces that database. What happens, then, with the applications expecting the bindery to be present? NDS provides an emulation called *Bindery Services* that fools these applications into thinking a bindery is there.

In an NDS environment, the server-centric bindery database has been replaced by a distributed hierarchical database, the DIB. However, not all applications (workstation-based utilities and server-based *NetWare Loadable Modules* [NLMs]) support NDS—at least not yet. Therefore, to provide backward compatibility with these tools and pre-NDS servers, NDS provides an emulation service, Bindery Services—that makes the NDS hierarchical database look like a flat bindery file to these utilities and servers. Prior to NetWare 4.10, this was known as *Bindery Emulation*.

How does a network administrator "flatten" the hierarchical NDS database to make it look like a bindery? This is accomplished, to some extent, using Bindery Services. With Bindery Services, however, rather than physically or even logically flattening the whole NDS structure, you ask the server to emulate a bindery using information from a limited number of containers—a "narrow view," if you will. This is done using the SET BINDERY CONTEXT console command on the NetWare server.

NOTE In order for a server to provide Bindery Services, it must hold a writeable copy (as in Master or Read/Write) of the replica holding the container to which the bindery context is pointing. The Server object itself does not have to be in the container to which its bindery context is set, however.

NetWare 4.10 and higher allows you to have 16 bindery contexts (each context points to a single container and that container only; subcontainers are not part of the context) per server, whereas previous versions of NetWare 4.0x only allow one. This enables you to "combine" the information from up to 16 containers into one emulated bindery.

TIP You can use either the complete naming convention or the typeless naming convention in setting the bindery context. SET BINDERY CONTEXT = OU=Markham.O=Toronto, for example, is the same as SET BINDERY CONTEXT = .Markham.Toronto.

Consider the [Root] partition of the NDS tree, that was presented in Figure 1.5, which contains five containers (not counting [Root]):

- ▶ O=Toronto
- ▶ OU=Richmond_Hill.O=Toronto
- ▶ OU=Development.OU=Richmond_Hill.O=Toronto
- ▶ O=Systems
- ▶ OU=Test.O=Systems

By setting the *bindery context* of the server TEST_NW51 (assuming it has either a Master or a Read/Write copy of the [Root] partition) to container OU=Richmond_Hill.O=Toronto, any bindery-based tool can retrieve only information that is in this (OU=Richmond_Hill.O=Toronto) container, and does not see anything outside of it. Those tools do not see any objects that are in O=Toronto or in OU=Development (even though OU=Development is located below OU=Richmond_Hill).

NOTE

You are not able to set a bindery context to OU=Markham.O =Toronto on the TEST_NW51 server, for example, as it doesn't have a copy of the Markham partition.

NDS-Related Traffic   Network traffic is an important consideration in any networking environment, with or without NDS. But because of the distributed nature of NDS and the capability to place replicas anywhere, NDS traffic optimization becomes a design consideration. This is especially critical when your WAN is composed of slower links (such as 56 Kbps leased lines) or expensive circuits (such as ISDN or Frame Relay where there may be per packet charges).

Several techniques were implemented in order for NDS to not overwhelm the network with its data synchronization and lookup traffic. Some of these techniques are as follows:

► **Sending delta change only.** When a partition is created, the partition root object receives a replica list. When changes are made to objects within a partition, those changes are sent to all other replicas of that partition using the replica list of the partition root object. Only *changes* — generally at the attribute level, not at the object level — are sent to other replicas. For example, if you add a new member to a Group object, only the new entry is sent, not the entire list of group membership. Similarly, if you delete a member from a Group object, only the removal request is sent.

► **Multi-master replication.** The master replica participates in the partition synchronization process by exchanging updates with other replicas, but it is not a controlling entity in this process. Similarly, each read/write replica synchronizes with the other replicas of the partition. Read-only replicas also synchronize with other replicas, but they receive updates only from other servers.

► **Traffic prioritization.** Some changes, such as changes to a user's password, are sent immediately to other replicas. Other less critical changes, such as a user's last login time, are collected locally for a short period of time before being sent out to the network.

NetWare 5.1 includes WAN Traffic Manager, a utility that enables you to manage your replica synchronization traffic across WAN links by using policies to limit NDS-related traffic to specific hours of the day.

▶ **Transitive synchronization.** Because servers that support only IP cannot communicate with servers that support only IPX, changes made on one replica in such an environment can't be synchronized to all other replicas. To resolve this, NDS v7 and higher includes *transitive synchronization*, which bridges the gap between IP-only and IPX-only servers. Transitive synchronization eliminates the requirement that all servers in a replica list must be able to communicate and synchronize with each server in the replica list. When an NDS change is made, a source server checks each target server. If the servers can't communicate with each other because of differing protocols, the source server doesn't continue to try to communicate the changes to the target. Instead, the target receives the updates through an intermediary server that uses both IP and IPX (see Figure 1.10). If a target server's replica is more recent than a source server's replica, the target server does not synchronize with the source server. This reduces synchronization traffic.

F I G U R E   1 . 1 0   *Synchronize DS changes through an intermediary.*

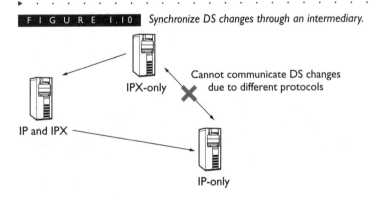

NDS Objects and Attributes

For each type of network entity and resource that exists on the network, you create an NDS object. This object may represent a real entity, such as a user, or it may represent a service, such as a printer.

Each NDS object contains one or more *attributes*, which are pieces of information that define that object. For example, a Group object contains attributes that list the users belonging to the group (the group membership attribute); a User object contains attributes that contain the user's full name, department, telephone number, and so on. Each type of object, such as a Server or Group object, may have different properties than another type of object. Each type of object, such as User or Print Queue, is referred to as an *object class*.

Categories of Object Classes

NDS object classes fall into three categories. They are as follows:

- ► **[Root] object.** The [Root] object is a special object created by NDS. [Root] is always the first object created for any NDS tree. [Root], sometimes referred to as Top, only does one thing: it contains all other objects in the NDS tree, either directly or indirectly. Each NDS tree has one and only one [Root], and unlike other objects in the tree, it can never be moved, deleted, or renamed.

- ► **Container objects.** Container objects contain other objects and are used to logically organize the objects in an NDS tree. Container objects that have other container or leaf objects in them are called parent container objects. Table 1.6 lists the possible container object types.

- ► **Leaf objects.** In the NDS tree, a leaf is at the end of the branch. Leaf objects represent the actual network resources, such as users, printers, servers, and so on, and cannot contain other objects.

T A B L E I . 6	*Container Object Types*	
NAME	ABBREVIATION	MANDATORY
Country	C	No
Locality	L	No
Organization	O	Yes
Organizational Unit	OU	No

NOTE

NetWare 5 introduces a few other container object types, such as those used by the Novell Licensing Services (NLS): Novell+ NetWare 5 Server Conn SCL+510 and Novell+NetWare 5 Server+510. But because you can't use them to organize network entities and resources, such as printers and users, NLS-related container types are not listed in Table 1.6.

You use the object class types listed in Table 1.6 to place your NDS objects into a manageable organization. The [Root] object resides at the top of the tree. The container objects form branches and subbranches. The leaf objects are the individual users, groups, printers, servers, and so on, that populate those branches.

Among the four container class types listed in Table 1.6, you find the most commonly used types are the Organization and Organizational Unit objects. The table also indicates that Country and Locality are optional. These two object types are primarily for X.500 naming specification compliance, and are seldomly used in NDS.

The Organization object is a required object. You must have at least one Organization object in your tree. You are probably going to want more — see Chapter 3, "Network Infrastructures, Resources, and NDS Design" for details. Organization objects must be created directly under [Root] or directly under a Country object, if you choose to use Country objects. Organization objects may contain Organizational Unit objects, Locality objects, or any type of leaf objects. Note that this is the first level of the tree which permits the creation of leaf objects. Leaf objects cannot be placed directly under [Root] or Country objects — Alias objects are an exception but they are not real objects.

Organizational Unit objects may contain other Organizational Unit objects, Locality objects, or any of the types of leaf objects, such as Users and Printers. You may "nest" Organizational Units as deep as you choose; however, making the tree structure too deep complicates user access.

Both the Organization object and Organizational Unit object may contain leaf objects. If you wanted to, for example, you could create a User object which is contained directly by an Organization object. This is analogous to a tree with a leaf sprouting directly from the trunk.

NDS Object Classes

An object class is like a skeleton for an NDS object. An NDS object is a class that has been instantiated with data. In other words:

```
Class + Data = NDS Object
```

When creating an NDS object, you select a class as a starting point. The class is like a request form for a specific type of NDS object. Once the class is selected, you, in a sense, complete the "request form" in order to provide essential and specific information on the new object.

Each class has a class name, an inheritance class (unless it is at the top of the class hierarchy), class flags, and a group of attributes. Classes are named like NDS objects—User, Printer, Queue, Server—yet they are just structure, no content. The inheritance class is a class that is used as a starting point. All of the attributes granted to the inheritance class are inherited by the classes that come below it in the class hierarchy. Shown in Figure 1.11 is the class inheritance of the User class in a NetWare 5.1 eDirectory environment; the list of User object's attributes are those defined for the following classes:

- ► User
- ► Organizational Person
- ► Person
- ► Top
- ► ndsLoginProperties

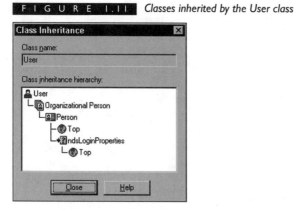

FIGURE 1.11 *Classes inherited by the User class*

Object classes are classified either as an *effective class* or a *noneffective class*. Simply put, effective classes can be used to create objects and noneffective classes cannot. For example, User, Group, and Printer are effective classes, while Person and Top are noneffective classes. The sole purpose of noneffective classes is to provide common attributes to the subordinate classes. NDS includes many (effective) object classes and Table 1.7 lists some of the most commonly used and encountered object classes available in NetWare 5.

T A B L E 1.7	*Commonly Used Object Classes*
OBJECT CLASS	**DESCRIPTION**
Alias	Points to the original object to make it possible to access an object from two or more places in the tree.
Application	A pointer to an application installed on the network. Different variations of this object exist depending on the type of application, such as Windows 98 or Windows NT.
Directory Map	Used to create drive mappings to frequently used applications. If the application is moved, only the map must be changed.
Group	A list of users used to assign rights to multiple users.
License Container	Contains licenses for applications enabled with NetWare Licensing Services (NLS). All NetWare 5 trees have these and may exist on NetWare 4.11 and higher trees.
License Certificate	Object represents a product license certificate to be used with NLS. All NetWare 5 trees have these and may exist on NetWare 4.11 and higher trees.
Locality	Optional container object that represents a location (State/Province or Locale).
LSP Server	Represents a License Service Provider server. It is used only if NLS is installed. All NetWare 5 trees have these and may exist on NetWare 4.11 and higher trees.
NetWare Server	Server running any version of NetWare. Server's location is recorded in the Network Address attribute.
Organization	Top-level container object. Generally used to represent a company.
Organizational Role	Represents a position, such as helpdesk, that various users can occupy. It enables you to assign rights to that position rather than to specific users. (Provides the same function as a Group object.)

(continued)

TABLE 1.7	Commonly Used Object Classes (continued)
OBJECT CLASS	**DESCRIPTION**
Organizational Unit	Lower-level container object. Generally used to represent divisions or departments within a company.
Print Queue	A print queue. Used in queue-based printing.
Print Server (Non-NDPS)	A NetWare print server that provides print services.
Printer (Non-NDPS)	A printer attached to the network.
Profile	Used to provide login script for users who need to share commands from the login script even though they are not located under the same container object.
User	People who use the network. Attributes include user name, address, telephone number, password, password restrictions, and so on.
Volume	Physical volume attached to a server. Attributes include which server the volume is located on, name, owner, space restrictions, and so on.

The NDS Schema

Like any good database, the NDS database has a *schema*. The NDS schema, in database parlance, is the overall plan that describes and defines the allowable types of NDS objects, their attributes, and the rules that govern their creation and existence. The schema also determines how objects can inherit attributes and rights of other container objects above it. In addition, the schema also defines how the NDS tree is structured — as in relationships between different objects — and how objects are to be named.

NOTE

As previously noted, each NDS server has a schema partition. When NDS is installed on a server, a copy of the schema is automatically placed on the server and any schema changes are automatically synchronized among the servers. Therefore, any changes made to the schema on one server are automatically reflected on all NDS servers in the tree.

NDS is supplied with an extensive set of objects and attributes. However, there might be times when you want to create certain object types or attributes for a particular need. Because NDS schema is extensible, this can be easily done.

If you're a programmer, using Novell's Directory Services APIs you can create new object types and attributes, as well as add new attributes to existing object classes. You can create a new attribute called When Employed for the User object, for example, that the Human Resources department can use to track the years of service of a given employee. If you don't have time to write codes, included with NDS Manager is a Schema Manager tool (see Figure 1.12) that enables you to define and add new object classes and attributes. Also available, as a free download, is ScheMax that can accomplish the same task.

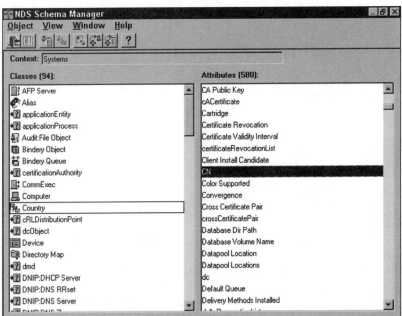

F I G U R E   1.12   *Access Schema Manager by choosing Object ⇨ Schema Manager from the NDS Manager pull-down menu.*

WARNING   Before you make any changes to your NDS schema, bare in mind that any extensions made to the base schema (the one that NDS originally installed) *cannot* be removed. For example, if you added the When Employed attribute to the User class, you can't remove it at a later time.

NDS Object Attributes

Attributes are the data fields in a database. If a class is like a form, then the attribute would be one question that's blank on the form. When an attribute is created, it is named (such as "Surname" or "Employee number") and given an *attribute syntax type* (such as "string A-Z, 0-9" or "number -999 to 999"). From then on, it is available in the attribute list. NDS supports 29 syntax types from which to choose, such as "Case Exact String," "Case Ignore String," and "Alpha-numeric." These are used to specify how you want data entered for each attribute. The syntax can only be specified when an attribute is created; you cannot modify it later. Shown in Figure 1.13 is the attribute definition for the Surname attribute.

► • ◄

F I G U R E   I . 1 3   *The Surname attribute is defined to be a "Case Ignore String" with no more than 64 characters in the name.*

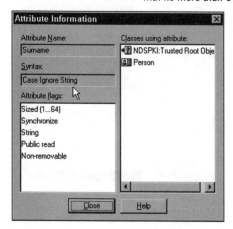

Each attribute can store one or more values, depending on its definition. Some attributes—known as *multi-valued attributes*—such as Telephone Number of a User object, can store one or more values. *Single-valued attributes*, such as the Password attribute of a User object, can store one and only one value.

NDS class attributes are of two basic varieties: mandatory and optional. *Mandatory* attributes, as the name implies, are required when an object is created, whereas *optional* attributes are not. Of the attributes listed for the Top class, only the Object Class attribute is mandatory. The rest of the attributes listed are optional. Another example of mandatory attributes is the Login

Name and Last Name fields for a User object. You must specify values for both attributes before a User object can be successfully created, otherwise, you receive a "missing mandatory" error. An optional attribute is one that can be completed if desired but can be left without content.

Working with NDS Objects

Once you've installed NDS on your server and have a Windows workstation configured with the Novell Client software, you can log in to the network and examine the NDS tree you've created so far. As you create new users and groups, or install new printers and servers, you can see the tree grow in size and complexity.

The primary tools for looking at the NDS tree, and for creating or modifying NDS objects, are the NetWare utilities called *NetWare Administrator* and *ConsoleOne*. The NetWare Administrator utility, commonly referred to as NWAdmin, is a 32-bit Windows application that runs on Windows 95/98, Windows NT, and Windows 2000. ConsoleOne, on the other hand, is a java application that also runs on Windows 95/98, Windows NT, and Windows 2000, provided you have java installed; ConsoleOne also runs on a NetWare 5.*x* server under the GUI interface.

TIP

NetWare Administrator is sure to be your preferred utility due to flexibility and speed. However, certain tasks and configuration of some products require ConsoleOne.

The following object management tasks can be performed using NetWare Administrator and ConsoleOne:

- ▶ Create new NDS objects (such as users and groups)
- ▶ Delete NDS objects
- ▶ Rename objects
- ▶ Move objects from one context to another within the same tree
- ▶ Change an object's attribute values
- ▶ Search for objects by particular attribute values (such as all users in the same Location)

Other tools and utilities necessary to manipulate and manage NDS are introduced as they are required in later chapters.

## CHAPTER 2

Installing NDS

One of the most important installation-related tasks is the design of your NDS tree structure, and we'll go over that in detail in the next chapter. Generally, this design work is done *prior* to installing a NetWare server or eDirectory on your system. However, there's nothing wrong with installing, testing, and becoming comfortable with your server before implementing your tree structure. Later, if you're not happy with the existing tree structure, you can make changes to your NDS tree easily — you're not locked into a static structure. So let's get started with the nuts and bolts — the installation.

A Word On Installation

Depending on the size of your network, number of users, and technical levels of your users, you can design an NDS tree in a number of ways. In this chapter, you learn how to use the basic design concepts necessary to implement a tree that fits your immediate needs, and yet is easy for future expansions. One of the topics covered is time synchronization. Although not part of NDS, time synchronization plays a critical role in the health and performance of NDS. Therefore, you should pay some attention to your time synchronization implementation; its implementation strategy is often considered part of the "tree design" process.

During the installation of NetWare 5.1 servers, you have the option of installing either NDS v7 (the "legacy" NDS) or NDS v8 ("eDirectory"); the default is NDS v8. You can choose to install NDS v7 initially and then upgrade to NDS v8 at a later time, without having to reinstall NDS as it is only the "backend engine" that's changed. On NetWare 5.0 servers, however, you don't have a choice between NDS v7 and NDS v8 during the initial installation — NDS v7 is installed. This is because NDS v8 was released after NetWare 5.0 shipped. Therefore, before diving into the NDS tree design topics, this chapter starts with a discussion about installing eDirectory on the following operating systems platform:

- NetWare 5
- Windows NT/2000
- Sun Solaris
- Linux

NOTE The discussions about NDS eDirectory installation in this chapter are based on product files downloaded from Novell's Web site. You can also get the product on CD-ROMs, in which case you don't need to extract any files before installation.

Upgrading to eDirectory on NetWare Servers

Upgrading the NDS on a NetWare 5 server to eDirectory is rather easy and straightforward. A few preinstallation steps need to be performed and they are as follows:

1. Check to ensure that your NetWare server meets the following *minimum* system requirements:

   • NetWare 5.0 or higher server

   • NetWare 5.0 Support Pack 2 or later; no Support Pack is required for NetWare 5.1 at the time of this writing

   • You have access to a user id that has administrative (Supervisor) rights to [Root] in order to modify the schema

   • If you're going to use ConsoleOne, your workstation should be a 200 MHz processor or faster and a minimum of 128MB of RAM

   • If you need ephemeral key support for SSL connections, you'll need the Novell Cryptography Support Modules (NICI 1.3 or later) available from Novell Products Web site at www.novell.com/products/cryptography/.

NOTE

eDirectory for NetWare runs only on NetWare 5.0 and higher servers. At the time of this writing, Novell has no plans to release a version of eDirectory for NetWare 4.11 or NetWare 4.2.

2. Download the latest version of eDirectory, including any updates, for NetWare from Novell's Web sites at www.novell.com/download/ #NDS and http://support.novell.com/misc/patlst.htm. You'll need a valid NetWare 5 serial number (found on the red product box or on the license diskette) to download the product but not the patches.

3. NDS eDirectory is available for download in a series of self-extracting files or a full self-extracting file (.EXE). All files must be downloaded and extracted before NDS eDirectory can be installed. Put these files into a temporary installation directory on the server on which you plan to install eDirectory (for example, SYS:EDIR). In the installation directory, extract each executable and follow the onscreen instructions.

4. You *must* run DSREPAIR.NLM before installing the first NDS eDirectory server in your tree if any one of the following conditions is true:

- A NetWare 5 server is running NDS 8 or you have NDS 8 NetWare Update anywhere in your tree.

- Your first installation of NDS eDirectory is on a NetWare 5 server that does *not* hold a writeable replica of the [Root] partition. For details, refer to the "Run DSREPAIR Before Upgrading" section that follows.

The appropriate version of DSREPAIR.NLM is included with the NDS eDirectory download. After you extracted the files from the download (as per the previous step), you find a \patches\netware\dsrepair directory under your installation directory.

5. If you're installing NDS eDirectory in an IP-only environment, load IPXSPX.NLM before loading NWCONFIG to start the installation. The reason is that NWCONFIG.NLM looks to Btrieve for the product list. Btrieve in turn requires an IPX NLM. Loading IPXSPX.NLM allows Btrieve to load. When you reboot the server, IPXSPX.NLM does not reload, so you have an IP-only environment again.

6. If you have SLPDA.NLM running on your NetWare server, you must unload it or else you'll receive an error and are unable to complete the install.

Once your system meets the preceding specifications, you then are ready to install the software by referring to the following "Installing NDS eDirectory" section. Otherwise, the following two sections cover the procedures necessary to run DSREPAIR and apply Support Pack on your NetWare server.

Installing Support Pack

If you're running NetWare 5.0, you need to install at least Support Pack 2 (later version preferred) before installing NDS eDirectory. The following steps outline how to install a Support Pack on a NetWare 5 server:

1. Download the latest version of NetWare 5.0 Support Pack from the Novell Support Connection Web site at http://support.novell.com/misc/patlst.htm#nw.

2. Run the downloaded self-extracting file and expand it into an installation directory on the NetWare server.

3. Run NWCONFIG.NLM on the server console.

4. Select Product Options ⇨ Install a Product Not Listed.

5. Press F3 (or F4 if you're using RCONSOLE) and specify the path to the expanded Support Pack files located on the server.

6. Follow the onscreen instructions to complete the setup.

7. Restart the server so the newly copied files are in effect.

Run DSREPAIR Before Upgrading

Depending on the version of NetWare and DS you currently have on the network, you need to select the appropriate version of DSREPAIR.NLM according to Table 2.1.

TABLE 2.1		Versions of DSREPAIR.NLM	
NETWARE VERSION	**DS VERSION**	**LOCATION OF DSREPAIR.NLM**	**DSREPAIR VERSION**
4.11	Any	Patches\netware\ nw4x\DSREPAIR.NLM	4.68
5.0	Pre-NDS 8	Patches\netware\ nw5x\DSREPAIR.NLM	5.21
5.0	NDS 8	Patches\netware\ nds8\DSREPAIR.NLM	6.32
5.0	NDS 8 NetWare Update	Netware\sys/system\ DSREPAIR.NLM	7.16

Once you located the appropriate DSREPAIR.NLM, copy it to the SYS: SYSTEM directory of the server containing the Master replica of the [Root] partition. At the server console, run DSREPAIR and select Advanced Options Menu ⇨ Global Schema Operations ⇨ Post NetWare 5 Schema Update. You are prompted for the Admin id (for example, .Admin.Company) and password. During the repair operation, you may see some errors associated with adding object classes, ignore those errors; DSREPAIR is simply applying the Post NetWare 5 Schema Update changes to each object.

TIP

Exit DSREPAIR before installing NDS eDirectory on the server. If DSREPAIR is loaded, the server might not restart.

Once you're done updating the schema, copy the appropriate updated version of DSREPAIR.NLM included with the NDS eDirectory download to each NetWare server in the tree to ensure that the schema needed for NDS eDirectory is properly maintained when DSRepair is run in the future. Use Table 2.1 to determine which version of DSRepair should be put on each server.

If you accidentally used an older DSREPAIR and selected Rebuild Operational Schema during a repair operation, schema enhancements made by the Post NetWare 5 Schema Update are lost. Reapply the Post NetWare 5 Schema Update to your tree if you are running off a server holding a writeable replica of the [Root] partition. If you are on a different server, you should click Advanced Options ⇨ Global Schema Operations ⇨ Request Schema from Tree to resynchronize the schema from the root of the tree. To prevent this problem, make sure you copy the appropriate version of DSREPAIR.NLM to each NetWare server in the directory tree.

Installing NDS eDirectory

The steps for installing NDS eDirectory are very similar to that of installing the Support Pack and other NetWare products:

1. Download the latest version of eDirectory and any updates from Novell's Web sites at www.novell.com/download/#NDS and http://support.novell.com/patlst.htm.

2. Extract the download files into an installation directory on the NetWare server.

3. If you're installing the server into an existing tree, check that all the replicas in the partition that you're installing the server into are in the ON state. This can be verified using NDS Manager.

4. Run NWCONFIG.NLM at the server console.

5. Select Product Options ⇨ Install a Product Not Listed.

6. Press F3 (or F4 if you're using RCONSOLE) and specify the path to the expanded NDS files located on the server.

7. Follow the onscreen instructions to complete the setup.

8. After the files are copied, the server automatically restarts.

9. After the server restarts, *make sure all volumes are mounted*. If you're not sure whether all volumes are mounted, issue the following command at the server console:

   MOUNT ALL

10. Switch to the NWCONFIG screen by pressing Ctrl+Esc and then select the number corresponding to the screen.

11. Enter the administrator login name (with context) and password. This installation step upgrades LDAP.

12. Press ESC to close the upgrade status log; a partial sample log file is shown as follows:

```
Begin NDS schema update for: SYS:\SYSTEM\SCHEMA\
NDS500.SCH
Schema attribute Partition Status already exists and is
identical.
Schema attribute dc already exists and is identical.
Schema attribute uniqueID already exists and is
identical.
Schema attribute Permanent Config Parms already exists
and is identical.
Schema attribute Timezone already exists and is
identical.
Schema attribute Bindery Restriction Level already
exists and is identical.
Schema attribute Transitive Vector already exists and
is identical.
Schema attribute Local Received Up To already exists
and is identical.
Schema attribute T already exists and is identical.
Schema attribute Purge Vector already exists and is
identical.
Schema attribute Synchronization Tolerance already
exists and is identical.
Schema attribute Password Management already exists and
is identical.
Schema attribute Used By already exists and is
identical.
Schema attribute Uses already exists and is identical.
Schema attribute Obituary Notify already exists and is
identical.
```

Schema attribute GUID already exists and is identical.

Schema attribute Other GUID already exists and is identical.

Schema attribute Auxiliary Class Flag already exists and is identical.

Schema attribute Unknown Auxiliary Class already exists and is identical.

Schema attribute AuxClass Object Class Backup already exists and is identical.

Schema class Organizational Person already exist and is identical.

Optional attributes specified for schema class NCP Server already exists and are identical.

Optional attributes specified for schema class Server already exists and are identical.

Optional attributes specified for schema class Partition already exists and are identical.

Schema class Tree Root already exist and is identical.

Optional attributes specified for schema class Partition already exists and are identical.

Optional attributes specified for schema class Resource already exists and are identical.

Optional attributes specified for schema class Top already exists and are identical.

Schema class domain already exist and is identical.

Added schema class dcObject.

13. You are prompted to restart the server.

14. Click Yes ⇨ Restart Now.

The server restarts, and the upgrade to NDS eDirectory is complete. You can verify that you're running NDS eDirectory by issuing a MODULE DS.NLM at the server console. You should see it report Novell Directory Services Version 8.

NOTE

If you did not configure LDAP for SSL during the initial OS installation, you will receive an error message when the server restarts. Refer to Novell Technical Information Document #10017683, "NLDAP Configuration (Quick Start)," for configuration information.

If you downloaded any patches for NDS eDirectory, apply them according to the documentation included with the patches.

Post Installation Checklist

Three tasks may need to be performed after the successful installation of NDS eDirectory. They are as follows:

► **Tuning NDS cache usage.** By default, NDS uses 8MB of RAM for cache. This setting allows NDS to run on servers without requiring more RAM. If you have sufficient RAM to increase the NDS and BULKLOAD cache size, you can significantly increase the efficiency of NDS for large databases by allocating more RAM to the NDS cache. The smallest cache size tested by Novell is 0 and the largest is 2 GB. NDS runs with either amount. To set the cache size, use the following command at the server console:

```
SET DSTRACE = !mb[bytes]
```

► **Running the backlinker process.** Because the internal NDS identifiers are changed when upgrading to NDS 8, the backlinker process has to update backlinked objects in order for them to be consistent. After upgrading to NDS eDirectory, Novell recommends that you force the backlinker to run by issuing a SET DSTRACE=*B command at the server console. If you don't manually force the backlinker to run, the process runs automatically after 50 minutes; but before it has completed, some objects might be in an inconsistent state. Therefore, forcing the backlinker to run right away speeds up the clean up. Running the backlinker is especially important on servers that do not contain a replica as they are the ones that are most likely to have backlinks.

► **Reassigning file system trustees on NFS Gateway volumes.** The NDS eDirectory installation process does not upgrade trustee assignments on NFS Gateway volumes. If you are hosting NFS Gateway volumes on a server upgraded to NDS eDirectory, those trustee assignments are mapped to nonexistent trustees, thus are useless. You need to first delete the inaccurate trustee assignments using the following steps, and then reassign them:

1. On the server, load UNICON.NLM and authenticate to NDS.

2. Select Start/Stop Services ⇨ NFS Gateway Server ⇨ Del. This stops the NDS Gateway Server service. Exit out of UNICON.

3. From a workstation, delete the file SYS:\NFSGW\SFS????.DAT.

4. At the server, load UNICON.NLM again and authenticate to NDS.

5. Select Start/Stop Services ⇨ NFS Gateway Server to restart the service.

Installing NDS on Non-NetWare Servers

At the time of this writing, NDS eDirectory supports the following non-NetWare platforms:

- ▶ Windows NT/2000
- ▶ Sun Solaris
- ▶ Red Hat Linux

TIP

As mentioned in Chapter 1, regardless of the platform, ensure the network time between the servers in the NDS tree is synchronized because consistent timestamping of NDS events is important for NDS health as well as security. As is described in Chapter 3, the Network Time Protocol (NTP) is the most common time synchronization implementation across different operating system platforms. Therefore, check the documentation for your particular operating system platform and enable NTP. It is okay if you're using a different method for time synchronziation as NDS *doesn't* depend on the protocol or method used for time synchronization, but only that network time is synchronized.

The following sections provide an overview of installing NDS eDirectory on these platforms.

Windows NT/2000

NDS eDirectory can be installed into a Windows NT/2000-only or a mixed Windows NT/2000/NetWare environment. NDS eDirectory for Windows

NT/2000 does not require a NetWare server to perform to full capacity. Therefore, you can have a *pure* Windows NT/2000 network and still take full advantage of NDS eDirectory.

The minimum system requirement for NDS eDirectory on Windows NT/2000 is as follows:

- ▶ Intel-based processor; Windows NT/2000 on DEC Alpha is not supported.

- ▶ Windows NT server 4.0 with Service Pack 3 or higher with Y2K patch; Service Pack 5 or higher is recommended.

- ▶ A static IP address.

- ▶ Pentium 200 with 128MB RAM and a monitor color palette set to a number higher than 16.

- ▶ Administrative rights to the Windows NT/2000 server and to all portions of the NDS tree that contain domain-enabled User objects. For the first NDS installation, you need administrative rights to [Root] of the tree in order to extend the schema.

- ▶ If you're running a mixed NetWare/NT/2000 environment and plan to share the NDS tree on these platforms, one of the following version of NetWare is required:

  - • NetWare 4.11 server with Support Pack 6 or higher. The DS.NLM version of NetWare 4.11 servers must be 5.99a or later.

  - • NetWare 4.2.

  - • NetWare 5.0 with Support Pack 3 or later.

  - • NetWare 5.1.

- ▶ Workstations running Novell Client for Windows 95 3.0 or higher or Novell Client for Windows NT 4.5 or higher.

Once your system meets the specification, you can download the latest version of eDirectory for Windows NT/2000 from Novell's Web site at www. novell.com/download/#NDS and any patches from http://support. novell.com/misc/patlst.htm. You'll need a valid serial number from a previously purchased NDS eDirectory, NDS eDirectory Corporate Edition, or NetWare 5.*x* product to download NDS eDirectory but not the patches. During the install, you are prompted for an NDS license. Use the license diskette that came with your copy of NDS eDirectory, NDS eDirectory Corporate Edition, or NetWare 5.*x*.

Like NDS eDirectory for NetWare, NDS eDirectory for Windows NT/2000 is available for download in a series of self-extracting files or a single full self-extracting file (.EXE). All files must be downloaded and extracted before NDS eDirectory can be installed. Put these files into a temporary installation directory (for example, C:\EDIR) on the Windows system that you'll be installing NDS eDirectory on. In the installation directory, extract each executable and follow the onscreen instructions.

If you're installing NDS eDirectory into an existing NDS tree where NetWare servers exist, one of the DSREPAIR.NLM modules provided with the product must be run on the server containing the Master of the [Root] replica. Refer to the "Run DSREPAIR Before Upgrading" section earlier to determine the version of DSREPAIR.NLM required and the steps to run DSREPAIR.

NDS eDirectory Corporate Edition

The procedure for installing NDS eDirectory Corporate Edition for Windows 2000/NT is very similar to the of NDS eDirectory for Windows NT/2000, except you have two more options to choose from in the opening screen: Integrate NT Domains with NDS and Integrate Microsoft Exchange Accounts with NDS.

It should also be noted that NDS eDirectory Corporate Edition (regardless of the platform) includes the following:

► NDS Server that allows you to place replicas of eDirectory locally on the server — Windows NT/2000 Primary Domain Controllers (PDCs) and Backup Domain Controllers (BDCs) , Solaris Sun server, and Red Hat Linux server.

► Windows-based NetWare Administrator and Java-based ConsoleOne to manage all your network users and resources.

► Windows-based NDS Manager to manage partitions, replicas, servers, and the eDirectory schema.

► Novell Client to provide users with access to all eDirectory features.

► LDAP server that provides an open structure for integration with applications written to the Internet standard.

► A bulkload utility that allows you to add millions of objects to the directory in one move using the LDIF data format.

- A repair utility (ndsrepair) to repair and correct problems with the eDirectory database, such as records, schema, bindery objects, and external references.

- A backup utility (ndsbackup) to back up and restore eDirectory objects and schema information.

The Installation Wizard

Being a Windows "application," NDS eDirectory uses an Installation Wizard, thus it is easy to install. The procedure for installing NDS eDirectory is as follows:

1. If the server is being installed into an existing NDS tree, ensure its time is synchronized with the servers in that tree before you proceed.

2. If you're installing the server into an existing tree, check that all the replicas in the partition that you're installing the server into are in the ON state. This can be verified using NDS Manager.

3. At the Windows NT/2000 server, log on as Administrator or as a user with administrative privileges.

4. Run SETUP.EXE from the extracted downloaded file.

TIP NDS eDirectory on Windows NT/2000 may be installed on a Windows NT/2000 Workstation, but NDS eDirectory Corporate Edition needs to be installed on a Windows NT/2000 Server if you wish to integrate the domain into NDS.

TIP During the installation, you can click Help for detailed information on each installation screen.

5. Select which components to install — NDS or ConsoleOne (see Figure 2.1). You can install the components separately or together. The following steps are based on installing both components at the same time.

NOTE The opening screen of the NDS eDirectory for Windows NT/2000 installation shows NDS for NT, which is the previous name of the product.

6. Check both the Install Novell Directory Services and Install ConsoleOne checkboxes. This installs NDS eDirectory and the Java-based ConsoleOne management utility.

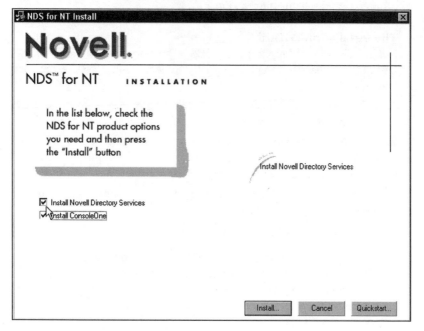

FIGURE 2.1   *When starting the NDS eDirectory installation for Windows NT/2000 note that only ConsoleOne is included with NDS eDirectory; NetWare Administrator and NDS Manager are not included.*

7. The installation process checks for the current release of the Novell Client software. If one is not found or an older version is detected, SETUP installs or updates it, and then restarts the server. Figure 2.2 shows the Novell Client installation dialog box. Click Custom Installation option and then select only the Client component for installation. The next screen prompts you to select a protocol option; available options are:

- IP only (remove IPX if present)
- IP with IPX compatibility
- IP and IPX
- IPX

F I G U R E   2 . 2   *Select Custom Installation so you can decide which*
components to install. Ensure only the Client component
is selected.

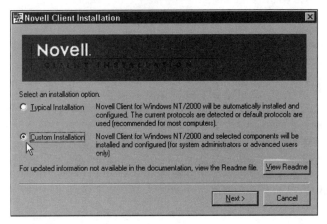

Select the desire option and click Next to continue. Click NDS
(NetWare 4.*x* or later) for the connection type. Then click Finish
to complete the client installation.

8. After the client is installed, click OK to restart your machine. The next
phase of the installation commences after you log in again — you now
see a Novell Client GUI instead of the Windows NT/2000 login interface. If you don't already have an NDS tree in place, perform a login to
Windows NT/2000 only by checking the Workstation only box.

9. The first step in the next phase is to select a setup language. Select the
desired one from the drop down list and then click OK to continue.

10. ConsoleOne is the first management utility to be installed. Follow the
Setup Wizard prompts to complete the installation.

11. After ConsoleOne has been installed, an Installation Wizard starts up
and runs you through the NDS eDirectory installation steps. You are
prompted for a license diskette. Use the license diskette that came with
your copy of NDS eDirectory, NDS eDirectory Corporate Edition, or
NetWare 5.*x*.

NOTE

If you choose to not install the license at this point, security services are not installed. That means any service that requires security services, such as SAS, PKI, and LDAP does not function. If you choose to install the license at a later time, you'll need to perform another NDS installation.

12. You are then given the option to either create a new NDS tree or install the server into an existing tree. Click the appropriate radio button and then click Next to continue. If you're creating a new tree, you are prompted to enter the related NDS information, such as tree name, server object name (which is based on your Windows NT/2000 computer name) and context, Admin username, context, and password. If inserting into an existing tree, you need to specify the tree name you wish to insert into and the server object name and context; you need to supply a username (normally Admin) and password that has rights to the tree.

13. The next screen shows that a total of six products are installed. They are:

    • NDS eDirectory

    • LDAP Services

    • WAN Traffic Manager

    • Secure Authentication Services (SAS) including SSL

    • Novell PKI Services

    • Storage Management Services (SMS)

    Click Finish to continue.

14. After the files are copied and products installed, you are prompted to restart the server. Click OK to reboot.

NOTE

When you're installing NDS eDirectory Corporate Edition and you selected only Installing Novell Directory Services as a component, the Domain Object Wizard, which integrates NT Domains into NDS, does not appear.

Upon restarting the server, a number of NDS-related services are automatically started (see Figure 2.3). You can use the NDS Services applet, found in Control Panel (see Figure 2.4) to manage these and other related services. You'll find a shortcut to ConsoleOne placed on your desktop.

FIGURE 2.3 The Bindery, DS, NLDAP, and PKI_SERVER services are automatically started upon server boot.

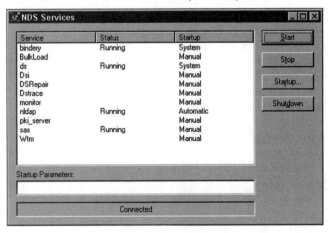

FIGURE 2.4 Use the NDS Services applet to manage NDS eDirectory-related services.

Also created, for both NDS eDirectory and NDS eDirectory Corporate Edition, is a Share called SYS: on the NT server (see Figure 2.5), using C:\NOVELL.

The default permission is Full Control for Administrator and Read for Everyone.

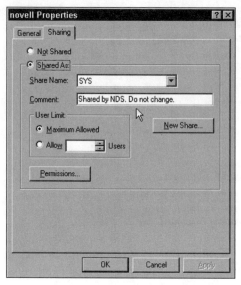

If you downloaded any patches for NDS eDirectory, apply them according to the documentation included with the patches.

Sun Solaris

NDS eDirectory on Solaris comprises the NDS server (with LDAP Services and Master replica support), SSL, and NDS server utilities (such as NDS Manager) which provide Read/Write replicas of NDS on the Solaris system. The NDS server component needs to be installed on all Solaris systems you want to place an NDS replica on.

Similar to NDS eDirectory on Windows NT/2000, NDS eDirectory on Solaris can be installed into a Solaris-only or a mixed Solaris/NetWare/Windows NT/ 2000/Linux environment. NDS eDirectory for Solaris does not require a NetWare server to perform to full capacity. Therefore, you can have a *pure* Solaris network and still take full advantage of NDS eDirectory.

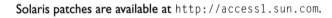

The minimum system requirements for NDS eDirectory on Sun Solaris are as follows:

- Solaris 2.6 or Solaris 7 (SPARC platform edition) with the latest recommended patches

  Solaris patches are available at http://access1.sun.com.

TIP

- A minimum of 64MB of RAM. To run the NDS server and LDAP server, a minimum of 128MB RAM is recommended
- Enabled for multicast routing; the steps are discussed later in this section
- 21MB of disk space to install the NDS server (including LDAP server and Novell Public Key Infrastructure PKI, services). Add 35 KB of disk space per 100 certificates and 3MB per 1000 User objects in the replica
- 3MB of disk space to install the NDS User Account Management (UAM) component
- Windows 95/98 or Windows NT/2000 workstation with 128MB of RAM and 125MB of disk space for the management utilities — you'll also need it to initially extract the necessary installation files from the download
- Novell Client for Windows 95/98 version 3 or higher, or Windows NT version 4.5 or higher

Once your system meets the specification, you can download the latest version of eDirectory for Solaris from Novell's Web site at www.novell.com/download/#NDS and patches from http://support.novell.com/misc/patlst.htm. You'll need a valid serial number from a previously purchased NDS eDirectory, NDS eDirectory Corporate Edition, or NetWare 5.x product to download NDS eDirectory but not the patches. During the install, you are prompted for an NDS license. Please use the license diskette that came with your copy of NDS eDirectory, NDS eDirectory Corporate Edition, or NetWare 5.x.

Like NDS eDirectory for NetWare, NDS eDirectory for Solaris is available for download in a series of self-extracting files or a single full self-extracting file (.EXE). All files must be downloaded and extracted before NDS eDirectory can be installed. Put these files into a temporary installation directory (for example, C:\EDIR) on a Windows machine that you'll be using to stage the installation of eDirectory. In the installation directory, extract each executable and follow the onscreen instructions.

If you're installing NDS eDirectory into an existing NDS tree where NetWare servers exist, one of the DSREPAIR.NLM modules provided with the product must be run on the server containing the Master of the [Root] replica. Refer to the "Run DSREPAIR Before Upgrading" section earlier to determine the version of DSREPAIR.NLM required and the steps to run DSREPAIR.

You need to perform two separate installs. One on the Solaris server to install eDirectory. After completing the installation on the Solaris host, you need to run the Windows Setup program on the Windows workstation that is going to be used for administration. This program installs the management tools.

NOTE
Like NDS eDirectory on Windows NT/2000, you can install the Solaris version on either the Server or Workstation. In the following discussion, the term "server" refers to both Solaris Server and Solaris Workstation, unless otherwise specified.

The procedure for installing NDS eDirectory on the Solaris server is as follows:

1. If the server is being installed into an existing NDS tree, ensure its time is synchronized with the servers in that tree before you proceed. Easiest is to use NTP to synchronize time; refer to the xntpd(1M) man page — online documentation — or the printed documentation, for more information.

2. Enable the Solaris server you are installing the product on for multicast routing. Enter the following command to check if the host is enabled for multicast routing:

   /usr/bin/netstat -nr

   The following entry should be present in the routing table:

   224.0.0.0 host IP address

   If it is not present, log in as *root* and enter the following command to enable multicast routing:

   route add -interface -netmask "240.0.0.0" "224.0.0.0" hostname

3. If you're installing the server into an existing tree, check that all the replicas in the partition that you're installing the server into are in the ON state. This can verified using NDS Manager.

4. If you don't have a product CD-ROM, you can either download the partial files or the full image file from Novell (www.novell.com/download/#NDS). If you downloaded the full file nds8sol.exe, you need to execute it on a Windows machine to create the nds8sol.tar.Z and nds8win.exe files. You then need to either FTP or somehow get your nds8sol.tar.Z file to the Solaris machine to be uncompressed.

5. Login to Solaris as *root*.

6. If you have the CD-ROM, insert the product CD-ROM, change to the Solaris directory on the CD-ROM and run nds-install — this is a shell script. Skip to Step 9.

7. Enter the following command to extract the NDS eDirectory installation files.

```
uncompress -c nds8sol.tar.Z | tar -xvf -
```

The files are extracted into the /EXPcdrom directory. The NICI Foundation key is extracted to the /opt/nds directory.

8. Change to the /EXPcdrom/Solaris directory and run nds-install — this is a shell script.

9. Choose to install the NDS Server. The installation program proceeds to add various packages of the NDS Server component.

NOTE

If the Install program cannot locate the NICI Foundation key file in the default locations, you are prompted to enter the complete path to the NICI Foundation key file. You are prompted if the path entered is not valid or the file cannot be located. If you skip the installation of NICI, you can not create certificates.

10. The program asks for configuration information. Although you can configure the product later using ndscfg, it is best that you configure now to ensure proper functioning of the product. Enter the following configuration parameters in the ndscfg.inp file, which is opened in the default editor:

- Name (with full context) of the user with administration rights to the root of the tree.

- Tree name.

- Server context.

- (Optional) DB files directory (default is /var/nds/dib).

- (Optional) To install NDS in a new tree, specify the value "Yes" for the Create NDS Tree parameter.
- (Optional) To install LDAP Services for NDS, specify the value "Yes" for the Install LDAP Services parameter.
- (Optional) If yes to install LDAP, enter a name with full context (for example, cn=yourldapgroup.ou=yourcontainer.o=yourorganization) for the LDAP Group object and specify the value "Yes" for the Create LDAP Group object parameter. If the specified context does not exist, the default LDAP Group object (LDAP Group *servername*) is created in the context where the server is located.

NOTE

The following code is a sample section of the ndscfg.inp. Enter the product configuration information in this file. This file is also displayed when you are installing and configuring the product using the ndscfg -install option. The current preferred values are displayed. If the parameter is required, replace the asterisks (*) with the required value.

```
#NDSCFG: Install Parameters
#Please enter the values for the following parameters
and save & quit the editor
The current or preferred values for the parameters are
displayed. You may change them.
Common Input parameters for Install


#ParamName: Admin Name and Context
#Description: The NDS name with context of the user
with
# admin rights to the root of the tree
#Example: Admin Name and
Context=CN=admin.OU=is.O=mycompany
#Required: Required
Admin Name and Context=*********


#ParamName: Tree Name
```

#Description: The name of the NDS tree the product
should be installed into
#Example: Tree Name=CORPORATE_TREE
#Required: Required
Tree Name=*********

#Parameters specific to NDS module

#ParamName: Create NDS Tree
#Description: Install a fresh NDS tree
#Example:Create NDS tree=NO
#Required: Optional
Create NDS Tree=NO

#ParamName: Server Context
#Description: The context in which the NDS server
object should reside.
If the context does not exist, it is created.
#Example:Server Context=ou=myContainer.o=myCompany
#Required: Required
Server Context=*********

#ParamName: DB Files Dir
#Description: The directory in which the NDS database
files are stored
#Example:DB Files Dir=/var/nds/dib
#Required: Optional
DB Files Dir=/var/nds/dib

#ParamName: Install LDAP
#Description: Install LDAP Services for NDS
#Example:Install LDAP=YES
#Required: Optional
Install LDAP=YES

```
#ParamName: LDAP Group Object
#Description: The distinguished name of the LDAP Group
object to which
# the LDAP Server should belong
#Example:LDAP Group
Object=cn=myLDAPgroup.ou=myContainer.o=myCompany
#Required: Optional
LDAP group Object=*********


#ParamName: Create LDAP group Object
#Description: Create the LDAP group Object if it does
not exist.
# If the specified LDAP Group Object is invalid, the
default group
# object is created.
#Example:Create LDAP Group Object=NO
#Required: Optional
Create LDAP Group Object=NO
```

I I. Save the information and close the editor.

I 2. Enter the password of the User with administration rights, when prompted.

TIP

If you need any help in the installation process, lookup the Quick Reference Card (in HTML format) available in the EXPcdrom directory, as well as the Administrator's Guide in PDF format. If you have the product CD-ROM, these files are located in the root directory of the CD-ROM.

After a successful NDS Server component install, the following daemons are running:

▶ **slpuasa** — the SLP (Service Location Protocol) User Agent and Service Agent daemon

▶ **ndsd** — the NDS server daemon

You can verify their presence using the ps command.

If you've installed LDAP services for NDS, then LDAP services will also run as part of NDS. In addition, the following configuration files are copied to the host:

▸ **/etc/nds.conf** — the NDS configuration file

▸ **/etc/slp.conf** — the SLP configuration file

If you need to install the NDS management tools, following these steps:

1. If you don't have a product CD-ROM, you need to either download the partial files or the full image file from Novell (`www.novell.com/download/#NDS`). If you downloaded the full file nds8sol.exe, you need to execute it on a Windows machine to create the nds8sol.tar.Z and nds8win.exe files. Run nds8win.exe to extract the contents.

   If you download the three files; nds8winsp1.exe, nds8winsp2.exe, and nds8winsp3.exe, save them to the same directory on the Windows system. Then execute the files to extract their contents.

2. Run WINSETUP.EXE to install the NDS management tools. If you have the product CD-ROM, it is located in the Windows directory on the CD-ROM.

3. You're presented with options (see Figure 2.6) to install ConsoleOne (which also and copies the NDS PKI and LDAP snap-ins) and NDS administration utilities (NDS Manger and NetWare Administrator). Select the desired option as you need to install one component at a time.

4. Follow the instructions given in the Setup Wizard.

5. If the Windows system didn't already have the Novell Client installed, you can install the necessary Novell Client DLL by running SETUP. EXE in the Install directory on the Windows system into which you have installed ConsoleOne (the default path is \Novell\ConsoleOne\x.x; where *x.x* is the version number of ConsoleOne and at the time of this writing, it is 1.2).

A "Novell (Common)" folder is created containing shortcuts to the various administration tools, such as NetWare Administrator, NDS Manager, and login utility.

NOTE

If you downloaded any patches for NDS eDirectory on Solaris, apply them according to the documentation included with the patches.

F I G U R E   2.6 *You'll have the option to install these NDS Management utilities either locally or to a NetWare volume.*

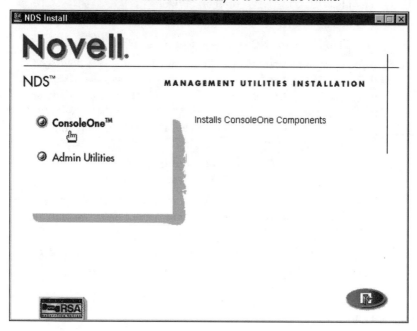

Using TIMESYNC.NLM

If you want to synchronize time on Solaris servers with NetWare 5 servers, use TIMESYNC.NLM version 5.09 or later. If the xntpd and ntpdate are running, kill the two processes. To set up the Solaris server as a TimeSync server, complete the following steps:

1. Edit /etc/inet/ntp.conf to include the following lines:

```
server 127.127.1.0
fudge 127.127.1.0 stratum 0
```

2. Run /usr/lib/inet/xntpd to restart the xntpd daemon.

3. Run ntptrace and the following information should be displayed after a few minutes:

```
localhost:stratum1, offset 0.000060. synch distance
0.01004, refid 'LCL'
```

The stratum number can be any number between 1 and 14.

To set up a Solaris machine as a TimeSync client, complete the following steps:

1. Edit /etc/inet/ntp.conf to include the following line:

```
server IP address of the TimeSync server
```

2. Use the date command to adjust the time on the Solaris machine to be as close to the TimeSync server as possible. Repeat the following command till the time is adjusted to the TimeSync server:

```
ntpdate IP address of the timesync server
```

3. Run /usr/lib/inet/xntpd to restart the xntpd daemon.

4. Run ntptrace and the following information should be displayed after a few minutes:

```
localhost:stratum 2, offset 0.000055, synch distance
0.02406 solaris server name: stratum 1, offset
0.000030, synch distance 0.01064, refid 'LCL'
```

The stratum number in the first line can be any number between 2 and 15. If the number is below 16, it means that the machine is synchronized with the machine named in Step 2.

Linux

NDS eDirectory on Linux comprises the NDS server (with LDAP Services and Master replica support), SSL, and NDS server utilities (such as NDS Manager) which provide Read/Write replicas of NDS on the Linux system. The NDS server component needs to be installed on all Solaris systems you want to place an NDS replica on.

Similar to NDS eDirectory on Windows NT/2000 and Solaris discussed earlier, NDS eDirectory on Linux can be installed into an Linux-only or a mixed Solaris/NetWare/Windows NT/2000/Linux environment. NDS eDirectory for Linux does not require a NetWare server to perform to full capacity. Therefore, you can have a *pure* Linux network and still take full advantage of NDS eDirectory.

NDS eDirectory for Linux provides the following features and utilities on Linux systems:

- NDS server component
- LDAP version 3 server (with SSL)
- User Account Management (UAM) module (part of Corporate Edition)
- ndsbulkload utility to load LDAP data (in LDIF format) into NDS

- ndstrace utility to trace the NDS activity
- ndsrepair utility to repair the NDS database
- ndsbackup utility to backup and restore NDS objects
- SLP User and Service Agents
- Java-based ConsoleOne utility and Windows-based NetWare Administrator to manage NDS objects
- Windows based NDS Manager utility to manage NDS partitions
- Novell Public Key Infrastructure (PKI) Services that allow you to protect confidential data transmissions over public communications channels such as the Internet

The minimum system requirement for NDS eDirectory on Linux is as follows:

- Linux kernel versions 2.2.12 or 2.2.15
- Linux glibc version 2.1.3
- A minimum of 64MB of RAM. To run the NDS server and LDAP server a minimum of 70MB of RAM is recommended
- 21MB of disk space to install the NDS server (including the LDAP server). Add 35 KB of disk space per 100 certificates in the replica
- Windows 95/98 or Windows NT system with 128MB of RAM and 125MB of disk space to install the Windows component
- Novell Client for Windows 95/98 version 3.2 or higher, or Windows NT version 4.7 or higher

Once your system meets the specification, you can download the latest version of eDirectory for Solaris from Novell's Web site at www.novell.com/download/#NDS and patches from http://support.novell.com/misc/patlst.htm. You'll need a valid serial number from a previously purchased NDS eDirectory or NDS eDirectory Corporate Edition product — unlike other versions of NDS eDirectory, you *can't* use a NetWare 5 serial number to download NDS eDirectory for Linux; no serial number is needed to download the patches. During the install, you are prompted for an NDS license. Please use the license diskette that came with your copy of NDS eDirectory or NDS eDirectory Corporate Edition.

Like NDS eDirectory for NetWare, NDS eDirectory for Linux is available for download in a series of self-extracting files or a single full self-extracting file (.EXE). All files must be downloaded and extracted before NDS eDirectory can be installed. Put these files into a temporary installation directory (for example, C:\EDIR) on a Windows machine that you use to expand the necessary eDirectory files. In the installation directory, extract each executable and follow the onscreen instructions.

If you're installing NDS eDirectory into an existing NDS tree where NetWare servers exist, one of the DSREPAIR.NLM modules provided with the product must be run on the server containing the Master of the [Root] replica. Refer to the "Run DSREPAIR Before Upgrading" section earlier to determine the version of DSREPAIR.NLM required and the steps to run DSREPAIR.

You need to perform two separate installs. One on the Linux system to install eDirectory. After completing the installation on the Linux host, you need to run the Windows Setup program on the Windows workstation that is going to be used for administration. This program installs the management tools.

NOTE

Like NDS eDirectory on Windows NT/2000 and Solaris, you can install the Linux version on either the Linux Server or Workstation. In the following discussion, the term "server" refers to both Linux Server and Linux Workstation, unless otherwise specified.

The procedure for installing NDS eDirectory on the Linux server is as follows:

I. If the server is being installed into an existing NDS tree, ensure its time is synchronized with the servers in that tree before you proceed. Easiest is to use NTP to synchronize time; refer to your main pages for more information.

2. Enable the Linux system you are installing the product on for multicast routing. Enter the following command to check if the host is enabled for multicast routing:

`/usr/bin/netstat -nr`

The following entry should be present in the routing table:

`224.0.0.0 host IP address`

If it is not present, log in as *root* and enter the following command to enable multicast routing:

`route add -interface -netmask "240.0.0.0" "224.0.0.0" hostname`

3. If you're installing the server into an existing tree, check that all the replicas in the partition that you're installing the server into are in the ON state. This can be verified using NDS Manager.

4. If you don't have a product CD-ROM, you can either download the partial files or the full image file from Novell (www.novell.com/download/#NDS). If you downloaded the full file ndslinuxfull.tar.gzyou then need to either FTP or somehow get this file to the Linux machine to be uncompressed.

5. Login to Linux as *root*.

6. Extract the contents using the following command:

`gzip -dc ndslinuxfull.tar.gz | tar xvfP -`

This creates the ndslinux.tar.gz and ndswin.exe files in the /WWcdrom directory. You need to later FTP or somehow transfer your ndswin.exe file back to a Windows machine.

7. Extract the installation files using the following command:

`gzip -dc ndslinux.tar.gz | tar xvfP -`

8. Change to the /WWcdrom/Linux directory and run nds-install — this is a shell script.

9. Choose to install the NDS Server. The installation program proceeds to add various packages of the NDS Server component.

NOTE

If the Install program cannot locate the NICI Foundation key file in the default locations, you are prompted to enter the complete path to the NICI Foundation key file. You are prompted if the path entered is not valid or the file cannot be located. If you skip the installation of NICI, you cannot create certificates.

10. The program asks for configuration information. Although you can configure the product later using ndscfg, it is best that you configure now to ensure proper functioning of the product. Enter the following configuration parameters in the ndscfg.inp file, which is opened in the default editor:

- Name (with full context) of the user with administration rights to the root of the tree.
- Tree name.
- Server context.
- (Optional) DB files directory (default is /var/nds/dib).
- (Optional) To install NDS in a new tree, specify the value "Yes" for the Create NDS Tree parameter.

- (Optional) To install LDAP Services for NDS, specify the value "Yes" for the Install LDAP Services parameter.
- (Optional) If yes to install LDAP, enter a name with full context (for example, cn=yourldapgroup.ou=yourcontainer.o=yourorganization) for the LDAP Group object and specify the value "Yes" for the Create LDAP Group object parameter. If the specified context does not exist, the default LDAP Group object (LDAP Group *servername*) is created in the context where the server is located.

11. Save the information and close the editor.

12. Enter the password of the User with administration rights, when prompted.

After a successful NDS Server component install, the following daemons are running:

- **slpuasa** — the SLP (Service Location Protocol) User Agent and Service Agent daemon
- **ndsd** — the NDS server daemon

You can verify their presence using the ps command.

If you install LDAP services for NDS, then LDAP services will also run as part of NDS. In addition, the following configuration files are copied to the host:

- **/etc/nds.conf** — the NDS configuration file
- **/etc/slp.conf** — the SLP configuration file

If you need to install the NDS management tools, follow these steps:

1. If you don't have a product CD-ROM, you need to either download the partial files or the full image file from Novell (www.novell.com/download/#NDS). If you downloaded the full file ndslinuxfull.tar.gz, you need to get the ndswin.exe created previously in Step 6 to a Windows machine and then run nds8win.exe to extract the contents.

If you download the three files; nds8winsp1.exe, nds8winsp2.exe, and nds8winsp3.exe, save them to the same directory on the Windows system. Then execute the files to extract their contents.

2. Run WINSETUP.EXE to install the NDS management tools. If you have the product CD-ROM, it is located in the Windows directory on the CD-ROM.

3. You're presented with options to install ConsoleOne (which also copies the NDS PKI and LDAP snap-ins) and NDS administration utilities (NDS Manger and NetWare Administrator). Select the desired option as you need to install one component at a time; you'll have the option to install the utilities locally or to a NetWare volume.

4. Follow the instructions given in the Setup Wizard.

5. If the Windows system didn't already have the Novell Client installed, you can install the necessary Novell Client DLL by running SETUP. EXE in the Install directory on the Windows system into which you have installed ConsoleOne (the default path is \Novell\ConsoleOne\ x.x; where x.x is the version number of ConsoleOne and, at the time of this writing, it is 1.2).

A "Novell (Common)" folder is created containing shortcuts to the various administration tools, such as NetWare Administrator, NDS Manager, and login utility.

 If you downloaded any patches for NDS eDirectory on Linux, apply them according to the documentation included with the patches.

NOTE

This chapter covered the upgrade and installation procedures of eDirectory on NetWare, Windows NT/2000, Sun Solaris, and Linux platforms. In the next chapter, you'll learn how to set up and design your NDS tree.

## CHAPTER 3

Network Infrastructures, Resources, and NDS Tree Design

The previous chapter covered the concepts of NDS design and some of the tasks you need to understand in order to have a successful NDS design. This chapter deals with the nuts-and-bolts of doing the design work. Depending on the size of your network, number of users, and technical levels of your users, a number of ways exist to design an NDS tree. This chapter shows you how to design a tree that fits your immediate needs and still facilitates future expansions. To help illustrate the process, a mid-size fictitious company, Universal Import, is used as an example to guide you through the design concepts presented in this chapter.

Also discussed in this chapter are time synchronization, NDS fault tolerance considerations, and the use of WAN Traffic Manager to manage your replica synchronization traffic across WAN links using WAN policies. Although not part of the NDS, time synchronization plays a critical role in the health and performance of NDS. Therefore, you should pay some attention to your time synchronization implementation.

▶ • ◀

NDS Directory Tree Design Tasks and Concepts

Several major tasks must be completed in a typical NDS design cycle. The flow chart shown in Figure 3.1 provides one possible NDS design cycle. This cycle involves both the organizational design and (high-level) technical design strategies. The cycle is a closed loop. As changes in the organization or its network occur, the design cycle begins again.

The work involved during the design approach phase includes the following tasks:

- ▶ Polling the users and network personnel most affected by the design

- ▶ Gathering business information related to network design

- ▶ Determining the scope of the design process

- ▶ Creating a preliminary schedule

These tasks help the project team set realistic expectations, based on business requirements. Then the design and implementation can proceed without unpleasant surprises. Organizing the project in this way also gives team members an idea of their roles, milestones, and responsibilities throughout the process.

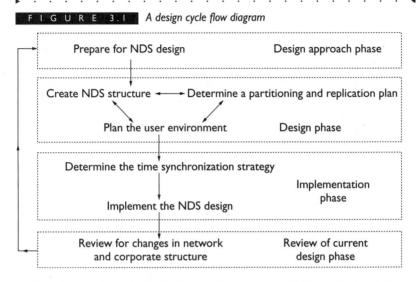

FIGURE 3.1   A design cycle flow diagram

The design phase is divided into three steps, which can be carried out simultaneously. However, changes in any one of these areas (NDS structure, partition and replication, and user environment) can and do affect and impact each other. For example, if some users require Bindery Services for a specific application, you'll have to think about the impact of placing an extra replica on these users' server, and that may have implication on how you best partition the tree, which may impact on the NDS structure design.

The actual implementation phase can be divided into two areas, depending on the actual rollout plan. Before you implement your NDS design, you need to configure time synchronization for all the servers on the network. Then you work with your team to roll out, monitor, and fine-tune your design.

NOTE

Chapter 8, "Managing Time Synchronization," explains how to make the time synchronization process fault tolerant without creating undue network traffic, and Chapters 5, "Creating Users, Groups, Aliases and other Object Types," and 7, "Managing Partition and Replication," outline the process of creating your NDS tree, user environment, and partitions and replicas based on the design standards you previously set forth.

If you have a test environment, it is best to implement your design in it before moving to production.

The review of current design is an ongoing process and should be part of the regular responsibilities of the network administrator. Evaluating and analyzing the organization and network use are often a natural result of such management tasks as creating users, configuring printing, determining security, and optimizing performance.

Creating an NDS Structure

Designing the NDS tree is the most important procedure in the design and implementation of an NDS network. Proper tree design provides the following benefits:

- Partitioning and replication can be completed successfully and easily
- The network can accommodate growth without complicated revisions or costly upgrades
- NDS trees can be merged more easily
- Other network services and network accessibility can be implemented more easily
- The NDS tree can be navigated more intuitively

Designing or creating the NDS tree structure includes setting a standard for NDS object names and values. This procedure also includes designing the upper and lower layers of the NDS tree. These tasks help you set up NDS so that it works efficiently, it is easy for network users to use, and it is easy for network administrators to manage. Furthermore, designing the NDS tree also lays a foundation for successfully completing the task for determining a partition and replica strategy.

The details of designing the upper and lower layers of the NDS tree is covered in Chapter 3, "Network Infrastructure, Resources, and NDS Design." The following sections cover naming related topics.

NDS Naming Conventions

Any solid and consistent design has a naming standard or convention. This also is true for NDS tree designs. A consistent NDS naming convention provides guidelines for naming objects such as Users, Groups, Printers, Print Queues,

Servers, and Volumes. Having a unified naming scheme greatly helps users identify available resources and navigate the tree.

In general, you should keep the names short, yet at the same time they should be simple and descriptive. One common practice is to shorten a word by removing all the vowels. For example, Provo becomes PRV. If a word has a well-known abbreviation, use it instead of removing the vowels. For instance, Toronto becomes TO or TOR, San Francisco becomes SFO, and LA for Los Angeles.

NOTE

Keep in mind that the maximum length for a distinguished name is 256 characters. This limit includes the typing characters, such as CN=, OU=, O=, and any embedded blanks.

Short User object names simplify logins for users — it is generally easier to remember a login name that's only three characters long rather than one that's 15. Short object names also help to reduce the amount of NDS data passed on the network. Consistency in use of capitalization is an effective naming scheme for differentiating between container and leaf objects — one convention is to use all caps for container objects and all lower case for leaf objects.

NDS treats blank spaces the same as underscores. Depending on the application, when referencing an NDS object that has embedded spaces, you may need to substitute each space with an underscore. Therefore, to minimize user confusion, you should avoid using blank spaces in NDS object names and use underscores instead.

To ensure consistent naming is used, you should create an NDS naming standards document containing the following:

▶ A list of each object used in the NDS tree.

▶ A specification of the standard you are using for each object, such as all Printer objects beginning with "PR_".

▶ An attribute naming standard for each object type. This specifies the object attributes that must be defined during NDS object creation. It should also define whether the attribute of an object is:

  • required

  • a system attribute value that is populated automatically by NDS

  • an optional attribute value you want your network administrator to define when an object is created

▶ A brief example for each object used.

For example, all User objects must have their Location and Telephone Number attribute entered by the network administrator during User object creation.

▶ A rationale for each object selected.

If you're not the network administrator that is also responsible for the day-to-day NDS object management, you should give a copy of the naming standard document to the network administrator or helpdesk people that are. Ensure the standard is adhered to.

TIP
You may choose to include other naming standards. For example, you can set standards for IP address deployment to routers, servers, and hubs/switches. This can simplify troubleshooting problems on your network.

Selecting a Tree Name

It may sound trivial that you have to assign a name to your NDS tree. However, keeping the following few considerations in mind when you're selecting a tree name saves you some headaches down the road:

▶ Use the name of the company in the tree name — for example, UNIVERSAL_IMPORT — but add "_TREE" to the end of it, as in UNIVERSAL_IMPORT_TREE (this way, any possible confusions, as outlined previously, can be easily avoided). The name of an NDS tree is limited to 33 characters, and should *not* include any trailing underscores.

▶ Ensure the name is unique within your network. For example, you should not have a tree called UNIVERSAL_IMPORT and a file server also called UNIVERSAL_IMPORT. This is because both resources advertise their presence on the network and having the same name can cause confusion.

▶ Ensure you don't have any top-level NDS object (such as an Organization) directly under [Root] that has the same name as the tree. This can cause some NDS applications to not function correctly because the API calls may get the two confused.

In some situations a company may have more than one NDS tree. In that case, you should name the trees such that their purpose is readily identified from the name. For example, a company may have a test tree in addition to the production tree for the purpose of testing without impacting production. In such a case, you should use TEST_TREE as part of the tree name for the nonproduction tree. In addition, when you have more than one NDS tree on the network, ensure the Preferred Tree parameter is correctly set in your workstation client properties (see Figure 3.2) to point to the right tree.

▶ . . . . ◀

F I G U R E   3 . 2 *Always set the Preferred Tree parameter if you have multiple NDS trees on your network.*

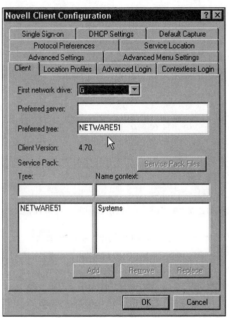

The Preferred Tree option forces the workstation to attach to the production tree, and not the test tree by mistake.

▶ . . . . ◀

Planning Considerations

In many respects, the planning of an NDS tree structure is very similar to planning your hard drive's directory structure — you want to keep your tree simple, not too flat, and the levels at no more than five to eight layers deep. Doing this makes your tree much easier to manage and navigate.

No "quick and hard" rules exist when it comes to designing your NDS tree because each installation is unique. Some common characteristics are shared by good tree designs, however. The following are some of the more common issues to consider when designing your NDS tree:

- ▶ Make network administration and maintenance (such as security assignments) simple.

- ▶ Keep your tree simple so that minimal to no user (re)training is required for the (new) environment.

- ▶ Keep the tree structure simple so that users can easily and efficiently find and access the various network resources. However, you should take advantage of the NDS security hierarchy when designing the tree — you'll read more about NDS security management in Chapter 9, "Troubleshooting Common Problems." In general, use a three to five layer design for a simple to medium-size tree, and five to eight levels for a complex tree design.

- ▶ If there's a need to support non NDS-aware applications, you need to give special consideration to tree partitioning and placement of replicas to enable Bindery Services; refer to Chapter 7, "Managing Partition and Replication." for detailed procedures on partitioning and replicating.

- ▶ Provide fault tolerance for the network. No one server down should prevent any users from accessing resources located on other servers.

NOTE

No right or wrong way exists to design an NDS tree. However, there always is a better way, and you only discover it after you have implemented your tree design and used it for a while. The NDS tree is not carved in stone once you implement it. You can always modify it at a later time if your needs change. However, beginning with a reasonably good, open, and scalable design reduces the changes you may need later.

While designing your NDS tree, consider the following questions:

- ▶ Do you have multiple departments?

- ▶ Do you have multiple locations/buildings?

- ▶ Do you have any department that is spread across multiple locations/buildings?

- ▶ Do your users travel between locations?

- ▶ Do your departments have their own file servers?

- ▶ Do you have applications that are not NDS-aware and thus require Bindery Services?

> ► Is the tree administrated centrally?
> ► What are the foreseeable future expansions plans for your company and network?

All these points influence how your NDS tree structure looks.

Let's consider a mid-size fictitious company called Universal Import. Universal Import has decided to jump on the NDS bandwagon to simplify the management of their network and prepare for e-commerce. Universal Import currently has only three departments — all located in the same building — and about 75 employees; the company does not really need multiple containers for its tree. However, plans are in the works to expand to two new remote locations, it has a number of departments and a couple of hundred users spread across three locations (possibly in different cities), its NDS tree would warrant a more complex design with multiple containers (to facilitate partitioning to cut down WAN traffic, for example).

Logical NDS Tree Structure

For networks of fewer than a couple of thousand objects (not necessarily User objects but NDS objects in general) with reliable LAN connections, you probably don't need to use the more advanced features of NDS (such as partitioning). NDS can take care of itself with its default settings. Some of these defaults are as follows:

> ► NDS keeps the tree as one single ([Root]) partition.
> ► NDS replicates the database to the first three NDS servers on the network. Those replicas are kept synchronized automatically.
> ► One tree is created, rather than multiple trees.
> ► A single Organization object is created (commonly named after your company).
> ► The Admin User object is created in the Organization container, as are the Server and Volume objects.

If you need to go beyond the defaults, an overall design goal to achieve for a good NDS tree structure is to have the tree resemble, to the extent possible, the shape of a pyramid. This pyramid structure (see Figure 3.3) means that you place few containers and objects near the top of the tree and should put most of your containers and objects at the bottom of the structure. The main advantage of this pyramid design is that the top levels are relatively static and they form the foundation upon which the bottom layers can be built. The bottom levels of the tree are more dynamic and allow for greater flexibility to change when your company organization changes.

► . . . . ◄

FIGURE 3.3 *A good NDS tree design should look like a pyramid where the majority of the objects are located at the bottom of the structure.*

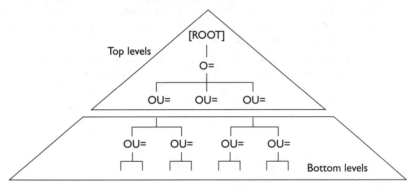

Another advantage of this pyramid structure is that it makes the partitioning of the tree much more natural and easy; it also helps to reduce the number of subordinate reference replicas from being created. For more information about subordinate reference and other replica types, refer to Chapter 1, "What is NDS and How Does It Work?"

NOTE

Subordinate reference, or SubRef, replicas are pointers between partitions and subordinate partitions and are automatically created and maintained by NDS. Because SubRefs participate in the synchronization process in a NetWare 4 environment (but not in a pure-NetWare 5 environment or in an eDirectory on non-NetWare environment), the number of SubRefs is more of a concern in NetWare 4 than it is in other configurations. However, the recommendation on keeping the tree structure as close to a pyramid structure as possible still holds even for NetWare 5 and eDirectory-based trees.

The alternative to the pyramid structure is to create a flat tree layout, as shown in Figure 3.4. A flat tree is generally *not* recommended because of the way it has to be partitioned and replicated. When the tree partition and replica layout becomes extremely flat (because the tree structure is flat), you can end up with many subordinate reference replicas because SubRefs are created on servers that have a copy of the parent partition but not the child partition; as a result, overhead is added to NDS synchronization traffic. These inefficiencies can result in poor performance (especially if you have replicas of the same partition located on servers separated by slow WAN links) and, thus, a less user-friendly environment for users and administrators.

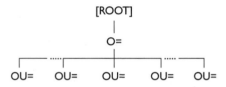

F I G U R E   3 . 4   *A flat structure is not as efficient as a pyramid one when the tree is of moderate size or larger. However, a flat layout is totally acceptable for a simple network.*

Three design approaches exist through which you can design your NDS tree structure: an organizational design which reflects a company's structure; a geographical approach that may be suitable if you have multiple locations or your departments are in different buildings or on different floors of the same building; and, a hybrid design that combines organizational and geographical information into the tree. The hybrid design is generally the more desirable of the three choices when working with medium to large installations.

These three different design concepts plus a 'simplistic approach' (which is ideal for small and medium sites) are discussed in the following sections.

Organizational Approach

When using the organizational approach, your tree structure reflects your company's organizational chart. Right under the object would be an Organization object to denote your company name. Underneath that, each department has its own Organizational Units (OUs) in the tree. This reflects how the company functions.

Under this model, Universal Import can design its tree as shown in Figure 3.5. Each of the three departments has its own OU. When the company later expands to include additional locations, additional OUs denoting the geographical locations may be created under the appropriate OU to indicate where the user is based. If more departments are created, additional OUs may be created under the O object to reflect the addition.

F I G U R E 3.5
An organizational approach for Universal Import's NDS tree design

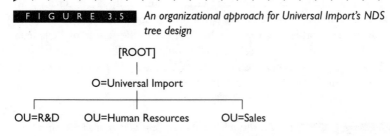

Care should, however, be taken when using this organizational-based implementation. It is often tempting to create an OU for every department you have in the company without giving much consideration to how many people actually works in that department. For example, it is not uncommon for a small or even mid-size company to have only one or two employees working in the Accounting department. It is not practical to create an OU for just a couple of users. In such cases, you should consolidate some departments together into a single OU, perhaps grouping those that have similar job functions, such as Accounting and Human Resources.

You should keep in mind such an approach can end up with a rather flat tree, which may not be desirable for reasons discussed at the beginning of this section. Another drawback of this design occurs if you have a department that is spread out across a number of locations (say, a number of different floors within the same building). It makes it difficult to determine the physical location of a given user from the User object.

Geographical Approach

If your company has many locations, you might want to consider turning the structure around a little by using a geographical approach instead of an organizational one. In a geographical model, instead of having the OUs directory under the Organization (O) for departments, the top level of the tree consists of Country (C) or Organization (O) containers for the different geographic locations; Locality (L) containers may be created at the lower levels to further denote various locations (such as L=East_Coast.C=US).

NOTE

Although defined within the schema, NetWare 4 did not provide the capability to create Locality objects using either NWAdmin or NETADMIN. You can, however, create the Locality containers using either NWAdmin or ConsoleOne shipped with NetWare 5, even on a NetWare 4-only tree.

Generally when using the geographical model, you don't "waste" the top level object (Organization) to identify the company. However, if the tree is shared by an organization that has multiple companies, then the use of Os to identify company names may be necessary.

Traditionally, one would generally use Os and OUs to denote the various geographic locations as shown in Figure 3.6. If your company has sites in different countries around the world, you can denote these locations using County containers under [Root]. For example, instead of having O=North_America and O=Europe to represent locations in Canada, the United States, Great Britain, France, and Italy, you can use Country objects to represent them, such as C=CA, C=US, C=BG, C=FR, and C=IT, respectively. A listing of the ISO (International Organization for Standardization) country codes may be found in Appendix A.

FIGURE 3.6 *A geographical approach for Universal Import's NDS tree design*

```
                          [ROOT]
                            |
        ┌───────────────────┼───────────────────┐
O=Future_Location_I   O=Head_Office      O=Future_Location_2
        ┌───────────────────┼───────────────────┐
  OU=3rd_Floor     OU=6th_Floor     OU=5th_Floor
```

The use of Country objects gives more (geographical) graduality to the tree. Of course, you can accomplish the same using Organization objects but the use of Country objects to represent countries and Locality objects to represent states and cities is more natural than using Organization or Organizational Unit objects.

NOTE When using Country objects to denote locations, you need to also keep in mind the company's operational policy. For example, if a company's operation is divided into a North American operation and a European operation, it may go against the company's view if Country objects are used as it would break down the locations too much.

WARNING Not all NetWare utilities, especially those of third party vendors, support the use of Locality object. Therefore, use Locality sparingly.

Similar to the organizational model, the geographical model works best for companies that have each of their separate divisions or departments — such as Sales — located at the same site. Otherwise, you are not able to easily tell if a given user is in Sales or R&D by simply looking at the location of the User object. This model can also suffer the flat-tree symptom if you are not careful.

A Hybrid Approach

In most cases, the best approach is to use a hybrid design that combines geographical and organizational information. Such a model doesn't have the drawbacks of either the geographical or organizational model discussed previously, such as difficulty in telling the location of a given user. Also, the hybrid approach is less susceptible to the flat-tree symptom.

When implementing a hybrid model, you need to determine the information pathways, and ways resources are shared within your company. You want to configure the tree to reflect the way people actually work and the resources they use, rather than reflect their location (geographical or organizational) within the company. In other words, the general implementation of this model is to have the top levels of your tree reflect your LAN/WAN infrastructure (generally based on location) and the lower levels a mixture of geographical and organizational structure.

Figure 3.7 shows a hybrid approach for Universal Export. At the very top level of the tree are three Os — O=Head_Office and two placeholder Os for future locations. The lower level indicates that the Research & Development department is spread across two floors in the building while the Sales and Human Resources departments are located on the same floor.

► · ◄

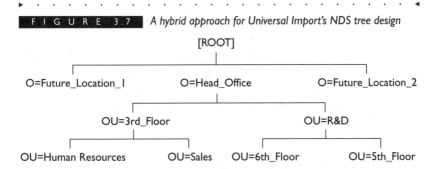

FIGURE 3.7 *A hybrid approach for Universal Import's NDS tree design*

This hybrid design concept generally results in an open and scalable tree. For example, if Universal Export's R&D department expands to more floors, an OU can be easily added. On the other hand, if more departments (such as Legal) are to be added, OUs can easily be added under OU=3rd_Floor or under O=Head_Office, depending on where they are located. You can see that it is much easier to design an open tree using the hybrid model than using either the organizational or geographical model.

NOTE The hybrid model works best most of the time. However, depending on internal company policy and politics, you might find that your design gravitates more toward the organizational approach than the hybrid one.

Remember, no matter which design model you used for your tree, you can always improve it.

The Simplistic Approach

In the case of companies that have only one location (such as the same building) and have fewer than a several hundred users (say, fewer than 500), you can save yourself a whole lot of work by using the simplistic model for your tree design — simply create an Organization object for the company and put all the NDS objects within this container.

The recommended partition sizes are as follows:

- ▶ 1,000–1,500 objects per partition for NetWare 4
- ▶ 5,000 objects per partition for NetWare 5 (NDS 7)
- ▶ "Unlimited" objects per partition for eDirectory (NDS 8)

That means for a typical small- and sometimes even a medium-size company, you can forgo having to worry about creating OUs for various locations and departments, and partitioning your tree. There's nothing wrong with just putting everything into a single container. That way, users won't have to browse or walk the tree in order to find resources, such as printers. What you do give up, however, is the immediate knowledge of where a given user is or which division a user belongs to by simply looking at the NDS object name.

NOTE You can compensate for the lost of geographical or organizational information in the NDS object name by populating the Location and Department attributes of the User object with the appropriate information.

No matter which design approach you take, keep the KISS—Keep It Simple, Stupid—concept in mind at all times. You want to make the tree easy for users to navigate and locate the necessary resources, yet at the same time easy for *you* and someone relatively new to your configuration to understand and manage. The reason that you want to make it easy for someone other than yourself to quickly make sense of your tree is that in the case of you hiring new staff, calling in a consultant, or perhaps having Novell dial-in to fix your tree, you don't have to spend too much time explaining things.

Time Synchronization Strategy

As was discussed in Chapter 1, NDS requires that the servers within your network all agree on a common time—it doesn't necessarily have to be the "correct" time but everyone's time has to be in synchronization with everyone else's. NetWare 5 provides two protocols that are used to synchronize time on a network. They are:

- ► TimeSync
- ► Network Time Protocol (NTP)

The TimeSync protocol is a Novell proprietary time synchronization protocol, available through the TIMESYNC.NLM on NetWare (it is the same protocol used by NetWare 4). In the past, the functionality of TimeSync was limited to IPX networks (as NetWare 4 doesn't support pure IP). However, with the introduction of NetWare 5, Novell enhanced its time synchronization service, with TIMESYNC.NLM (v5.08 and later), to function over IP natively and to interoperate directly with NTP based time sources. In other words, TIMESYNC.NLM can handle both IP and IPX related communication and provides Novell TimeSync protocol, NTP client, and NTP server capability.

NOTE   Also included with NetWare 5 is a NTP.NLM which implements the NTP definition RFC1305. But because the newer TIMESYNC.NLM inter-operate directly with NTP based time sources, no real need exists to use the NTP.NLM.

A number of differences exist between TIMESYNC.NLM included in NetWare 4.x (TIMESYNC.NLM version 4.15 and earlier) and TIMESYNC. NLM included with NetWare 5.1 (TIMESYNC.NLM version 5.14 and later). Table 3.1 illustrates the differences between each version.

TABLE 3.1	Difference Between TIMESYNC.NLM Versions 4.15 and 5.14	
CATEGORY	**NETWARE 4.X**	**NETWARE 5.1**
Protocol supported	IPX	IPX, IP
Time server types	Single Reference, Reference, Primary, Secondary	Single Reference, Reference, Primary, Secondary
Time server auto-discovery	Yes, through SAP	Yes, through SAP for IPX networks and through SLP for IP networks
NTP support	No	Yes
DNS support	No	Yes

NOTE

In Table 3.1, SLP stands for *Service Location Protocol*, and is an Internet standard.

The original TIMESYNC.NLM version included with NetWare 5.0 contained the same functionality as the version of TIMESYNC.NLM that ships with NetWare 5.1 except for time server auto-discovery functionality over IP networks. However, this shortcoming was addressed with one of the NetWare 5.0 service packs.

Instead of time server "types" (such as Single Reference) used by Novell, the Network Time Protocol (NTP) uses the term *stratum* to indicate the accuracy of a time source. The stratum ranges from *1* to *16*. 1 stands for the time source itself, 2 stands for the first server referencing that time source, 3 stands for the server referencing stratum 2, and so on. An NTP server at stratum "n+1" is one that accepts time from an NTP server at stratum "n." Thus a server at a lower stratum is accepted as a server that is more accurate than one at a higher stratum.

NOTE

Internet time sources are typically public domain NTP time sources that are at stratum *1* or *2*.

NTP is very strict in considering a time source. If a time source is more than 1,000 seconds (17 minutes) away from the local clock, NTP rejects the time source and labels it as *insane*. Because of its refusal to accept *insane* time sources, NTP time sources are usually very reliable. More information about NTP can be found at www.eecis.udel.edu/~ntp/database/html_ntp-4. 0.72c/index.htm.

When NTP is loaded on a NetWare server, NTP becomes the time source for all IP servers. NTP can be used as a time source for IPX networks if the Reference server has both IP and IPX bound to their own network boards *or* if the Reference server is running a Compatibility Mode Driver (CMD). When NTP is loaded on an IP server, NTP also becomes the time source for all IPX servers, so IPX servers must be set to Secondary time servers.

Therefore, depending on your environment, you need to first make a decision on if you want to use TimeSync or NTP. You can use either method in a pure NetWare environment. However, if you have non-NetWare servers on the network, such as UNIX servers, then NTP would be what you should implement.

 NOTE If you're implementing eDirectory on a mixture of NetWare and non-NetWare platforms, such as Solaris, you have no other option but to use configure NTP because NTP is the most common time synchronization protocol supported by various operating systems.

When using TimeSync, you can start with the default configuration options (which means you don't have to do anything special). When your network grows to about 35 NetWare servers or more *or* when you need more control over the time synchronization-related traffic and relationships between the time servers, should you then consider using the custom method for TimeSync? More details about time synchronization management are discussed in Chapter 8, "Managing Time Synchronization."

Determining a Partition and Replica Strategy

The following items can help you to determine the direction of your partition and replication strategy, as part of your overall network design:

- Considering factors that affect partitions and replicas
- Determining partition boundaries
- Determining replica placement

Factors that Affect Partitions and Replicas

Before creating a partition and replication plan, you should be aware of how the following actions and factors affect partitions *and* the number of replicas you'll have per partition:

- Installation of NetWare servers
- Merging of NDS trees
- Upgrading bindery (pre-NetWare 4) servers to NetWare 4 or NetWare 5
- Working with WAN environments

When the first NetWare server is installed in a new NDS tree, the first partition ([Root]) is automatically created. The [Root] partition's Master replica is placed on that server. This server does not receive special rights or considerations. If you like, this replica of [Root] can be removed at any time or can be changed to a Read/Write replica after other servers are placed in the NDS tree. For subsequent server installations in an existing NDS tree, the following default partitioning and replicating rules apply:

- When you install a new NetWare server on an existing NDS tree, the server is installed in an existing partition; no additional partitions are automatically created.

- The second and third new servers installed in a partition receive a Read/Write replica of the partition. The fourth and subsequent servers do not receive replicas. The second and third new servers receive replicas only of the partition they are installed in.

NOTE

An exception to fourth and subsequent servers not automatically receiving replicas occurs when you upgrade bindery-based servers. Whenever a NetWare 3 server is upgraded to NetWare 4.x or 5.x, the server automatically receives a Read/Write replica of the partition containing the NetWare server's bindery context.

When a server is installed, NDS determines whether enough replicas — three copies — exist for fault tolerance. In the absence of at least a Master and two Read/Write replicas, NDS places a replica on the new server. Consider this example. A network with seven servers and one ([Root]) partition, the Master replica is on server A and Read/Write replicas on servers B and C. Servers D through G hold no replicas. The network administrator decides to remove server C from the network and then add server H. When the network administrator installs server H, NetWare finds that not enough replicas exist — there's only Master and one copy of Read/Write — for fault tolerance and therefore places a Read/Write replica on server H. Although server H isn't the third server in the network, it is the third server needed for fault tolerance purposes.

In all other cases, if you want a replica created on a server, you must add it manually.

NOTE

When you merge NDS trees, a server from one NDS tree is the source and a server from the other NDS tree is the target. The source and target servers must each have the Master replica of its NDS tree's [Root] partition. During the merge, the Master replica on the target server becomes the Master replica of the new partition, and the contents of the two [Root] partitions are combined. Any servers in the target server's original NDS tree that held replicas of the old [Root] partition are given replicas of the new, combined, [Root] partition.

The main thing to note here is that the source server loses the Master replica of its old [Root] partition and is given a Read/Write replica of the new [Root] partition. Any servers in the source server's original tree that held replicas of the old [Root] partition lose their copies and do not receive copies of the new [Root] partition. Any server containing a replica of the new [Root] partition receives Subordinate References to child partitions of the new [Root] partition. To reduce the number of SubRefs, you need to (re)evaluate partition boundaries and replica placement after merging NDS trees.

In conclusion, merging trees affects partitions and replicas in the following ways:

▶ All first-level containers in the source tree [Root] partition become independent partition roots. All source tree servers that held a replica of the source tree [Root] partition lose the [Root] replica, but maintain replicas of the new first-level partitions.

▶ The server that contained the master replica of the source tree [Root] receives a read/write replica of the new [Root].

▶ All servers in the target tree that held replicas of the target [Root] receive replicas of the new [Root].

▶ Subordinate References for new partitions under the [Root] are added to servers holding replicas of the new [Root].

If, after tree merge, the final NDS tree structure is very different than the original, you might experience serious naming problems in login scripts and workstation name contexts.

WARNING

The following planning guidelines can help you to minimize the impact of merging NDS trees:

▶ Choose the appropriate tree to be the source tree. In general, the source tree should be the tree with fewer objects at the [Root].

▶ Gather the full name and password for a user object with Supervisor object rights at the [Root] of each tree being merged.

▶ Modify the NDS trees so that they have the same or very similar first-level structures.

▶ At the time of the merge, change the names of the first-level containers of one NDS tree to unique names as you can't have, for example, a O=Sales in the source tree and a O=Sales in the target tree.

▶ After the merge, move subcontainers below the first-level containers to recreate the original structure, if necessary.

For example you're merging two trees that have the same first-level structures, HumanResources.Company and Marketing.Company in TreeA *and* Sales.Company and Engineering.Company in TreeB. Before the merge, rename the Company container in TreeA to TempCompany (assuming TreeA is the source tree). After the merge, move HumanResource and Marketing from TempCompany to below Company. This recreates the original structure (HumanResource.Company and Marketing.Company) in the merged tree. This process avoids having to update all the name contexts for users in the HumanResource and Marketing containers. It also avoids the need to change object names in the HumanResource and Marketing container login scripts.

When a NetWare 3 server is upgraded to NetWare 4.x or 5.x, it automatically receives a Read/Write replica of the partition containing the NetWare server's bindery context. Should you not want the replica, you need to manually remove it afterwards. There's no way to prevent the replica from being placed there during the upgrade process. Therefore, if you're upgrading a bindery server into a large partition, allow ample time for the replica to be placed on it.

WAN environments greatly affect how you design partitions and replicas — you don't want to have unnecessary traffic crossing your WAN (because its slow, as compared to the LAN, and could be expensive depending on the type of link as there could be a packet charge). The beauty of NDS is that it enables you to divide your tree via partitioning. Therefore, you can partition the database around slow or unreliable WAN links to ensure only necessary NDS-related traffic cross these links.

TIP

You should try not to enable a partition to span a WAN link as this causes unnecessary NDS traffic across the link. For example, if you have a partition that contains users from Toronto and Vancouver, chances are good that you'll place a replica of this partition at each site for fault tolerance and performance in NDS lookup. However, traffic arising from changes to Toronto-based User objects has to cross the WAN link to Vancouver as the replicas need to synchronize, and vice versa. The point is that Vancouver-based users don't care about changes to Toronto-based users and the partition boundary should be created around WAN links and keep your replicas stored on local servers. Then WAN traffic is optimized.

At times you may need to replicate across a WAN link. In such instances, try to keep the size of the replica small and use a high-speed, reliable, link.

Determining Partition Boundaries

The primary reason for partitioning and replicating the NDS database is to increase efficiency for users and to create fault tolerance. In most cases, you should design partition boundaries around the physical layout of your network infrastructure. This coincides with the approach used in designing the upper and lower layers of the NDS tree. When creating partitions, you should determine:

- ▶ Partition boundaries for upper layers of the NDS tree
- ▶ Partition boundaries for lower layers of the NDS tree
- ▶ Partition size and number of replicas

If you design your NDS tree in a pyramid shape as recommended, with fewer container objects in the upper layers and more container and leaf objects in the lower layers, your partition structure should also resemble a pyramid. Your partition structure has few partitions at the top of the tree and more partitions as you move toward the bottom. Such a design creates fewer subordinate references than an NDS tree structure that has more partitions at the top than at the bottom. This pyramid design can be achieved if you always create the partitions relatively close to the leaf objects (particularly the users). An exception is the [Root] partition, created during installation of the first server.

When designing the partitions for the upper layers of the NDS tree, keep the following points in mind:

- Design upper-layer partitions around Organization or Organizational Unit container boundaries that represent locations or organizational structures.

- In a WAN environment, define upper-layer partitions (below the [Root] partition) according to the physical locations within your organization and the network infrastructure. Take for example, Universal Import's tree shown in Figure 3.7 earlier. It has multiple sites located across the country and the upper-layer partitions should be established at each site as shown in Figure 3.8. If your organization is contained at one site, create your upper-layer partitions to reflect the structure of your organization.

- If WAN bandwidth is an issue, create smaller partitions and replicate them in fewer locations with fewer child partitions. This produces less network traffic when synchronizing across WAN links.

FIGURE 3.8 *Upper-layer partitions for Universal Import*

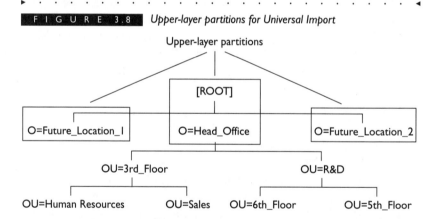

When designing the partitions for the lower layers of the NDS tree, keep the following points in mind:

- Define lower-layer partitions by organizational divisions, departments, and workgroups, and by their associated resources. It is not unheard of that each of the OUs in the lower-layer of the tree becomes its own partition.

► Partition so that all objects in each partition are at a single location. This ensures that updates to NDS can occur on a local server.

Partition size (such at the number of objects contained within that partition and the type of objects — Alias objects don't take up much space but an Application object would) can significantly affect the synchronization and responsiveness of the system. As you plan partitions, regulate the size and number of partitions.

The general guidelines for size and number of partitions are based on a Pentium 100 with 128 MB of RAM on an average network. Faster servers and networks can accommodate larger numbers; slower servers and networks can accommodate smaller numbers. Following are some guidelines based on experience with NDS 7:

► Maintain small partitions. Typically, a partition should have fewer than 3,500 objects. (If Application objects exist in the partition, depending on the type of application, you may want to have fewer than two thousand.)

► Maintain as few child partitions as possible. Typically, a partition should have fewer than 35 child partitions per parent. Any partition operation, such as creating, merging, or deleting a partition, affects child partitions. Minimize the number of child partitions linked across unreliable WAN connections to other replicas of the same partition.

► Avoid creating unnecessary partitions. Partition only when necessary, based on the other guidelines.

NDS eDirectory allows for substantially more scalability and better performance. NDS 8 has changed partition design guidelines in the following ways:

► Trees can store an unlimited number of objects (Novell has load tested to 1 billion objects)

► Partitions can contain an unlimited number of objects (Novell has load tested to 100 million objects)

► The number of child partitions is unrestricted (Novell has load tested to 75 partitions)

Although NDS eDirectory has radically increased the scalability of NDS, WAN and hardware restrictions are still a factor to be considered. Communication speeds, data input/output speeds, and disk size still limit the size and scalability of your tree — even though it is starting to be more common place to see 10 Mbps ATM networks linking WAN sites and 100 Mbps full-duplex Ethernet to servers and desktops. Unless you have lots of experience with NDS, it is best to initially observe the lower limit guidelines based on NDS 7. When you're more comfortable working with NDS, you can then increase the complexity and size of your tree based on experience with your network's performance.

Determining Replica Placement

Many reasons exist for the need to create replicas of a particular partition. Your replica placement strategy should enable the network to efficiently meet the following objectives:

- ▸ Meet workgroup needs
- ▸ Create fault tolerance
- ▸ Manage the number of replicas (especially the number of SubRefs)
- ▸ Replicate the [Root] partition
- ▸ Replicate for administration
- ▸ Meet Bindery Services needs

Replica tables (essentially spreadsheets) are one tool available to help you visually determine replica placement, and is discussed in Appendix A. Your replica placement should also enable you to efficiently walk the tree and to manage WAN traffic.

You should place replicas of each partition on servers that are physically close to the workgroup that uses the information in that partition. For example, if your Accounting group has their own server, it would follow that you partition the Accounting container and place a copy of that container on their home server.

Before you start placing additional replicas out on your network, you should consider the following:

- ▸ Where the replica is placed
- ▸ How many objects are in the replica
- ▸ How static the data is in the replica
- ▸ How users access objects

The advantage of placing additional replicas strategically throughout the network is increased performance, fault tolerance, and navigation. Too many replicas, however, can cause excessive traffic. Therefore, before creating a replica placement strategy for your NDS tree design, determine the best balance of advantages and disadvantages.

To minimize network traffic and login time, users should have a Read/Write replica containing their context on a server physically near them. (Read-Only replicas can't be used for authentication as certain User attributes need to be updated during the login process.) This enables faster login authentication and access to network resources.

If users on one side of a WAN link often access a replica, stored on a server, on the other side of the server, place a replica on a server located near the group of users. This means that a replica is stored on servers on both sides of the WAN link.

TIP

Place replicas in the location of highest access by users, groups, and services. For example, if groups of users in two separate containers need access to the same object within another partition boundary, you should place the replica on a server that exists in the container one level above the two containers holding the groups — as the tree-walking process tends to walk up the branch towards [Root].

To meet fault tolerance needs, you should have at least three or more strategically placed replicas of each partition. If your network encompasses multiple locations, at least one replica should be stored offsite (even at the expense of some synchronization traffic across a WAN link).

At a minimum, place three replicas of each partition on the network whenever possible. Of course, if the network has fewer than three servers, this is not possible. More copies of replicas might be necessary, depending on network topology or performance, but should not place more than ten replicas of a single partition. NDS eDirectory allows for an unlimited number of replicas per partition, but the amount of network traffic increases as the number of replicas increases.

TIP

If your network is comprised of fewer than three servers, you may consider doing the following for NDS fault tolerance. The cost of hardware, especially a no-name brand system, is inexpensive. If you wish to have three replicas for each partition, you can set up one or two dedicated NDS servers that do nothing except hold replicas. Such a server doesn't need much disk space, RAM, or a very high speed processor — a PII-200 with 2GB of disk space and 128 MB of RAM should be sufficient.

Be sure to balance fault tolerance needs with network performance needs as you plan the number and placement of replicas. More locations might also be necessary because of the disaster recovery plan used by the organization. The major work of rebuilding the NDS network after a loss of a server or location can be done using partition replicas — it is always best to recover NDS data using existing replicas rather than going to backups as the NDS information on backups are inevitably always out-of-date.

TIP

The key to determining the maximum replicas for a given partition, is to look at the amount of time it takes to fully synchronize these replicas. The process must complete within the time interval of the start of background synchronization process — on NetWare 4 its 30 minutes and NetWare 5 is 60 minutes; this means NetWare 4 initiates a synchronization process every 30 minutes, and NetWare 5 every hour. So, if you have 15 replicas but they can finish synchronziation in, say, 15 minutes, then there's nothing to worry about. On the other hand, if you have 5 replicas and it takes 45 minutes to complete (and you're running NetWare 4), you need to reduce the number of replicas or upgrade the link speed between the servers holding these replicas.

WARNING

As Subordinate Reference is simply a pointer and does not contain objects other than the partition root object, do not depend on it for fault tolerance and do not count it as one of the three recommended copies.

As previously discussed, when a change is made to an NDS object, that change is communicated to all replicas in the replica list. The more replicas in a replica list, the more communication, thus network traffic is required to synchronize changes. The time cost of synchronization is greater when the servers keeping a replica list are separated by relatively slow WAN links. Therefore, the limiting factor in creating multiple replicas is the amount of processing time and traffic required to synchronize them. It is recommended that you *initially* observe the following guidelines:

- No more than 10 replicas per partition
- No more than 20 replicas per server — a dedicated NDS server can handle up to 50 replicas, depending on the hardware

As mentioned before, NDS eDirectory allows for an unlimited number of replicas per partition, but network traffic increases as the number of replicas increases. Again, be sure to balance fault tolerance needs with network performance needs. If you plan partitions for many geographical sites, some servers receive numerous Subordinate Reference replicas. You can distribute these Subordinate References among more servers by creating regional partitions.

The partition that includes the [Root] is the most important partition of the NDS tree — as the [Root] object facilitates tree-walking among other functions — be sure to replicate the [Root] partition. If the only replica of the [Root] partition becomes corrupted, users experience impaired functionality on the network until the [Root] partition is repaired or the NDS tree is completely rebuilt. Also, you are not able to make any tree design changes involving [Root]. However, you must balance the cost of synchronizing Subordinate References with the number of replicas of the [Root] partition.

Because partition changes only originate at the Master replica, you should place the Master replicas of your various partitions on servers near the network administrator. Generally, when a change is made to a replica, only the updated information is sent across the network. However, when a replica is created, the entire replica is copied to the target server. Typically, each object takes up roughly 5 KB of space (some newer objects, such as ZENworks and DNS/DHCP objects, can take up more). Therefore, if you have a large replica to copy (more than 500 objects), perform the task during a low-traffic time.

Making changes to a few objects does not create much synchronization traffic. However, making changes to many objects at once or making changes in partition boundaries (particularly merging partitions) can slow a network considerably because it generates a lot of traffic and can drive the server CPU utilization high. Again, reserve these high-cost activities for times when network use is low.

If your users or applications require access to a server through Bindery Services, that server must contain a either a Master or Read/Write replica which contains the bindery context — the context set by the SET BINDERY CONTEXT statement in the AUTOEXEC.NCF file. However, to reduce the number of unnecessary replicas, consider centralizing the various Bindery Services onto a small number of servers.

Using WAN Traffic Manager

As NDS synchronizes partition replicas, it creates network traffic. If this traffic crosses WAN links unmanaged, it can increase costs and overload slow WAN links during high-use periods. WAN Traffic Manager (included with NetWare 5) enables you to manage *NDS-related* traffic across WAN links (or over LAN links between any servers in an NDS tree), thus, reducing network costs. WAN Traffic Manager enables you to do the following:

- Control server-to-server traffic generated by NDS
- Restrict traffic based on cost of traffic, time of day, type of traffic, or a combination of these
- Control periodic events initiated by NDS, such as replica synchronization

  Note that WAN Traffic Manager *does not* control NDS events initiated by administrators or users (such as traffic due to tree-walking or creation of a replica) nor does it control non-NDS server-to-server traffic such as time synchronization.

WAN Traffic Manager is made up of the following three components:

- **WTM.NLM.** WTM.NLM resides in SYS:SYSTEM on each NetWare 5 server. Before NDS sends server-to-server traffic, WTM.NLM reads a WAN traffic policy and determines whether that traffic is sent.
- **A snap-in module.** The snap-in is the interface to WAN Traffic Manager and can be accessed through NetWare Administrator or ConsoleOne. It enables you to create or modify policies, to create LAN area objects, and to apply policies to LAN area objects or server objects.
- **WAN Traffic Policies.** These traffic policies are rules that control the generation of NDS traffic. They are stored as NDS attribute values on the NetWare server object, the LAN area object, or both.

When WAN Traffic Manager is installed, the schema is extended to include a LAN area object. The snap-in module adds three new detail pages (LAN Area Membership, WAN Policies, and Cost) for the NetWare server object (see Figure 3.9).

A LAN area object enables you to administer WAN traffic policies for a group of servers. If you do not create a LAN area object, you must manage each server's WAN traffic individually. After you create a LAN area object, you can add servers to or remove servers from the LAN area object. When you apply a policy to the LAN area, that policy applies to all servers in the LAN area.

A WAN Traffic Policy is a set of rules that control the generation of NDS traffic. A policy is text stored as an NDS attribute value on the Server object, the LAN Area object, or both. The policy is interpreted according to a simple processing language. The attribute in which this text is stored is Wanman: Wan Policy. This is a multi-valued attribute so multiple policies can be stored.

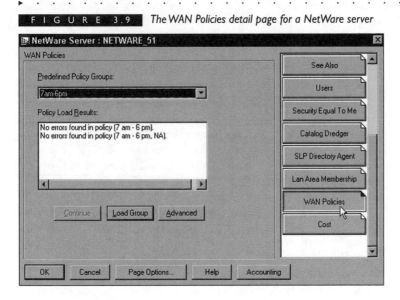

F I G U R E   3 . 9   The WAN Policies detail page for a NetWare server

Ten predefined policy "groups" (see the following list) are distributed with WAN Traffic Manager in NetWare 5.1. Each policy group contains the following two types of policies:

▶ **Policy, NA.** Limits or prevents the checking of such things as backlinks, external references, and login restrictions to a specified parameter.

▶ **Policy.** Limits or prevents all other traffic to a specified parameter.

You must apply all policies in a group for all traffic specific to that group to be prevented or limited to a specified parameter. For example, if you wish to restrict all NDS-related traffic to between 1 and 3am, apply *both* the 1-3am, NA and 1-3am policies.

Predefined WAN Traffic Manager policies included with NetWare 5.1

Many policies for the WAN Traffic Manager are predefined and included with Netware 5.1. I've broken these groups down and described each subset here, starting with the policy group and then a description of each policy within its group.

- **1–3 am policy group.** The policies in this group limit the time traffic can be sent to between 1 and 3 a.m. (To restrict all traffic to these hours, both policies must be applied.)

  - **1–3 am, NA.** This policy limits the checking of backlinks, external references, login restrictions, the running of janitor or limber, and schema synchronization to these hours.

  - **1–3 am.** This policy limits all other traffic to these hours.

- **7am–6pm.** The policies in this group limit the time traffic can be sent to between 7 a.m. and 6 p.m. (To restrict all traffic to these hours, both policies must be applied.)

  - **7am–6pm, NA.** This policy limits the checking of backlinks, external references, and login restrictions, the running of janitor or limber, and schema synchronization to these hours.

  - **7am–6pm, NA.** This policy limits all other traffic to these hours.

- **CostLT20.** The policies in this group allow only traffic to be sent that has a cost factor below 20. (To prevent all traffic with a cost factor of 20 or more, both policies must be applied.)

  - **Cost < 20, NA.** This policy prevents the checking of backlinks, external references, and login restrictions, the running of janitor or limber, and schema synchronization unless the cost factor is less than 20.

  - **Cost < 20.** This policy prevents all other traffic unless the cost factor is less than 20.

- **IPX.** The policies in this group allow only IPX traffic.(To prevent all non-IPX traffic, both policies must be applied.)

  - **IPX, NA.** This policy prevents the checking of backlinks, external references, and login restrictions, the running of janitor or limber, and schema synchronization unless the traffic that would be generated is IPX.

  - **IPX.** This policy prevents all other traffic unless the traffic is IPX.

- **TCP/IP.** The policies in this group allow only TCP/IP traffic. (To prevent all non-TCP/IP traffic, both policies must be applied.)

  - **TCP/IP, NA.** This policy prevents the checking of backlinks, external references, and login restrictions, the running of janitor or limber, and schema synchronization unless the traffic that would be generated is TCP/IP.

- **TCP/IP.** This policy prevents all other traffic unless the traffic is TCP/IP.

▶ **SameArea.** The policies in this group allow only traffic in the same network area. A network area is determined by the network section of an address. In a TCP/IP address, Wan Traffic Manager assumes a class C address; addresses whose first three sections are the same are in the same network area. In an IPX address, all addresses with the same network portion are considered to be in the same network area.

  - **Same Network Area, NA.** This policy prevents the checking of backlinks, external references, and login restrictions, the running of janitor or limber, and schema synchronization unless the traffic that would be generated is in the same network area.

  - **Same Network Area, TCP/IP.** This policy restricts TCP/IP traffic unless that traffic that would be generated is in the same TCP/IP network area.

  - **Same Network Area, IPX.** This policy restricts IPX traffic unless that traffic that would be generated is in the same IPX network area.

▶ **ONoSpoof.** The policies in this group allow only existing WAN connections to be used. (To prevent all traffic to existing connections, both policies must be applied.)

  - **Already Open, No Spoofing, NA.** This policy prevents the checking of backlinks, external references, and login restrictions, the running of janitor or limber, and schema synchronization except on existing WAN connections.

  - **Already Open, No Spoofing.** This policy prevents all other traffic from using existing WAN connections.

▶ **OpnSpoof.** The policies in this group allow only existing WAN connections to be used but assume that a connection that hasn't been used for 15 minutes is being spoofed and should not be used. (To prevent all traffic from using existing connections that are opened for fewer than 15 minutes, both policies must be applied.)

  - **Already Open, Spoofing, NA.** This policy prevents the checking of backlinks, external references, and login restrictions, the running of janitor or limber, and schema synchronization except on existing WAN connections that have been opened for fewer than 15 minutes.

- **Already Open, Spoofing.** This policy prevents other traffic from using existing WAN connections that have been opened for fewer than 15 minutes.

▸ **NDST Typs.** (Over a dozen policies.) The policies in this group are sample policies for various NDS traffic types. They contain the variables NDS passes in a request of this TrafficType.

▸ **TimeCost.** A combination of five existing policies: Cost < 20, Disallow everything, NDS Sychronization, Start rest. procs, NA, and Start unrest. procs, 1–1:30, NA.

NOTE

NA indicates that this is a policy that contains a NO_ADDRESSES statement. Five of the NDS Traffic Types require NO_ADDRESSES statements. These are NDS_Backlinks, NDS_Janitor, NDS_Limber, NDS_Schema_Sync, and NDS_Check_Login_Restrictions.

Cost or Cost Factor is used by WAN policies to determine the relative expense of WAN traffic. In policies, you can use DestCost to determine whether to send traffic or not.

For more details about these and other terms, see the online help for WAN Traffic Manager.

You can use these policies as they are, you can modify these policies, or you can write new policies. You create or apply policies from the WAN Policies page of the Server object or of the LAN Area object. You can apply policies to individual servers or, via the LAN Area objects, you can make policy assignments to several servers at once.

The use of WAN Traffic Manager is optional, and you should only consider using it if you have slow WAN links or if you're being charged for usage based on time-of-day or based on number of packets.

## CHAPTER 4

Special-Purpose
NDS Objects

Many of the object types defined in NDS are self-explanatory. However, NDS includes a number of powerful special-purpose objects that can make your life and your users' lives a lot easier. This chapter covers how, why, and when to use the following object types:

- ▶ Alias
- ▶ Organizational Role
- ▶ Profile
- ▶ Directory Map
- ▶ Template

This chapter also discusses the use of NDS container objects versus the use of Group objects.

Aliases

Unless you have taken the simplistic design approach discussed in Chapter 3 where you placed all your objects in a single container, you should take full advantage of the NDS alias capability whenever possible. An *alias object* is simply a pointer that links back to an object located elsewhere in the tree — if the other object is in the same location as the Alias object, there's generally no need to create an alias for it. An Alias object can point to either a container object (such as an OU) or a leaf object (such as a User). This enables the users to access resources, such as Volumes and Printers, much more easily while the user can still maintain the standard naming convention. The object being aliased is known as the *primary object*.

TIP

An alias also can serve as a nickname to another object. This enables you to use a much shorter name to reference an object that has a long name. A Volume object in NDS — ANDROMEDA_DATA, for example — is automatically named by combining the volume's name (DATA) and the server's name (ANDROMEDA) on which it is located. You can create an Alias simply called DATA to access this object instead and save yourself some typing.

In NetWare Administrator, no indication is given if an object has any Aliases pointing to it. However, an Alias object is shown with the proper object class icon (such as a User) and immediate to its right, a black mask. Figure 4.1 shows three objects that are Aliases:

- ▶ Tasha_Alias1 (a User alias)

▶ Tasha_Alias2 (a User alias)

▶ Markham (an OU alias)

Alias objects are shown with a black mask icon in NetWare Administrator.

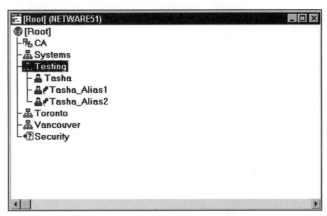

Under ConsoleOne, Alias objects are shown with a dotted-arrow to the right of the object class icon.

As a crude analogy, aliasing is like the drive mapping we use so often in NetWare. Instead of a user having to know that a file is in ANDROMEDA_ DATA:STARCHART\SECTOR5, he can simply go to drive S which is mapped to this directory. The user does not have to know the actual location — just the pointer.

NOTE

Alias objects are most often used for Users, Volumes, Printers, and Print Queue objects to simplify user lookups.

TIP

Under NetWare 4.x, it was possible to do a DOS mapping to a Volume alias object. However, in NetWare 5, you are no longer able to do that. You must instead create a Directory Map object pointing to the Volume object; then grant the users Browse object right and Read & Compare property rights to the container that holds the Volume object to which the Directory Map object points. Directory Map objects are discussed later in this chapter and NDS rights are covered in detail in Chapter 6, "Assigning NDS Security Rights."

Using Alias Objects to Facilitate Printing

Consider Figure 4.2. To facilitate easy printing of reports to the Vancouver location, a Print Queue alias is created in the Toronto container so that the Toronto users need only to issue the command CAPTURE Q=LASER2 instead of CAPTURE Q=.LASER2.VANCOUVER to print to Vancouver.

▶ · ◀

F I G U R E 4 . 2   *Using Print Queue alias object to ease printing to remote location*

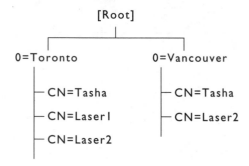

Simplifying Logins for Travelling Users

If you have travelling users, User aliases are very helpful in simplifying logins. As shown in Figure 4.2, for example, user Tasha frequently travels between Toronto and Vancouver. Without the use of aliases, you have two options: create two User objects for Tasha: one in O=Toronto and one in O=Vancouver or while Tasha is visiting Vancouver, she has to log in using the full NDS name (.Tasha.Toronto). The first option could pose problems for Tasha as she needs to remember two sets of passwords and, at the same time, login script and NDS/file system rights assignments get complicated. The alternative option requires her to remember a longer name. Neither option can be considered user-friendly. The best solution is to create a User alias in O=Vancouver for Tasha (as Toronto is her home-base). With a User alias, Tasha needs only one password and she can login in while in Vancouver in exactly the same way that she does in Toronto.

Some caveats do exist with login scripts when using User aliases. These issues are discussed in the "Login Scripts" section of Chapter 5.

NOTE

Container aliases can be used if you're modifying the structure of your tree. Suppose you need to rename a container from OU=Testing to OU=Production. Because you haven't had the time yet to go over all the login scripts and batch files to point at the new container name, you can create an Alias called OU=Testing that points to OU=Production. That way, any references to OU=Testing are actually references to OU=Production. You can then take your time in updating all the login scripts and batch files to reflect the change.

NOTE

If you delete the primary object, any alias objects associated with it are automatically deleted from the tree. If you deinstall a NetWare server from the NDS tree, for example, all its Server and Volume alias objects are automatically removed. On the other hand, removing an Alias object does *not* remove the primary object.

Avoiding Alias Loops

Given the power and versatility of Alias objects, you must be careful not to create "alias loops." Although it is impossible to do with leaf objects, such as Users and Groups, creating alias loops is possible with containers.

When an object alias points to another alias, the resulting alias object actually points to the primary object. This is known as *dereferencing*. Consider the case in which Shirley is the primary User Object: Alias1 points to Shirley, and Alias2 points to Alias1. When examining the use of NetWare Administrator, Alias2 actually points to Shirley rather than Alias1. Thus, as far as leaf objects go, aliases do not create loops.

WARNING

If an Alias object is made to point at a Group object, the Group alias *cannot* be used in testing for group membership in a login script. For example, if you have a Group object called MAIL_USERS.Toronto. Company, and an Alias object called MAIL_USERS.Dallas.Company which points to the MAIL_USERS group in Toronto.Company, you may not use the login script command "if member of MAIL_USERS" in the Dallas container script. You must use "if member of .MAIL_ USERS.Toronto.Company" to correctly test for membership in order for the script commands within the IF-block to work.

The situation is different with containers. Consider the NDS tree illustrated in Figure 4.3, in which two different alias loops exist. First, under OU=Testing is an alias to its parent container OU=Markham. You can easily notice the problem with this type of a container alias loop. When you double-click in NetWare Administrator on the alias Markham.Testing.Markham.Toronto, it is dereferenced to a point in the original. When trying to expand the tree display, NetWare Administrator encounters the alias, which points to the parent container, which contains the alias. Fortunately, NetWare versions 4.10 and higher don't allow you to alias a parent container; however, earlier versions of NetWare 4 do.

F I G U R E   4 . 3   *An example of two types of container alias loops*

[Root]

O=Toronto

OU=Markham

OU=Testing

alias to

OU=Markham

OU=Richmond_Hill

alias to

OU=Markham

OU=Richmond_Hill

alias to

1

2

NOTE   Although NetWare versions 4.10 and higher don't allow you to alias a parent container, if you inadvertently try to do it, NetWare Administrator returns the following error message: *xxxx* is of an object class that cannot be contained by the destination object, where *xxxx* is the parent container name you're trying to alias to.

The second type of container alias loop is a little more subtle and more difficult to detect. But given some hints, it is easy to spot.

When you expand the tree in NetWare Administrator, the effect of the second type of container alias loop is very noticeable (see Figure 4.4). However, this is not readily obvious using NETADMIN (the DOS version of NetWare Administrator is not included with NetWare 5). If you have a container loop, NETADMIN simply "drops" you into the dereferenced primary container without informing you. So, if you're not paying attention to the Context heading at the top of the menu screen, it is not immediately apparent that you're going around in circles. Given these reasons, you might want to avoid creating container aliases as a shortcut.

FIGURE 4.4
*The effect of a container alias loop as shown in
NetWare Administrator*

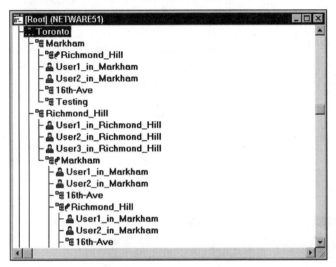

WARNING

Because Aliases are NDS objects and have no bindery counterparts,
they are not accessible by bindery clients.

TIP

If the name of the Alias doesn't reflect its primary object, you can
view its details using NetWare Administrator by right-clicking the
object and selecting Details. The name shown in the Identification
tab (the Login Name attribute for User objects or the Name field
for OUs, for example) is that of the primary object. ConsoleOne,
unfortunately, doesn't show you this information.

Chapter 6, "Assigning NDS Security Rights," discusses some security issues
related to Alias objects.

Special Purpose Objects

There are several object types that will make things a lot easier both for you
and for your users. I've defined these special purpose objects here.

Organizational Role Objects

If you've used previous versions of NetWare, you might be familiar with the use of groups in the NetWare environments. In NDS, there's an Organizational Role (OR) object that works very similarly to the Group object.

Functionally, there's no difference between a Group object and an Organizational Role object. A conceptual difference exists, however, and in some situations it makes more sense to create an OR instead of a Group. In general, group objects are used in login scripts (as in IF MEMBER OF group) and are activity oriented (such as for granting file system trustee rights to an application on your server). Groups tend to have many members. Organizational Roles, on the other hand, generally are used to create administrative groups that contain a small number of users. The OR object has an attribute known as *role occupant*. Instead of being referenced as members, users belonging to ORs are called occupants (see Figure 4.5).

► · ◄

FIGURE 4.5 *An occupant list as displayed by NetWare Administrator*

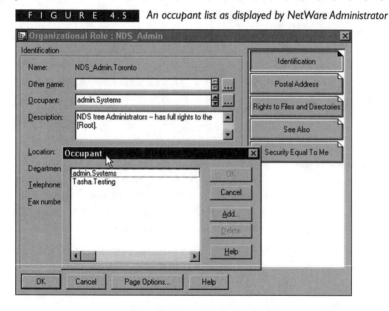

You can create an OR called NDS Admin that has Supervisor object rights over [Root]. Any occupants of this OR are then able to perform NDS management functions. As shown in Figure 4.5, Admin and Tasha have all rights over the whole NDS tree.

TIP

Organizational Role is a very powerful method of creating subadministrators for your NDS tree. Make use of ORs if your tree is not centrally administrated. Refer to Chapter 6, "Assigning NDS Security Rights," on setting up special administrators.

Profile Objects

NetWare 2.*x* and 3.*x* contain two levels of login scripts — unless NetWare Naming Services is used, in which case three levels exist. NetWare version 4 and higher, however, use the following three levels of login scripts:

- ▶ Container login script
- ▶ Profile login script
- ▶ User login script, or the default login script if a user login script isn't present

The *Profile* object is used as a scripting object. The Profile object can provide special drive mappings (via the login script) and file system rights to a group of users. Each User object has a profile attribute (see Figure 4.6). When the user logs in to the network, the login script of the Profile object to which this attribute is pointed is executed.

You can use profile login scripts in three ways:

- ▶ As a global login script
- ▶ As a location-dependent login script
- ▶ As a special-purpose login script

If you want to have a global login script (similar to the System Login Script in NetWare 2.*x* and 3.*x*), you can assign the same Profile object to each user. Therefore, everyone executes the same set of (profile) login script.

TIP

You can use a Template (discussed in Chapter 5, "Creating Users, Groups, Aliases, and other Objects Types") to automatically assign a profile to a new user.

If you later want to globally update each User object with a profile setting, you can use either the UIMPORT utility or the NetWare Administrator.

A profile can be used to assign site-specific CAPTURE and drive mappings (using Directory Map objects; see following). If you're using a geographical design for your NDS tree, for example, each container can have its own Profile object that is specific for the particular location.

In NetWare Administrator, the profile attribute is found on the same tab as Login Script.

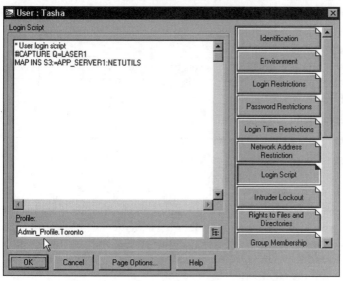

You can create profiles based on job functions. You can, for example — instead of creating a group and testing for group membership within the login script — create a Profile object for the Word Processing group, which maps those in the group to the word processing application, and captures to printers located near them. You can have a separate Profile object for the Engineering department that captures their LPT2 to a plotter.

If you're wondering whether this is different than creating groups and using IF MEMBER OF *group* in the container login script, it is not. You can use this command in the container login script or use a profile script. However, if you have many groups, your container login script can become very long and users might experience a performance slow down during login. This is because the login process must parse the whole script and check every IF MEMBER OF conditional statement. If you use profile script instead, no checking occurs. You either execute that particular set of script or you don't. In general, users find themselves using a combination of both the container and the profile login script.

TIP

If you have a Group object that has many members and you're only using this group for the IF MEMBER OF checking, consider switching to using a Profile instead. The IF MEMBER OF check reads every member entry in the Group object *sequentially* and for large groups, this can be time consuming. If the group contains users from different containers located across WAN links (that you don't have a local replica of), the scanning of the members can be *very* time consuming.

Directory Map Objects

The *Directory Map* (DM) object works somewhat like the familiar drive pointers. A DM object points to a specific volume and directory path on a NetWare server (see Figure 4.7). You can then create a drive mapping, but instead of using the full server name, volume name, and directory path, use a DM object name instead.

FIGURE 4.7   *Creating a Directory Map object using NetWare Administrator*

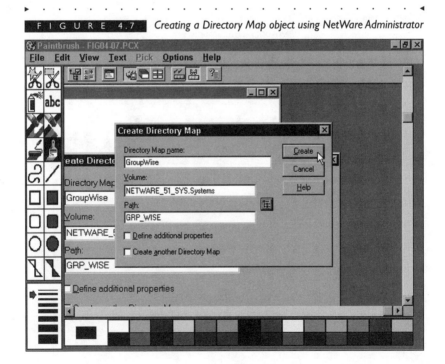

For instance, in the example shown previously in Figure 4.7 a DM called GroupWise was created, pointing to the SYS:GRP_WISE directory on the server NETWARE_51. In your login script, reference it as MAP INS S1:= GROUPWISE, assuming the DM object is located in the context in which you're logging in. You may wonder "what's the big deal about this?" Imagine you later need to move the GroupWise application to another volume because of disk space issues. With the use of DM objects, you simply need to change the reference path in NDS; no need to change any login scripts.

TIP

A Directory Map object shows up in Window's Network Neighborhood as a regular folder (see Figure 4.8). Therefore, if any of your users are using permanent drive mappings in Windows, the use of DM objects would also save on reconfiguration work should you change volume and directory names for one of your applications.

FIGURE 4.8

A DM object shows up as a regular folder in Network Neighborhood.

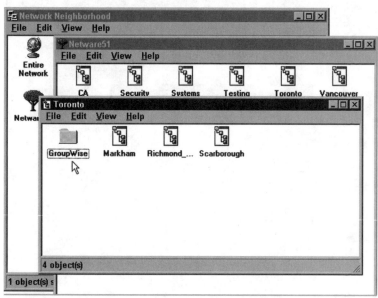

A word of caution about using Aliases with Directory Map objects. Consider the example shown in Figure 4.9 where there is a DM object in OU=Markham, pointing to a drive mapping and an Alias object in OU= Richmond_Hill pointing back to the DM object in OU=Markham. You get an error saying "Volume or Directory Not Found" if you try to map a drive using the Alias. This is because a Directory Map object is a pointer, pointing to a directory on a volume, and an Alias object is a pointer pointing to another NDS object. An Alias of a Directory Map object would be a pointer pointing to another pointer, which doesn't get dereferenced correctly. Therefore, it doesn't make sense to use an Alias for the Directory Map object.

FIGURE 4.9 *You cannot use a DM alias to map drives.*

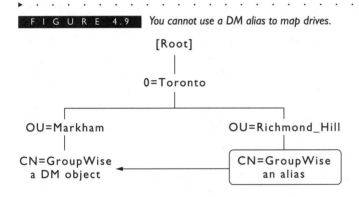

[Root]

O=Toronto

OU=Markham

CN=GroupWise
a DM object

OU=Richmond_Hill

CN=GroupWise
an alias

Template Objects

A Template object is an object that provides a base set of properties and setup procedures for creating new User objects. Templates can't be used to apply changes to existing users. When a new User object is created based on a Template object, the properties of the Template object are copied to the new User object. This new Template class of objects was introduced in NetWare 4.11; in previous versions of NetWare 4, this was known as the *USER_ TEMPLATE* object.

NOTE

USER_TEMPLATE is not an object type like the other special objects (such as Directory Map) discussed earlier in this chapter. It simply is a special User object with the name USER_TEMPLATE.

In NetWare versions prior to 4.11, you can have only one USER_TEMPLATE in any given container. If you need to have multiple templates (say, one for Sales and another one for Engineering), you need to reference a dummy User object (say, SALES_TEMPLATE) and rename it to USER_TEMPLATE before you can use it. This is cumbersome at best if you have a number of these templates. NetWare 4.11 introduced the Template object class so you can more easily manage the various templates and no renaming is needed prior to using them.

The idea behind Templates (or USER_TEMPLATE for that matter) is similar to the default account restrictions setting found in SYSCON under NetWare 2.x and 3.x — you can pre define a set of restrictions (such as Login Time Restriction), and this set is automatically applied to any new User objects created. Templates take the function one step further by allowing you to also assign user login scripts, profile settings, and all user-associated attributes (such as Location and Group Memberships).

Any information you enter for the Template object is copied over to the new user you create using the template. You can even use Template objects to assign NDS rights and file system trustee rights to the newly created User objects.

Refer to Chapter 5, "Creating Users, Groups, Aliases, and other Object Types," for more information about using Template objects to create new users.

The Use of Groups Versus Containers

A Group object is often used when many User objects need the same file system trustee assignments. This is so that rather than making many trustee assignments, you only need to make one trustee assignment to all users who belong to the group by making the trustee assignment to the Group object itself. Network administrators have been doing this since the NetWare 2.x era and many continue to do so with NetWare 4 and NetWare 5. However, with NetWare 4 and higher, the use of groups may not always be necessary — as NDS containers function as "natural" groups (also known as "super groups").

In the NDS environment, any User object within a container is automatically considered a "member" of that container, without having to be explicitly assigned. That means, if you grant file system trustee rights to a container, all users within that container have access. Furthermore, container "memberships" are inherited, meaning that if you grant file system rights to, say, O=Toronto, then all users in O=Toronto, OU=Markham.O=Toronto, *and* OU= Richmond_Hill.O=Toronto automatically inherit the same file system rights.

When you're using Group objects to assign file system trustee rights, you have to manually update the Group object with new users created (unless you're using Templates). But if you use containers instead, any new users are automatically granted the rights as they are automatically made "members" of the container. Therefore, you should take a good look at your file system security requirements and use NDS containers as trustees instead of groups whenever possible.

A more detailed discussion about how file system rights work with NDS is given in Chapter 6, "Assigning NDS Security Rights."

## CHAPTER 5

Creating Users, Groups, Aliases, and Other Object Types

After you've installed a brand-new network, you'll need to create a user account for each of your network users. By default, the only User object that exists in your NDS tree upon a new installation is the Admin User object. As a general rule, each person should have his or her own user account and not use a shared ID. In some environments, shared user IDs can lead to potential security issues, including lack of accountability for changes to documents.

Therefore, to facilitate use of the network, you (as the network administrator) must create accounts for each user. In addition, performing several other configuration and setup tasks makes life easier for your users. Some of these tasks are as follows:

- ▸ **Create user accounts.** You can create user accounts following a standard naming convention that you've developed for naming NDS objects (refer to Chapter 2, "Installing NDS and Designing Trees," for some naming convention guidelines and recommendations).

- ▸ **Create Group objects.** You may need to create some Group objects, and organize the users into these groups. Groups enable you to manage security, printer assignments, and so on, much more easily and efficiently; but keep in mind the "containers versus groups" discussion in Chapter 4, "Special-Purpose NDS Objects," so that you don't over use Group objects.

- ▸ **Create login scripts.** To make accessing network resources (such as applications) easier for your users, create login scripts that automatically set up the necessary drive mappings and printer capturings for your users. See later in this chapter for more about login scripts.

- ▸ **Set up Organizational Role objects.** If someone other than you is responsible for administrating the network, you should consider setting up some Organizational Role objects to facilitate the assignment of management rights—such as NDS security.

This chapter discusses the various methods and steps for creating users, groups, aliases, and containers; this chapter also has discussions about various types of login scripts that you can implement.

Creating a User

Creating a user's account means creating, for the user in question, a User object in NDS. However, it is not enough to simply create the object. Often you also need to configure one or more of the following settings:

- ▶ Information associated with a user, such as full name, location, telephone number, fax number, and so on.

- ▶ The user's group memberships. This is generally done so that the user has the appropriate file system trustee rights, printer settings, and drive mappings to the specific applications and data files the user needs to access as part of his or her job.

- ▶ A home directory for the user's personal files or files that are not shared with other users.

- ▶ User-specific login script to further customize his or her work environment.

- ▶ NDS rights that govern how the user can see, use, and manage other NDS objects in the tree.

- ▶ File system trustee rights that determine the files and directories the user has access to, and what actions they can take on these files and directories.

- ▶ Account restrictions, if necessary, to control when and where the user can log in, how often the user must change passwords, the minimum length of a password, and so on.

- ▶ Access to network printers.

NDS security and file system security are explained in Chapter 6, "Assigning NDS Security Rights."

X-REF

A number of different methods exist for creating one or more User objects in NDS. In a typical business environment, you generally only need to create a new User periodically. However, in an academic setting, for example, you'll need to have the ability to bulk create a large number of users when new students arrive.

The following sections describe how to create users with the various tools included in NetWare:

- ▶ NetWare Administrator
- ▶ ConsoleOne
- ▶ UIMPORT
- ▶ BULKLOAD
- ▶ Web Manager

Using NetWare Administrator

NetWare Administrator (often referred to as NWAdmin) is a Windows application that can run on either Windows 95/98 or Windows NT/2000. NetWare Administrator lets you control the security and efficiency of your network by editing the contents and configuration of NDS. NetWare Administrator is like a control console. It has a default set of controls known as the *browser*. Other sets of controls, known as *tools*, can be installed for specific purposes, such as to configure Novell Licensing Services (NLS); see Figure 5.1

FIGURE 5.1 *NetWare Administrator's controls are accessed through pull-down menus.*

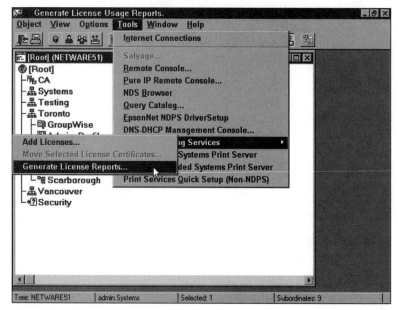

NOTE

Different versions of NetWare have different versions of NetWare Administrator. For example, NetWare 4.10's version is called NWADMIN.EXE while later versions of NetWare 4 have NWADMN3X.EXE, NWADMN95.EXE and NWADMNNT.EXE, for the different Windows platforms. Around the time when NetWare 5.0 shipped, Novell released NWADMN32.EXE, a 32-bit version of NetWare Administrator that runs on Windows 9x and higher—the support for Windows 3.x was dropped. Although designed and shipped with NetWare 5, you can use the latest version of NetWare Administrator with NetWare 4 and have no ill effects, except that some of the tools are not supported on NetWare 4.

Unless otherwise specified, the version of NetWare Administrator discussed in this book is NWADMN32.EXE, found in SYS:PUBLIC\WIN32 directory.

TIP

You can start NetWare Administrator either from the command line or by double-clicking its icon if one is present as a result of a shortcut created on your Windows desktop or delivered by NAL. Normally, you simply launch NetWare Administrator without any command-line options, such as NWADMN32. However, NetWare Administrator supports two command-line options that enable you to specify where its settings are to be stored: NWADMN32 [/N | /F*file*].

The /N causes your preferences to be registered in your User object in the Directory (see Figure 5.2), and the /F causes your preferences to be registered in the specified file. If you don't include a path, the local Windows directory is assumed. Omitting the parameter causes your preferences to be registered in the local Windows registry.

For example,

```
NWADMN32
```

registers your preferences in the local Windows registry.

```
NWADMN32 /N
```

registers your preferences in your User object in the Directory; and,

```
NWADMN32 /Fh:\admin\nwadmn32.ini
```

registers your preferences (see Table 5.1) in the file H:\ADMIN\ NWADMN32.INI. Therefore, if you need to run NetWare Administrator on different workstations, consider using either the /N or /F option so you get the same preferences regardless of which workstation you're using.

FIGURE 5.2 *NetWare Administrator adds five keys to the NetWare Registry attribute associated with the User object.*

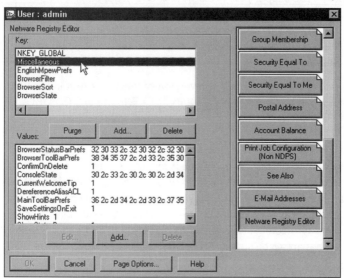

TABLE 5.1 *Registry Keys Used by NetWare Administrator*

REGISTRY KEY	DESCRIPTION
Miscellaneous	This key controls miscellaneous settings, such as displaying the Welcome ToolTip, or saving settings upon exit.
BrowserFilter	This key controls hiding certain object classes from display.
BrowserSort	This key controls the order in which object classes are displayed. The key value is the decimal equivalent of the object class names.

REGISTRY KEY	DESCRIPTION
BrowserState	This key stores the state of the browser (name of NDS tree, context, and so on) when you exit NetWare Administrator so that the same window is displayed next time.
EnglishMPewPerfs	This key controls the order of the information tabs (Identification, Environment, and so on) associated with various object classes.

To create any new NDS object, including users and groups, you must be logged in as Admin, or as another user that has sufficient rights to create or modify NDS objects (see Chapter 6 for more information about security rights). Before creating a new User object, prepare answers to the following questions:

▶ Where should the new User object be located within the NDS tree?

▶ Should the user have a home directory? If yes, where should it be placed (that is, on which server and volume, and along which directory path)?

▶ Is the user going to be subjected to any account restrictions, such as login time restriction? If yes, which of the restrictions apply and what are the settings going to be?

NOTE

Very often, a network administrator creates a directory, called USERS or HOME, on a server's volume. Then, the administrator creates a home directory for each user under USERS or HOME. Users have all rights to their home directory, so they can store and manage files there. Once you've created this top-level directory (USERS), you can then specify if a home directory is created underneath it for each new user you add to NDS.

To create a new User object, complete the following steps:

I. Start NetWare Administrator. The NetWare Administrator's browser window should appear, as shown in Figure 5.3. (If the browser window doesn't appear, select Tools ⇨ NDS Browser. Select the tree you want by using the tree button or choose from the list of available trees. Then, type or choose the complete name of the container object that you want to place at the top of the view, or choose the browse button to choose from the available containers; then click OK.)

F I G U R E   5.3   *NetWare Administrator's browser window*

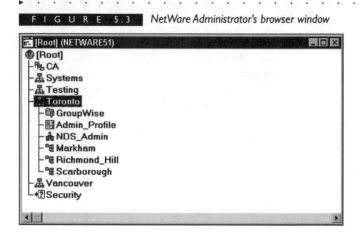

2. Select the container object (an Organization or Organizational Unit object) to hold the new User object. If the desired container is inside another container, double-click the parent container to display its subordinate objects. If the desired container is in a different subtree branch, select View ⇨ Set Context, then type or choose the complete name of the container object that you want, or choose the browse button to choose from the available containers, and then click OK.

3. Select Object ⇨ Create. (Alternatively, you can simply press the Insert key, right-click the container, and choose Create, or click the Create User object icon on the toolbar.)

4. From the New Object dialog box (see Figure 5.4), highlight User and then click OK.

5. In the Login name field (see Figure 5.5), type a name for the new object. The name you enter is the name the user enters to log in. Make sure you follow standard object naming conventions.

6. In the Last Name field, type the user's last name.

7. If you have Template objects defined and would like to use them, check the Use template box. Then click the Browse button (which has a directory structure icon) located to the right and browse to locate the desired Template object — Template object is a leaf object that provides a base set of properties and setup procedures for creating new user accounts; more details about it can be found later in this chapter.

FIGURE 5.4 The list of objects shown in the New Object dialog box varies depending on the parent object you've selected.

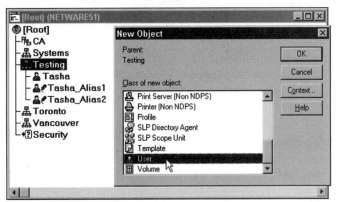

FIGURE 5.5 The Login Name and Last Name are mandatory attributes of a User object. If either one of these fields is not filled in, the Create button remains grayed out.

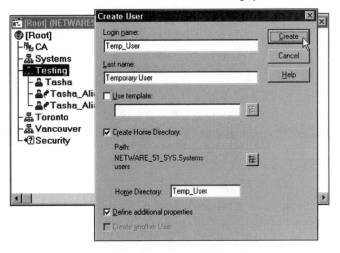

8. To create a home directory for the new user:

  a. Check the Create Home Directory checkbox.

  b. Click the Browse button (which has a directory structure icon) located to the right of the word "Path" and above the words "Home Directory."

  c. From the Select Object dialog box, on the right-hand panel double-click the Volume object name that will hold the user home directories (you may need to navigate the NDS tree to locate the desired Volume object).

  d. When the top level of the user's home directory (such as USERS) appears on the left panel of the dialog box, select that directory and click OK. The path to that directory should now appear in the Create User dialog box (refer to Figure 5.5).

WARNING By default, the name of the user's home directory is the same as the login name. If your naming standard for user login names allows names exceeding eight characters, ensure that the volume you're creating the home directories in supports long names.

9. Check the Define additional properties checkbox. (This enables you to see and modify more information about the User object after you create it in the next step.)

10. Click Create.

11. The user's identification page is displayed, as shown in Figure 5.6. This identification page is displayed every time you use NetWare Administrator to view this User object's details. A large number of attributes are associated with a User object and they are grouped into different categories by NetWare Administrator (under different "tabs" or "pages"). You can fill in none, some, or all of the information on these pages, depending on your needs. Click OK when finished.

TIP If you have entered new information or modified existing data in one of these property pages, the turned-down corner of the button appears black.

After you've created a new User object, that User object appears in NetWare Administrator's browser window.

Should you need to create multiple users, you can check the Create another user checkbox at the bottom of the Create User dialog box. However, you can only choose either Define additional properties *or* Create another user, but not both. If you need to do both, you should consider using Templates.

Many "tabs" or "pages" are associated with a User object. Click the tab button (which has a turned-down corner) to display additional information.

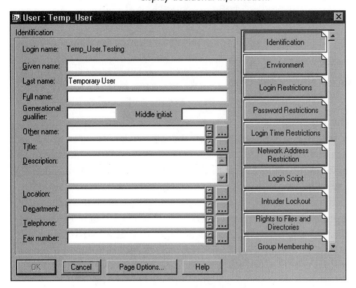

Templates

As previously discussed in Chapter 4, Template objects are special-purpose NDS objects that contain the 'mold' from which you can create one or more User objects. A Template object provides a base set of property values (such as Location and fax number information) and setup procedures for creating new User objects. When a new User object is created based on a Template object, the property values defined in the Template object are copied to the new User object.

The following steps illustrate how to create a Template object:

I. Right click the container where you want to create the Template, and then choose Create.

2. In Class of New Object, choose Template, and then click OK.

3. In Name, type a name for the new object.

4. Click Create.

TIP

You can create a new Template based on an existing Template or User object. Then you only need to make minor changes for the new setup. To do that, check the Use template or User checkbox, and then use the browse button to choose the Template or User object.

In addition to automating the set up of the network environment for users, such as working directories and files, Templates can also set up accounting charges and balances if you need them. If you prefer, you can set up these resources manually, without using a Template.

Use the following steps to prepare the network environment for a user:

1. Choose the desired Template.

2. Double-click the object to view its details.

3. Choose the Environment page and fill in the following fields:

   a. Language. This is an optional, single-valued property that lists, in order, the languages in which the user prefers to work. Each entry can be up to 256 characters (bytes) long, but in practice should correspond to one of the NetWare Client32 language (NWLANGUAGE) values documented in *NetWare Client for MS Windows User Guide*, such as English. (The supported languages are: Chinese, Danish, Dutch, English, Finnish, French, German, Italian, Japanese, Korean, Norwegian, Portuguese, Russian, Spanish, and Swedish.) If the user logs in and then runs a program that checks this property (some NetWare utilities do), the program displays text in the language of first preference, if the language is installed. If it isn't installed, the second preference is used, and so on.

   b. Default server. This is a mandatory, single-valued property that specifies the NetWare server associated with the User object. The value must be a complete name, such as NETWARE_51.Systems. You can either type the name in the available field or use the browse button to browse the available NetWare server objects. The default server is used to retrieve messages, such as those sent by Client32's Send Message option. If a user doesn't have a default server defined, he or she will not be able to receive such messages.

   c. Home directory. This is an optional, single-value property that specifies the location (volume and path) and name for the user's home directory (working area on the server). This field is automatically filled in if you chose to create home directory when the User object was created.

4. Check the Run setup and enter the commands to perform the tasks in Setup script. The Setup script attribute specifies a setup script for the Template object. You can use this script to perform user setup tasks that aren't taken care of by the other properties of the Template. For example, you can copy files to the user's home directory. The syntax rules for the setup script are the same as for login scripts. The setup script is processed by the login script processor on your workstation immediately after each new User object is created, if Run setup is checked.

NOTE

For detailed information on setup (login) script commands and variables, see the online documentation CD-ROM that came with your copy of NetWare or from the Web at www.novell.com/documentation.

TIP

The following is a sample setup script that copies a set of INI files to the user's home directory.

```
WRITE "Setup script begin"
WRITE "Copying important files to user's home directory"
MAP K:=server1\sys:users\%LOGIN_NAME
#XCOPY c:\setup\*.ini k:
WRITE "Setup script end"
```

5. Click OK to save the changes.

Using ConsoleOne

ConsoleOne is a graphical Java utility that runs on a Windows workstation (if it has Client32 and a JVM — Java Virtual Machine — installed) or a NetWare 5.*x* server for centrally managing and administering network resources. It is designed like a file manager utility: in the left pane you browse containers, and in the right pane you work with the resources in those containers (see Figure 5.7). With ConsoleOne you can perform the following tasks:

▶ Manage NDS and the file system from within a single application. Using the Schema Manager tool in ConsoleOne, you can change NDS object rules.

▶ Browse large trees (NetWare Administrator is restrained by the workstation's available memory).

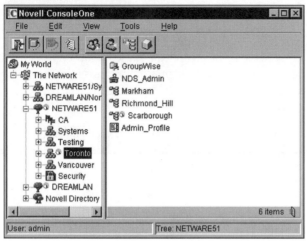

ConsoleOne has the look and feel of a file manager utility.

▶ Extend the NDS schema to include new object classes.

▶ Administer large numbers of objects.

▶ Administer objects at your server as well as at your workstation.

The procedure for creating a User object using ConsoleOne is very similar to that of NetWare Administrator, yet with some significant differences. The following steps outline how to use ConsoleOne to create a new User object:

I. Launch ConsoleOne on your NetWare server or Windows workstation. On the server, if the GUI desktop is running, click the Novell button at the bottom of the screen and select ConsoleOne; otherwise enter **C1START** at the server console prompt. You need to log in to the NDS tree using ConsoleOne on the server.

TIP

> To install ConsoleOne on your desktop, run SETUP.EXE, which is located in the SYS:PUBLIC\MGMT\ConsoleOne\1.2\INSTALL directory. A shortcut is created on your desktop and you can launch ConsoleOne by simply double-clicking the icon.

2. Select the container object (an Organization or Organizational Unit object) that will hold the new User object. Expand the tree by clicking the plus icon, if necessary.

3. Click the User icon on the toolbar (the icon with a single person) to bring up the New User dialog box, as shown in Figure 5.8. Alternatively, you can right click the container and choose New ⇨ User (see Figure 5.9), or select File ⇨ New ⇨ User from the pull-down menu.

FIGURE 5.8 *ConsoleOne's New User dialog box looks similar to that of NetWare Administrator's; however, the Unique ID field is not available in NWAdmin.*

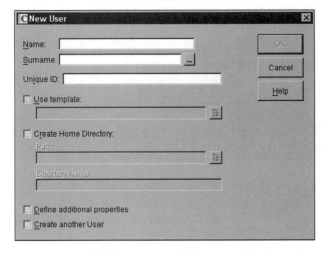

4. In the Name field, type a name for the new object. The name you enter is the name the user enters to log in. Make sure you follow standard object naming conventions.

5. In the Surname field, type the user's last name.

6. The value of the Unique ID field defaults to that of the Name. The Unique ID field enables you to enter an identifier to enable Lightweight Directory Access Protocol (LDAP) access for the user. The identifier *must* be unique for each user in the NDS tree. It can be up to 64 characters long.

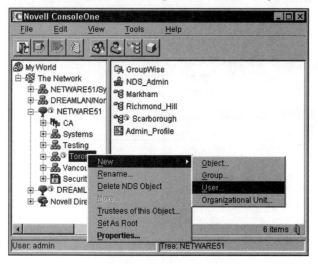

ConsoleOne enables you to create Users and Groups without having to select them from object class list.

7. If you have Template objects — these are leaf objects that contain the 'mold' from which you can create one or more User objects (see the preceding "Templates" section) — defined and would like to use them, check the Use template box. Then click the Browse button (which has a directory structure icon) located to the right and browse to locate the desired Template object.

8. To create a home directory for the new user:

   a. Check the Create Home Directory checkbox.

   b. Click the Browse button (which has a directory structure icon) located to the right of the word "Path" and above the words "Home Directory."

   c. From the Select Object dialog box, double-click the *right-hand* panel on the Volume object name that will hold the user home directories (you may need to navigate the NDS tree to locate the desired Volume object).

   d. When the top level of the user's home directory (such as USERS) appears on the left panel of the dialog box, select that directory and click OK. The path to that directory should now appear in the Create User dialog box.

9. Check the Define additional properties checkbox. (This enables you to see and modify more information about the User object after you create it in the next step.)

10. Click Create.

11. The Create Authentication Secrets dialog box is then displayed. Fill in the Create Authentication Secrets dialog box (see Figure 5.10) and then click OK.

All fields except the New password field are automatically filled in. Enter the password for the User object. (This is known as the authentication secret.) For security, only asterisks (*) are displayed as you type. If you don't want the User object to require a password, leave this field blank.

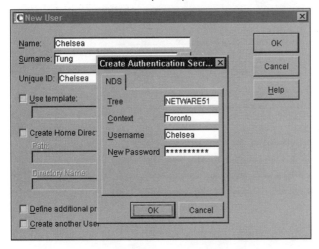

If the Create Authentication Secrets dialog box appears and you cancel it, an object-key pair (password) won't be created for the user account and the user won't be able to log in. If you don't want to set a login password right now, just click OK in the Create Authentication Secrets dialog box without filling it in. This creates an object-key pair with a null (empty) password. You can change the password later by going to the Password Restrictions property page of the User object.

NOTE

12. The user's identification page is displayed, as shown in Figure 5.11. This general identification page is displayed every time you use ConsoleOne to view this User object's details. A large number of attributes are associated with a User object and they are grouped into different categories by ConsoleOne (under different "tabs"). You can fill in some, none, or all of the information on these pages depending on your needs. Click OK when finished.

F I G U R E 5.11
The way object attribute information is displayed in Console One is different from that of NetWare Administrator.

Properties of Chelsea

| General ▾ | Restrictions ▾ | Memberships ▾ | Security Equal To Me | Login Script | NDS Rights ▾ | Other | Rights t |
| Identification |

Given name:
Last name: Tung
Full name:
Qualifier: Middle initial:
Other name:
Title:
Description:
Location:
Department:
Telephone:
Fax Number:
E-Mail Address:

ConsoleOne is to replace the NetWare Administrator utility in the future and the version of ConsoleOne found in NetWare 5.1 is a transitional version between using NetWare Administrator and ConsoleOne for all your administrative needs. At the time of this writing, certain NDS management tasks are still best performed using NetWare Administrator; for example, defining a Template object.

In most cases, either tool works fine. However, ConsoleOne has some limitations on the user properties you can define in a Template. Specifically, you must use NetWare Administrator to define rights assignments, scripted environment setup, and volume space restrictions in a user template.

On the other hand, when it comes to the creation of an NDS object, you'll find ConsoleOne to be a lot more flexible and powerful. ConsoleOne can create any object type defined in your schema, including new types you've added. NetWare Administrator can only create object types for which it has custom snap-ins (such as those listed in the New Object dialog box).

Using UIMPORT

In some occasions you may need to create a large number of users. It would be very inefficient to use NetWare Administrator or ConsoleOne for such a task. UIMPORT (User Import) is a Novell-supplied utility shipped with NetWare 4 and NetWare 5. Its function is the same as the MakeUser application included with earlier versions of NetWare — to create users in a batch mode.

UIMPORT uses two text files for input: a control file containing keywords that specify how the objects are to be created and how the data file is formatted, and an ASCII data file containing user object information.

NOTE

DS changes from NetWare 4.10 to 4.11 (and higher) included a change for the user template. In NetWare 4.10, the user template was simply a User object called USER_TEMPLATE; in NetWare 4.11 and higher, it is a separate object (of the Template class) and you can have multiple Templates in a container, whereas in NetWare 4.10 and below, you could have only one. Unfortunately, UIMPORT was not updated to support the new Template class, therefore the Template objects can't be used with UIMPORT. However, you can still create a User object called USER_TEMPLATE and UIMPORT takes settings from it when creating new users.

The following is a sample control file for UIMPORT. For a complete listing of supported keywords and attributes, enter **UIMPORT /? ATTR** at the DOS prompt.

```
IMPORT CONTROL
    CREATE HOME DIRECTORY = Y
    HOME DIRECTORY PATH = "\USERS"
    HOME DIRECTORY VOLUME = "NETWARE_51_SYS.SYSTEMS"
    IMPORT MODE = C
    NAME CONTEXT = "TORONTO"
    REPLACE VALUE = N
```

```
         SEPARATOR = ;
         USER TEMPLATE = Y
     FIELDS
         NAME
         LAST NAME
         GROUP MEMBERSHIP
         PASSWORD REQUIRED
         MINIMUM PASSWORD LENGTH
         PASSWORD EXPIRATION INTERVAL
```

NOTE

Note that Name and Last Name are mandatory User attributes while the rest are optional. Also note that the UIMPORT keywords and attributes are not case-sensitive.

TIP

By changing the IMPORT MODE from C (create) to R (remove), the list of users specified in the data file is deleted from NDS. So, you can also use UIMPORT as a user clean up tool. In this mode, you only need to specify NAME and LAST NAME in the data file.

Note that the IMPORT CONTROL and FIELDS headings are required. The following is a sample data file that contains the values to be created for each field listed in the preceding control file specification. The values for each user are entered on a single line and are separated by semicolons, as follows:

```
Tasha; Golden; Admin.Toronto; y; 6; 30
Chelsea; Golden; Sales.Toronto; y; 6; 30
Test1; "Test User #1"; Demo.Testing; n; 5; 45
Test2; "Test User #2"; Demo.Testing; n; 5; 45
```

After building the control and data files, ensure your workstation's current context is set to where the User objects are created, and then run UIMPORT as follows:

```
cx .Toronto
uimport demo.ctl demo.dat
```

You should have at least 500K of free memory for UIMPORT to run correctly.

WARNING

Because UIMPORT is a DOS application, it cannot create user home directories with long file name support. When users home directories are created via UIMPORT, they are truncated to eight characters.

For more information about UIMPORT, consult your documentation CD-ROM or the Novell Web site www.novell.com/documentation.

Using BULKLOAD

If you have installed eDirectory (NDS8) and have configured an LDAP (*Lightweight Directory Access Protocol*) server, you can then use BULKLOAD. NLM (see Figure 5.12) to create users en masse. BULKLOAD uses *LDAP Data Interchange Format* (LDIF) files for batch processing, which can be generated from most e-mail programs and directory services (such as Netscape). Therefore, you can easily generate the necessary LDIF data file for import into NDS.

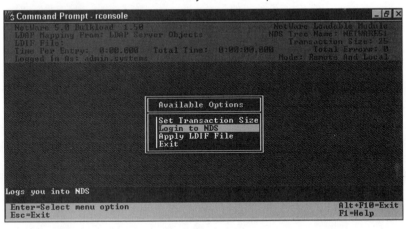

FIGURE 5.12   *Other than creating objects, BULKLOAD can also modify and delete NDS objects in a batch process.*

NOTE

BULKLOAD.NLM is installed as part of the upgrade to eDirectory. On non-NetWare platforms, such as Windows NT/2000 and Solaris, BULKLOAD is also included as one of the utilities.

An LDIF file is a text file with blocks of data. Each block of data, separated by a blank line, is called an LDIF entry; these entries describe either an object in the directory or a modification to the directory. Each LDIF file contains either object definitions or object modifications, never a mixture of both. Different files can be used to represent definitions and modifications. Files with object definitions, for example, can be used to describe a subset *or* the entire contents of a directory or naming context.

Each LDIF entry is written as one or more lines of text. A given line typically describes one attribute of an object; the attributes can be specified in any order, with the exception that dn must come first. Long attribute specifications can be continued on additional lines that begin with a single space. LDIF entries in the file are separated with at least one blank line. Comment lines begin with a pound sign (#).

The first entry in an LDIF file should begin with an LDIF version number. The current specification for LDIF is version one (which allows for adding, modifying, and deleting objects). Therefore, the first line of the file should be:

```
version: 1
```

If this line is omitted, BULKLOAD assumes that the file is version 0, and that all objects in the file are to be added. Following is a sample LDIF version 0 file:

```
dn: cn=Tasha Golden, o=Toronto
cn: Tasha
sn: Golden
objectclass: inetorgperson
givenname: Tasha
telephonenumber: +1 905 555 1212
title: Administrator

dn: cn=Chelsea, o=Toronto
cn: Chelsea
sn: Golden
givenname: Chelsea
objectclass: inetorgperson
telephonenumber: +1 905 555 1212
title: Sales
```

LDIF version 1 files may contain additions, modifications, and deletions in the same file. Following are sample data for adding entries:

```
version: 1
dn: cn=Tasha Golden, o=Toronto
changetype: add
cn: Tasha
sn: Golden
objectclass: inetorgperson
givenname: Tasha
telephonenumber: +1 905 555 1212
title: Administrator

dn: cn=Chelsea, o=Toronto
changetype: add
cn: Chelsea
sn: Golden
givenname: Chelsea
objectclass: inetorgperson
telephonenumber: +1 905 555 1212
title: Sales
```

Following is an example of entry modifications. The hyphens are required to terminate each change:

```
version: 1
dn: cn=Tasha, o=Toronto
changetype: modify
add: postaladdress
postaladdress: 1234 Main Street E $ Sometown, ON $ Canada
-
delete: description
-
replace: telephonenumber
telephonenumber: 1-905-555-1212
-
```

Deleting entries is done by specifying the specific names to be deleted with no leading qualifier, as shown following:

```
version: 1
dn: cn=Test1, o=Testing
changetype: delete

dn: cn=Test2, o=Testing
changetype: delete
```

BULKLOAD can produce keypairs (a password) for each user when the userPassword field is included. To run BULKLOAD, you must first create your LDIF file using a text editor. After you have created your LDIF file, follow these next steps (assuming we're dealing with a NetWare server):

1. Copy the LDIF file to the server — it can be placed anywhere.

2. Start BULKLOAD.NLM at the server console by entering **BULKLOAD** or **LOAD BULKLOAD** at the console prompt.

3. Select Login to NDS from the menu and log in as a user with the NDS rights needed to perform the desired operations (such as add, delete, or modify objects and properties).

4. Select Apply LDIF File from the menu and enter the file name of your LDIF file, including the path.

> **NOTE**
> For more information about **LDIF** file formats, see www.ietf.org.

> **NOTE**
> The process runs considerably slower when you include the user Password field.

The results, including any errors encountered, are written to a log file named after the LDIF file (see Figure 5.13). For instance, if the LDIF file is DEMO.TXT, the log file is called DEMO.LOG.

F I G U R E 5.13 *The log file is created in the SYS:SYSTEM directory, regardless of where DEMO.TXT is located.*

```
MS Command Prompt - rconsole                                    _ [] X
NetWare 5.0 Bulkload  1.50                    NetWare Loadable Module
LDAP Mapping From: LDAP Server Objects        NDS Tree Name: NETWARE51
LDIF File: SYS:DEMO.TXT                        Transaction Size: 25
Time Per Entry:  0:00.000   Total Time:  0:00:00.000   Total Errors: 0

                   View Log File: "SYS:\SYSTEM\DEMO.log"

/*****************************************************************************/
Netware 5.0 Bulkload 1.00
Log file for tree NETWARE51
Bulkload Applying LDIF FILE Status Screen
Processing LDIF File: SYS:DEMO.TXT
Transaction Size: 25
Total entries to be processed: 2
Start:  Tuesday, May 16, 2000  10:32:01 pm Local Time
Total Time:  0:00:00.000
Time Per Entry:  0:00.000
Total Errors: 0
End:  Tuesday, May 16, 2000  10:32:02 pm Local Time
*** END ***

Esc=Exit the editor              F1=Help              Alt+F10=Exit
```

The following is the sample LDIF used to create two test users; the details of one of these users is shown in Figure 5.14.

```
version: 0
dn: cn=ldif_user1, o=testing
cn: ldif_user1
sn: ldif
description: created by ldif
objectclass: inetorgperson

dn: cn=ldif_user2, o=testing
cn: ldif_user2
sn: ldif
objectclass: inetorgperson
description: created by ldif
```

The sn (surname) field in LDIF is shown as the Last name field in NetWare Administrator.

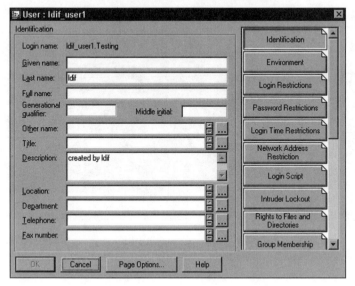

For more information about BULKLOAD, see `www.novell.com/documentation/lg/nds8/docui/index.html` under the Contents ➪ Utilities Reference ➪ Bulkload section.

Using NetWare Web Manager

New in NetWare 5.1 is the NetWare Web Manager, a browser-based management tool that enables you to configure and manage a number of Novell Internet Services, such as the FTP server and Web server. As a side benefit, the NetWare Web Manager also enables you to perform some simple NDS object management tasks, such as creation and modification of objects and their attributes, via a standard Web browser. Through the Web Manager, you can create, delete, and modify containers, users, and groups — however, the Web Manager, as shipped with NetWare 5.1, doesn't support other NDS object classes; for example, it is *not* shown user Alias objects.

You need to install the NetWare Enterprise Web Server in order for the Web Manager to be installed.

NOTE

Use the following steps to create a new User object using the NetWare Web Manager:

1. Start your Web browser and specify the secure URL (such as https instead of http) of your NetWare 5.1 server, using the port 2200 (the default port).

2. If your workstation doesn't already have the site certificate (a certificate is a unique digital ID that can be used to verify the identity of a person, Web site, or JavaScript/Java applet) for your server, you'll be prompted to accept it.

3. Login with a username that has sufficient NDS rights to perform object creation in the tree. (Use the absolute naming convention, such as .admin.systems.)

4. Click the Users and Groups link under the General Administration heading, or the button with the name of your server under Novell Directory Service (NDS), as shown in Figure 5.15.

FIGURE 5.15 *Internet services that are installed have either the On or Off button lit beside the server name button; services that cannot be turned on or off have both buttons darkened.*

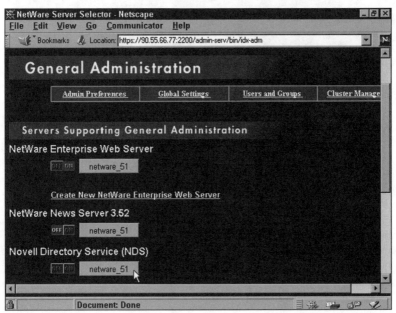

5. Click the container in which you wish to create the new User object.

6. From the Organization Contents form, click the New User link on the left of the screen (see Figure 5.16).

► . . . . ◄

F I G U R E 5 . 1 6   *Containers (such as Organization and Organizational Units), Users, and Groups are the only NDS object types you can create using the NetWare Web Manager.*

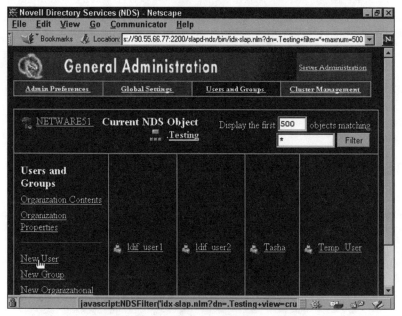

7. Type in the new user information in the displayed form (see Figure 5.17). You must enter a surname and User ID (this is the user login name). By default, the User ID is the same as the surname.

8. Enter the password.

9. Optionally, enter one or more e-mail addresses. When entering more than one e-mail address, separate each address by pressing Enter on your keyboard.

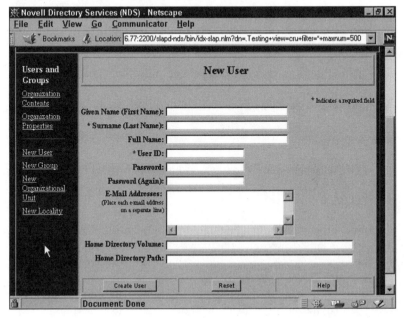

F I G U R E   5.17   *The use of Template is not supported by the NetWare Web Manager.*

10. If you want a home directory to be created for the user, in the Home Directory Volume field, type the name of the NDS object in the form of servername_volume.context, as in **netware_51_sys.systems**. Then, in the Home Directory Path field, type **/USER/username**.

11. Click Create User to add the new user to the NDS tree.

A JavaScript Application status box is displayed, informing you whether the object was successfully created. Click OK to continue.

NOTE

If you need to change any of the User object's attributes, such as the password, click the User object and then select User Attributes or User Password on the resulting form.

You'll find that the NetWare Web Manager is not as powerful as NetWare Administrator or ConsoleOne. However, because all you need is a standard browser and IP connectivity from your workstation to the NetWare server, the NetWare Web Manager is a nice tool should you find yourself having to create a new user or reset a user password and you don't have ready access to a Windows workstation.

Creating a Group

Creating a Group object is similar to creating a User object. The following procedure shows how to create a Group object using NetWare Administrator.

NOTE

> The remainder of the chapter uses NetWare Administrator as the preferred tool to illustrate the procedures for creating other objects.

1. Start NetWare Administrator. The NetWare Administrator's browser window should appear. (If the browser window doesn't appear, select Tools ⇨ NDS Browser. Select the tree you want by using the tree button or choose from the list of available trees. Next, type or choose the complete name of the container object that you want to place at the top of the view, or choose the browse button to choose from the available containers. Then click OK.)

2. Select the container object (an Organization or Organizational Unit object) that holds the new Group object. If the desired container is inside another container, double-click the parent container to display its subordinate objects. If the desired container is in a different subtree branch, select View ⇨ Set Context, then type or choose the complete name of the container object that you want, or select the browse button to choose from the available containers, and click OK.

3. Select Object ⇨ Create. (Alternatively, you can simply press the Insert key, right-click the container and choose Create, or click the Create Group object icon on the toolbar.)

4. From the New Object dialog box, highlight Group and then click OK.

5. In the Create Group dialog box (see Figure 5.18), enter the name for the new Group object. Make sure you follow standard object naming conventions.

6. Click Create.

You have two ways to associate User objects to Group objects and they are discussed in the following two sections.

F I G U R E   5 . 1 8 *If you want to add members to this Group object right away, check the Define additional properties checkbox.*

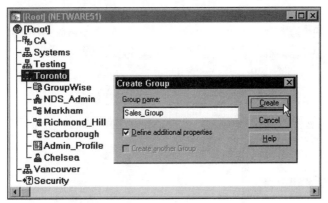

Making Users a Group Member

Generally you'll assign group members at the same time you're creating the new Group object. If you checked the Define additional properties checkbox during the Group object creation process, the Group's identification page is displayed. If not, double-click the Group object to display its details. You'll see that a Group object's identification page has fewer "tabs" or "pages" than a User object's identification page.

TIP

You should fill in some of the information on the Identification page, especially the Description field. Without adequate documentation, over time you'll find a large number of Group objects with no clear purpose. Use the Description field to indicate why the Group object was created, so you know if it can be safely removed later.

Use the following steps to add members to a Group object:

1. Display the details of the Group object using NetWare Administrator by double-clicking the object.

2. Click the Members page button.

3. Click Add.

4. From the screen that follows (see Figure 5.19), specify any existing users who should be members of this group. From the right panel, open the container that holds the user(s) you want. From the left panel, select the user and click OK. (You can also double-click the User object instead.)

F I G U R E 5.19 *Select users that are to be added to the group using this screen.*

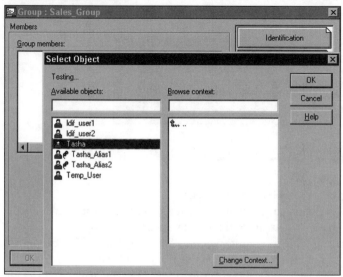

NOTE

You can also select user Aliases and they are deferred to the real objects when you save the changes.

TIP

You can select multiple users to be added by using Shift+click or Ctrl+click.

5. Click OK to save the selections.

Assigning Group Memberships to a User

If you need to add a user to multiple groups, the method discussed previously is not the most convenient, as you need to perform the steps for every Group object. Instead, you can assign memberships to a user with the following steps:

 I. Display the details of the User object using NetWare Administrator by double-clicking the object.

 2. Click the Group Membership page button.

 3. Click Add.

 4. From the screen that follows, specify any existing groups to which the user should belong. From the right panel, open the container that holds the group(s) you want. From the left panel, select the group and click OK. (You can also double-click the Group object instead.)

> **You can select multiple groups to be added by using Shift+click or Ctrl+click.**

TIP

 5. Click OK to save the selections.

Creating an Alias

An Alias object enables a user to access an object outside of the user's normal working context, without having to tree-hop to locate the actual resource. You'll find examples of the appropriate times to use an Alias in Chapter 4. Because an Alias is simply a pointer, the steps to create an Alias are very simple:

 I. Start NetWare Administrator. The NetWare Administrator's browser window should appear. (If the browser window doesn't appear, select Tools ⇨ NDS Browser. Select the tree you want by using the tree button or choose from the list of available trees. Then, type or choose the complete name of the container object that you want to place at the top of the view, or choose the browse button to choose from the available containers. Then click OK.)

2. Select the container object (an Organization or Organizational Unit object) that holds the new Alias object. If the desired container is inside another container, double-click the parent container to display its subordinate objects. If the desired container is in a different subtree branch, select View ⇨ Set Context, then type or choose the complete name of the container object that you want, or choose the browse button to choose from the available containers, and then click OK.

3. Select Object ⇨ Create. (Alternatively, you can simply press the Insert key, right-click the container and choose Create, or click the Create a new object icon — looks like a 3-D blue cube — on the toolbar.)

4. From the New Object dialog box, highlight Alias and then click OK.

5. In the Create Alias dialog box (see Figure 5.20), enter the name for the new Alias object into the Alias name field. Make sure you follow standard object naming conventions.

FIGURE 5.20 *An Alias object is simply a pointer to the real object.*

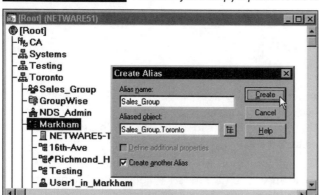

6. In the Aliased object field, enter the full name of the real object. Alternatively, you can click the Browse button (which has a directory structure icon) located to the right and browse to locate the desired object.

7. If you wish to create more than one Alias object, check the Create another Alias checkbox.

8. Click Create.

Creating a Container

Container objects are used to help organize the objects in your NDS tree by grouping relevant objects together. Typically one uses an Organization object (O) to denote a company, an Organizational Unit object (OU) to represent a workgroup or department within the company, a Country object (C) to indicate the country where network sites are located, and the Locality object (L) designates the location of this portion of the network. For example, if a company that is based in Canada has offices on both the east and west coast, its NDS tree may look similar to the one shown in Figure 5.21.

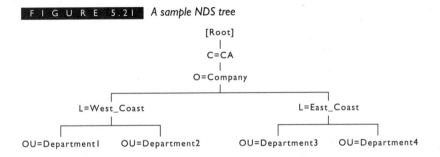

FIGURE 5.21 *A sample NDS tree*

NOTE

The Country object is always found at the top of the Directory tree (directly below the [Root] object). This object is not often used, but it is available for compliance with the X.500 standard.

When creating container objects, you need to be aware of the NDS object containment rules shown in Table 5.2. As a result of the containment rules, NetWare Administrator and other tools (such as ConsoleOne) show only certain types of container objects in the New Object dialog box depending on the parent container you selected.

NOTE

An additional container class exists, Licensed Product (LP). But because you can't use LPs to organize NDS objects such as Users and Groups — they are for license certificates only — one normally doesn't think of LPs as containers.

TABLE 5.2	NDS Object Containment Rules
PARENT CONTAINER TYPE	ALLOWED CHILD CONTAINER TYPES
[Root]	Country Organization
Country	Locality Organization
Locality	Locality Organization Organizational Unit
Organization	Locality Organizational Unit
Organizational Unit	N/A

The following steps outline the procedure for creating container objects:

1. Start NetWare Administrator. The NetWare Administrator's browser window should appear. (If the browser window doesn't appear, select Tools ⟿ NDS Browser. Select the tree you want by using the tree button or choose from the list of available trees. Then, type or choose the complete name of the container object that you want to place at the top of the view, or choose the browse button to choose from the available containers. Then click OK.)

2. Select the parent container object that will hold the new container object. If the desired container is inside another container, double-click the parent container to display its subordinate objects. If the desired container is in a different subtree branch, select View ⟿ Set Context, then type or choose the complete name of the container object that you want, or choose the browse button to choose from the available containers, and then click OK.

3. Select Object ⟿ Create. (Alternatively, you can simply press the Insert key, right-click the container and choose Create, or click the Create a new object icon — looks like a 3-D blue cube — on the toolbar.)

4. From the New Object dialog box, highlight the desired container type (such as Organizational Unit) and then click OK.

5. In the Create dialog box, enter the name for the new container object. Make sure you follow standard object naming conventions.

NOTE

When creating a Locality object, you can specify if the object is a Locality, State, or Province. From a usage point of view, the options function the same way and NetWare Administrator (or ConsoleOne) shows them the same way. However, if you examine the object in detail using DSVIEW.NLM (for NetWare 4) or DSBROWSE.NLM (for NetWare 5), you'll find that the object with the Locality radio button clicked during creation has an L attribute while the object with the State or Province radio button clicked during creation has an S attribute. This means that if you have an NDS-aware utility that searches the tree for Locality objects, you may get different results depending on whether the utility looks for the L or S attribute in the object.

6. If you wish to create more than one container object, check the Create Another checkbox.

7. Click Create.

Generally you don't need to check the Define additional properties checkbox unless you need to define a container login script (discussed in the following section), enable intruder detection security, or modify printing-related settings. You can access a container's details by right-clicking the container object and choosing Details — do *not* double-click the object because it "opens" the container and lists its subordinate objects instead.

Creating an Organizational Role

An Organizational Role (OR) object is a leaf object in the NDS tree that represents a position or role, such as Team Leader or Accounting Resources Manager, that can be filled by any designated user. Although it functions much like a Group object, using it can simplify NDS rights management — you grant rights to the Organizational Role object, and the current occupant(s) automatically gets security equivalence to the Organizational Role object, something you can't do with Group objects.

The following steps outline the procedure for creating Organizational Role objects:

1. Start NetWare Administrator. The NetWare Administrator's browser window should appear. (If the browser window doesn't appear, select Tools ➪ NDS Browser. Select the tree you want by using the tree button or choose from the list of available trees. Then, type or choose the complete name of the container object that you want to place at the top of the view, or select the browse button to choose from the available containers. Then click OK.)

2. Select the container object (an Organization or Organizational Unit object) that will hold the new OR object. If the desired container is inside another container, double-click the parent container to display its subordinate objects. If the desired container is in a different subtree branch, select View ➪ Set Context, then type or choose the complete name of the container object that you want, or select the browse button to choose from the available containers, and then click OK.

3. Select Object ➪ Create. (Alternatively, you can simply press the Insert key, right-click the container and choose Create, or click the Create a new object icon — looks like a 3-D blue cube — on the toolbar.)

4. From the New Object dialog box, highlight Organizational Role and then click OK.

5. In the Create dialog box, enter the name for the new OR object. Make sure you follow standard object naming conventions.

6. If you wish to create more than one OR object, check the Create another checkbox.

7. Click Create.

Generally you'd want to check the Define additional properties checkbox in order to add occupants to the object. Use the following steps to add occupants to an OR object:

1. Display the details of the OR object using NetWare Administrator by double-clicking the object.

2. Click the browse button located to the right of the Occupant listbox.

3. Click Add.

From the screen that follows, specify any existing users who should be occupants of this OR object. From the right panel, open the container that holds the user(s) you want. From the left panel, select the user and click OK. (You can also double-click the User object instead.)

Login Scripts

Login scripts are tools similar to batch files that you can use to set up a user's workstation environment automatically. Each time a user logs in, the login script is executed (unless the Run Script option is disabled in the workstation's client software). Login scripts are often used to set up frequently used drive mappings, printer capturing, display system messages (such as notices from the network administrator) on the screen, and perform other types of tasks for the user.

NOTE

In NetWare, you can assign a drive letter (such as F or H) to point to a specific network directory. This is similar to having drive E point to the CD-ROM on your workstation. When you assign a drive letter to a directory, it's called *mapping a drive*. The resulting drive assignment is called a *drive mapping*.

Types of Login Scripts

Four types of login scripts exist:

- **Container login scripts.** The container login script (called *the system login script* in NetWare 2.x and NetWare 3.x) is an attribute of a container object. All the commands in the container script execute for every user within that container who logs in. Therefore, container script is an excellent place to put commands that are common to all users within the container.

NOTE

Container login scripts are not nested. This means users in OU=Markham.O=Toronto will only execute the login script defined for OU=Markham and not execute the container script from O=Toronto.

- **Profile login scripts.** The profile login script is associated with a Profile object and can be applied to several users who don't necessarily have to be in the same container. Profile login scripts can be a type of *group login script*. Note that each user can have only one profile login script defined.

- **User login scripts.** Each User object has a Login Script attribute where you can define specific drive mappings or other commands that are unique to that user. If the user doesn't have a specific user login script, a default login script will execute instead, setting up the most basic drive mappings.

▶ **Bindery login scripts.** Container, profile, and user login scripts are stored in NDS. However, when a user connects to a NetWare server using a bindery connection, instead of any of the NDS login scripts, a set of bindery login scripts is executed. Bindery login scripts are executed for every bindery user. The bindery login script is stored in a file called NET$LOG.DAT in the SYS:PUBLIC directory, and is unique to each NetWare server.

TIP If you have users that will be making both NDS and bindery connections to the network, you need to synchronize the bindery script with the NDS-based scripts so the users will have the same working environment when they log in.

The discussions in the following sections will focus on the NDS-based login scripts.

When a user logs in, the login scripts are executed in the following order:

1. Container login script

2. Profile login script

3. User login script (or the default user login script, if a user login script doesn't exist)

All three login scripts are optional. If one of them doesn't exist, the login process will skip to the next in the list. Therefore, if no login script is defined, the default user login script (which maps a search drive to SYS:PUBLIC on the user's default server) will be the only one that runs when a user logs in. You should be careful here though — if the container and profile scripts exist and are run without a user login script, the default user login script will run and possibly overwrite mappings set up in the other scripts.

Creating a Login Script

You can use NetWare Administrator to create login scripts just as you assign any other attribute values to NDS objects.

TIP Windows 95 and higher users can use the Network Neighborhood and permanent mappings to customize their workstation environments. However, if you have a large number of Windows workstations, you should consider doing their customization centrally through login scripts as it makes future modifications much easier and eliminates the need to touch each and every workstation. It also makes troubleshooting a lot simpler.

TIP

Instead of setting up drive mappings via the login scripts, you can use the NetWare Application Launcher (NAL) that's part of the ZENworks package included with NetWare 5. Using NAL, you can set up icons on users' desktops that point directly to network applications. Then, the users can simply launch the applications from their desktops without having to know where the applications are located, or which drive letters to map, and so on.

The following steps apply equally to creating container, profile, and user login scripts:

1. Locate the desired container, Profile, or User object using NetWare Administrator.

2. Open the object's Details page — double-click the Profile or User object *or* right-click the container object and then select Details.

3. Click the button for the Login Script page.

4. You're presented with a blank screen, or the previous login script if one already exists (see Figure 5.22).

5. Enter your login script commands.

6. Click OK to save changes.

F I G U R E   5.2 2   *Sample container login script*

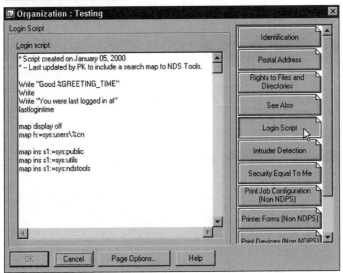

Details about login script commands and troubleshooting tips can be found in NetWare Administrator's online help — after clicking the Login Script button, click Help, and then click Login Script Help. You can also consult the online documentation either on the CD-ROM included with your copy of NetWare *or* on the Web at www.novell.com/documentation.

In general, ordinary users can only modify their own login scripts. The Admin user, or equivalent, can change login scripts for other users and for containers.

Assigning Profile Login Scripts to Users

To create a profile login script, you first create a Profile object as outlined in an earlier section in this chapter. Create its script in the Profile object's login script attribute as described previously. After you have created the script, you must then assign it to individual users. To do this, complete the following steps:

I. Use NetWare Administrator to select the desired User object.

2. Double-click the User object, and then click the Login Script button.

3. Enter the complete name of the Profile object (such as **Admin_Profile.Toronto**) in the Profile field located at the bottom of the window. Alternatively, you can click the Browse button (which has a directory structure icon) located to the right and browse to locate the desired Profile object.

4. Click OK to save the changes. If the selected Profile object is located in a container other than where the User object is, the following warning message will be displayed:

```
The user does not have Read rights to the Profile's
login script. You have to grant the user Read rights to
execute the Profile's login script. Do you want to save
the Profile assignment?
```

Click Yes to continue.

You might not receive this warning message if you've previously granted the necessary NDS rights.

5. Locate the Profile object using the browser, right-click, and then select Trustees of this Object.

6. In the Trustees window that appears, click the Add Trustee button and then enter the complete name of the User object that will use this profile login script. Ensure the Browse object rights and Read property rights checkboxes are checked (see Figure 5.23). Click OK to save the changes.

F I G U R E   5.23 *Granting a user Read rights to the Profile object*

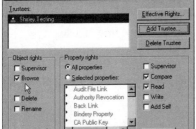

If you're getting a –609 error from NetWare Administrator when trying to assign a trustee to a Profile object, check to see if the Login Script attribute of the Profile object has any commands defined.

TIP

Refer to Chapter 6, "Assigning NDS Security Rights," for more details about object trustee assignments.

Caveats about User Alias Objects

Two caveats exist with login scripts and user Alias objects. By default, when a user logs in using a user Alias object, the container login script where the actual User object exists is the one that executes, not the container script where the user Alias object resides. You can address this by adding the following commands to the container login script where the User object exists so that the Alias object's container login script(s) can be executed. This example provides for multiple Alias objects, located in different containers.

```
IF "%LOGIN_ALIAS_CONTEXT" = "Y" THEN
INCLUDE %REQUESTER_CONTEXT
EXIT
END
```

The IF-THEN condition tests that if the LOGIN_ALIAS_CONTEXT login script variable is "Y" (which is as if logging in using a user Alias) the container script of the Alias object is executed (via the INCLUDE command). The "Exit" statement prevents control from being returned to the User's container login script and executes any commands in the script that may follow the preceding commands. This example works with LOGIN.EXE (for DOS), Windows 95 clients v3.0 and above, and the Windows NT GINA logins.

The second caveat relates to the profile login script. During the login process, the profile login script associated with the primary object is executed. Therefore, if the primary User object and its Alias object are located in replicas separated by WAN links, there may be drive mapping and print queue capturing commands resulting in unnecessary WAN traffic.

## CHAPTER 6

Assigning NDS
Security Rights

In NetWare prior to version 4, system security is tied closely to the Supervisor user. Only the Supervisor or a user with equivalent rights can perform certain management functions, and you cannot assign only certain network management functions (such as the ability to change passwords but nothing else) to a user. These limitations stem from the fact that the security division for the earlier releases of NetWare is not *granular*, as is the case for NetWare 4 and above.

As discussed previously in Chapter 1, "What is NDS and How Does It Work?" a set of attributes is associated with each NDS object. One of the attributes for a User object, for example, is a Telephone number. NDS enables you to grant a user full access to one or more attributes of a given object. You can, therefore, set up an administrator to manage the Telephone number attribute of your users and nothing else.

You cannot easily set up an administrator in pre-NetWare 4 such that the user can only manage other users without having full access to the file system. In order for someone to have full user-management capability, that user needs to be Supervisor equivalent. That also means the same user is to have full file system access. In situations for which you want to grant only user management privileges and not file system rights, the NetWare option is not desirable.

NDS enables you to separate user management rights (NDS object rights) from file system rights. You also can have multiple administrators such that each manages a different portion of the NDS tree. On the other hand, you can still have a central administrator who can perform management functions on both the NDS objects and file systems, much like the pre-NetWare 4 environment.

This chapter discusses what NDS rights are, how they are assigned, and how you can implement them for your particular needs. A quick review of security concepts opens the discussion.

▶ · ◀

Basic Security Concepts

Before getting into the details of NDS rights and how to assign them, you need to have a basic understanding of the following NetWare-based security concepts:

- ▶ Trustees and trustee assignments
- ▶ Inherited rights
- ▶ Inherited rights filters
- ▶ Security equivalence
- ▶ Effective rights

These concepts apply to both file system and NDS security. A solid understanding of them, therefore, is imperative. The discussion in the following sections uses the more familiar directory — the file system — as an example.

NOTE

Once you've mastered how NDS security works, you have a good
grasp of how NetWare file system rights function as well, or vice
versa.

Trustees and Trustee Assignments

In any shared-resources configuration, protecting files from unauthorized
access is important. NetWare users must be granted rights in order to access
resources — such as applications. Users are *not* given any rights by default in
NetWare except for a few (such as Read and File Scan file system rights to
SYS:PUBLIC) "low access" rights if certain conditions are met; refer to the
"Default NDS Rights" section later for more details. For a user to access a directory, for example, that user must be made a *trustee* of that directory.

The administrator also determines what types of rights are given to the
trustee (for example: what action the user can perform on the file or directory).
One trustee might only have read access, though another can write to the directory. These rights are known as *trustee assignments*. In order for Shirley to read
from and write to the SALES:DATA directory, she must be made a trustee of this
directory, and be given Read and Write trustee assignments (see Figure 6.1).

F I G U R E 6 . 1   *Shirley has Read and Write rights to SALES:DATA (and below)
but not to SALES:FORECAST.*

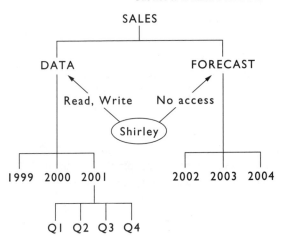

Inherited Rights

Assigning each user rights to every directory and their subdirectories is impractical. To circumvent this problem, NetWare uses the idea of *inheritance* — the "flow down" of rights. That is to say, if Shirley is given Read and Write rights to SALES:DATA, she automatically receives Read and Write (inherited) rights to all its subdirectories (refer to Figure 6.1). These rights may be removed or changed by explicitly granting a different trustee assignment.

Figure 6.2 offers an example of Shirley's trustee assignment being reassigned at a lower level of the directory structure. According to the figure, she now has Read, Write, and Erase access to SALES:DATA\2001\Q4, but, due to inheritance, Shirley still has only Read and Write access to the other three directories (Q1, Q2, and Q3) in SALES:DATA\2001.

F I G U R E   6 . 2   *A reassignment of trustee rights at a lower level changes the trustee rights for Shirley.*

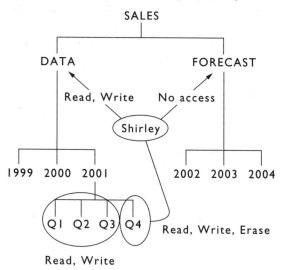

Inherited Rights Filter

You can prevent rights from flowing down a directory through the use of an *inherited rights filter* (IRF). The IRF specifies which rights are allowed to pass through the subdirectories, and affects *all* users' inherited rights, except for Supervisor. In essence, when you have an IRF, you need to perform a logical AND between the IRF and your inherited rights. Figure 6.3 illustrates the effect of an IRF on users Shirley and Peter. Shirley is granted Read and Write rights at the top level of the directory (SALES:DATA), and Peter is granted Read and Write rights to SALES:DATA\2001.

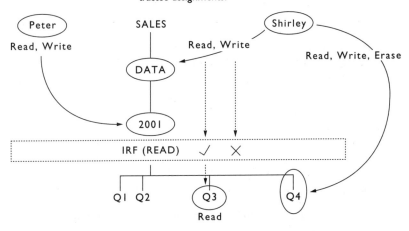

F I G U R E   6.3   *An IRF of Read blocked Shirley's Write access to SALES:DATA\2001\Q1 through SALES:DATA\2001\Q3 but not to SALES:DATA\2001\Q4. The IRF has no effect on Peter's trustee assignments.*

NOTE   If you're famililiar with pre-NDS versions of NetWare, the IRF was known as an Inherited Rights Mask (IRM) under NetWare 3, and the Maximum Rights Mask (MRM) under NetWare 2.

An IRF of Read is placed at the SALES:DATA\2001 level. Shirley, therefore, has only Read rights in SALES:DATA\2001 and, consequently, SALES:DATA\2001\Q1 through SALES:DATA\2001\Q3. But because she has an *explicit* trustee assignment to SALES:DATA\2001\Q4 of Read, Write, and Erase rights, she retains the same rights there. Peter has an *explicit* trustee assignment to SALES:DATA\2001; he, therefore, is not affected by the IRF at all.

NOTE

An IRF only affects inherited rights. Users with explicit trustee assignments at the level where an IRF is placed are unaffected.

Mathematically, the following indicates what happened with Shirley's rights in directory SALES:DATA\2001\Q3:

```
Shirley is given           Read, Write to SALES:DATA

Inherited Rights Filter of [Read,        ] is applied at
SALES:DATA\2001

Apply logical AND, we have (Read)         as Write is
filtered out by the IRF
```

Security Equivalence

Security equivalence is a User object attribute that lists other objects. When you make User A security equivalent to User B, User A receives all rights to which User B has explicit assignments. Security equivalence is *not* transitive, however. That means, if you make User A security equivalent to User B, and User B security equivalent to User C, User A is *not* security equivalent to User C through User B. Security equivalence only grants User A those rights that User B is explicitly granted.

Also, security equivalence is unidirectional. Making User A security equivalent to User B does not give User B access to any of User A's rights, unless User B is made security equivalent to User A.

NOTE

In pre-NetWare 4 environments, administrators often make users security equivalent to the Supervisor so those users can manage other users and file systems.

Although not explicitly mentioned in any of the NetWare documentation, any member of a group is security equivalent to the group. If you belong to the group ACCOUNTING, and the group has a trustee assignment to ACCT:DATA, you have the same access rights to this directory, through security equivalence.

Effective Rights

Effective rights are what rights a given user has after taking into account all the aforementioned items. Figure 6.4 illustrates a flow diagram to assist you in determining the effective rights of a user.

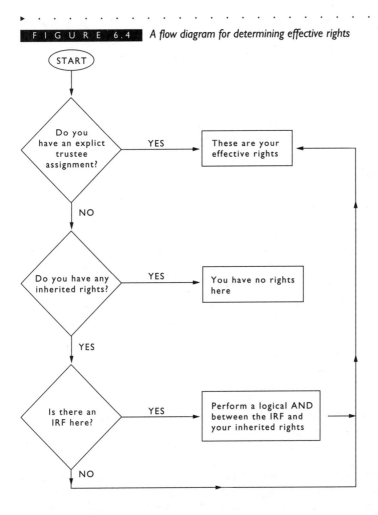

A flow diagram for determining effective rights

NDS Rights

Analogous to file system rights (which determine the directories and files over which you have control), NDS rights dictate what you can see, use, and manage within the NDS tree. Just as NetWare file system rights have separate directory rights and file rights, NDS rights also are divided into two categories: *object* rights and *attribute* (or *property*) rights.

NOTE

Novell documentation and utilities (such as NetWare Administrator) use the terms attribute and property interchangeably. In this book, however, the term attribute will be used whenever possible.

Object Rights

Each object in the NDS tree has a set of rights associated with it. These rights govern what other objects (not necessarily User objects) in the tree can do to the specific object. The following object rights are available:

- **Supervisor (S).** Grants all object *and* attribute access privileges to an object.

- **Browse (B).** Enables you to see the object in the NDS tree. Can be compared to the File Scan file system rights.

- **Create (C).** Enables a new object to be created under the specific container object in the NDS tree.

- **Delete (D).** Enables you to remove leaf and container objects from the tree. Note that a container must be empty before you can delete it.

- **Rename (R).** Enables you to change the name of an object. This right is much like the Modify file system rights.

- **Inheritable (I).** Enables the trustee assignment made of a container object to be inherited to objects, and containers below this object in the NDS tree. This applies to object rights, rights to all properties, and rights to specific properties.

NOTE

The Inheritable right feature only applies to container objects. This feature is functional only with versions of NDS that ship with NetWare 5 or later.

To use a resource (such as print queue) in the tree, a user needs the Browse right, and sometimes also the Read attribute right, to the resource. Later, this chapter discusses the various default rights assignments.

A User object does not need Browse rights to himself or herself in order to log in; he or she simply needs to specify the distinguished (fully qualified) name. The Browse right is granted by default, however, so the user can see his or her own object in the tree.

It is customary to denote the object rights as [SBCDRI]. If you have Browse and Create object rights, and then they are represented as [BC]. Similar conventions are applied to attribute rights (discussed in the following section). NETADMIN (a DOS-based utility shipped with NetWare 4) shows the rights in much the same order, except S is listed last — [BCDRS], and it does not show the Inheritable right assignment.

NETADMIN is not included with NetWare 5 or higher, and because the Inheritable right was introduced with NetWare 5.0, it follows that NETADMIN neither shows nor supports the Inheritable right flag.

NOTE

Attribute Rights

Each object has one or more attributes. Each attribute can have one or more values. Many attributes are multivalued. Figure 6.5, for example, shows the Location attribute for User object Chelsea to have two values. Using NetWare Administrator, a list button (and up/down arrows) falls on the right-hand side of the first value of a group of multiple values (see Figure 6.6); ConsoleOne uses a list icon with a down arrow to indicate multivalued attributes.

F I G U R E 6 . 5 *A User object's Location attribute can be multivalued.*

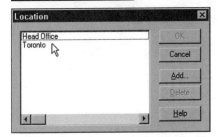

When rights are applied to a given attribute, they are applied to all the attribute's values. That means, if two entries (values) exist in the Location attribute, a User with Read right may read both values from the attribute.

Similar to object rights, attribute rights control what other NDS objects can do to the specific attribute. The following list explains the six attribute rights:

▶ **Supervisor (S).** Grants all rights to the attribute.

▶ **Compare (C).** Enables you to compare a value to the value of the attribute. A response of True or False is returned on comparison. You cannot, however, see the value of the attribute unless you have the Read attribute right.

▶ **Read (R).** Enables you to read values of an attribute. The Compare right is implied when a Read right is granted.

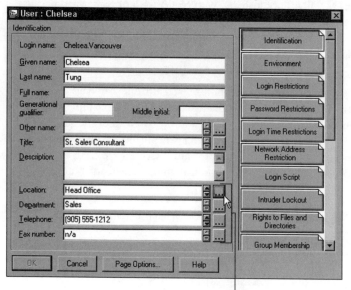

F I G U R E 6.6 NetWare Administrator uses list buttons to indicate an attribute can support multiple values.

Indicates multiple values possible

- ► **Write (W).** Enables you to add, delete, or change any values of the attribute.

- ► **Add/Delete Self (A).** Enables you to add or remove yourself as a value from the attribute. This right is only useful for attributes such as mailing lists that use object names as values. The Write right includes the Add/Delete Self right.

- ► **Inheritable (I).** Enables the trustee assignment made of a container object to be inherited to objects and containers below this object in the NDS tree. This applies to object rights, rights to all properties, and rights to specific properties.

NOTE

As mentioned previously, the Inheritable rights only apply to container objects and are functional only with versions of NDS that ship with NetWare 5 or later.

NOTE

The Supervisor object right also grants you Supervisor rights for all attributes.

Attribute rights can be assigned individually or through the All Properties option in NetWare Administrator (see Figure 6.7). The All Properties rights are applied to all attributes, but individual attribute right assignments override that default. An All Properties rights assignment of [CR], for example, and a Telephone number right assignment of [CRW] mean a trustee has Compare, Read, and Write rights to the Telephone number attribute, but only has Compare and Read rights to the other attributes. Similarly, file system rights assigned to individual files override those assigned to the directory in which the file resides.

▶ • ◀

F I G U R E   6 . 7   *Assigning object and attribute rights using NetWare Administrator*

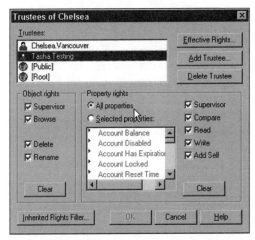

NOTE

Attribute rights can be assigned to all attributes of an object, or only to specific attributes of an object. The assignment of attribute rights is *not* all or nothing.

Attribute rights can be assigned selectively (that is, different rights to different attributes). A user might have [CR] to Group Membership, for example, but [CRW] to his Login Script and Print Job Configuration attributes.

NOTE

Again, object and attribute rights apply only to NetWare NDS objects, and *not* to the file systems (with one exception to be discussed later in the "NDS and File System Rights" section of this chapter).

Access Control List

An attribute called *Access Control List* (ACL) is associated with every NDS object. This attribute is worth special mentioning here because it controls access to both the object and the object's attributes.

NOTE

The ACL for NDS objects resembles the Directory Entry Tables (DETs) for file systems. DETs contain directory and file trustee assignments (among other information), and the ACL stores NDS trustee assignments.

The ACL attribute is listed as "Object Trustees (ACL)" when viewed using NetWare Administrator; and ConsoleOne lists it as "ACL."

The ACL is simply a list that stores who has rights (trustees) and what those rights are (trustee assignments). It does not, however, list what the object may have rights to. This concept is important to keep in mind. If you want to grant a user rights to a container, you must go to that container and make the user a trustee of it, with the appropriate rights. You do not go to the User object and make the container a trustee of that user.

An ACL value can specify rights for one of the following:

▶ A specific attribute, such as Telephone number

▶ The All Properties attribute of an object

▶ The object itself

Because the ACL is itself an attribute of an object, the ACL can have (as one of its values) a trustee assignment to itself. If a trustee is granted the Write right to the ACL (which in turn means the object itself), that trustee is allowed to modify *any* of the rights of the object. This Write right access is similar to granting the Supervisor trustee right to the object. *It can be a security risk.*

In practice, granting the Supervisor right is preferable to granting individual ACL access rights because the Supervisor right grants *both* the object and (all) attribute rights to an object via a single assignment. The use of ACL, however, does come in handy at times. This chapter discusses an example of its use in the section "Special Security Examples."

Inherited Rights for NDS Security

The concept of inherited rights for NDS security is very similar to that of the file system. Rights flow down an NDS tree. Under NetWare 4, however, the only rights that can be inherited are the object rights and the special All Properties right; individual attribute rights are not inherited. With NetWare 5, though, with the introduction of the Inheritable right flag at the container level, it is possible to grant rights to a specific attribute (at the container level) and have it be applied to all the objects in that container and below.

Similar to file system rights, only one specific trustee assignment is in effect at a time. That is to say, when multiple trustee assignments are made to the same user at different points in the NDS tree, the rights assignment made at the lowest level of the tree is the one that gets inherited (see Figure 6.8).

FIGURE 6.8 *The lowest rights assignment is the assignment that gets inherited.*

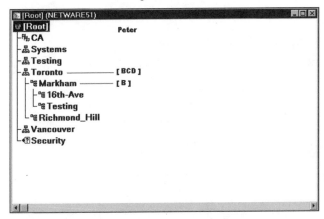

User Peter is granted the following object rights:

▸ [BCD] at O=Toronto

▸ [B] at OU=Markham.Toronto

At OU=Richmond_Hill (under O=Toronto), Peter inherits [BCD] rights, but for OU=Testing and OU=16th-Ave (both under OU=Markham.O=Toronto), he gets only [B] rights. Only the rights at the lowest portion of the tree are inherited. Therefore, you can easily control the rights inheritance by making multiple assignments.

Inherited Rights Filter for NDS Security

The IRF controls which rights can be inherited. It works in much the same manner as the IRF for file system security. The IRF in NDS security, however, applies to object rights, the All Properties right, and individual attribute rights.

NOTE The one main difference between how IRF works in NDS and the file system is that in file system security, you cannot use an IRF to block Supervisor rights to a file or directory. However, you can use IRF to block NDS Superivsor rights to an object or an attribute.

A little confusing at first, the situation is clarified by a simple example (see Figure 6.9). User Tasha is granted [BC] object rights and [CRW] All Properties rights to O=Toronto. An IRF of [SB DR] has been placed on object rights (meaning no Create right is to be inherited), and an IRF of [SCR A] has been placed on All Properties rights (meaning no Write right to All Properties is to be inherited) at OU=16th-Ave. Furthermore, User Jacques imposed an IRF of [SC] to the Login Script attribute.

FIGURE 6.9 *A simple NDS IRF example*

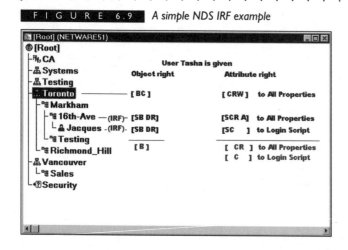

NOTE No Inheritable flag exists within the IRF. Any inherited rights from higher containers (granted through the Inheritable flag) may be blocked by the IRF.

Note that because Jacques is a leaf object, the Create object right does not apply to it. Thus, it is not a valid IRF option.

As a net result of inheritance and IRF, user Tasha has only Browse rights to the Jacques User object, and has Compare and Read rights to all attributes *except* for Login Script, to which she has only Compare rights.

Under NDS security, it is possible to use an object IRF to filter out Supervisor object rights from a branch of the tree. If you do this without first granting the Supervisor object rights to this portion of the tree to a separate object, you have no effective way of managing this section of the tree! This same precaution should be taken if you are deleting an object that has Supervisor object rights to other objects.

It is strongly recommended that when you grant Supervisor object rights to an object, you also grant the other object rights so that if the Supervisor rights are blocked by an IRF, you can still manage the tree. The granting of the Supervisor rights only *implies* the granting of the other rights. You should assign the other rights explicitly as a safety measure. IRFs for attributes provide one exception: Supervisor object rights grant all attribute rights, and an attribute IRF *cannot* block Supervisor object rights.

Two Special Trustee Objects

NDS introduces two special trustee objects. You cannot see these objects within the NDS tree, but nevertheless, they exist for your use. These objects are similar in concept to the *phantom Supervisor* user under Bindery Services.

At the top of every NDS tree is an object called [Root]. In NetWare Administrator, the [Root] object is represented by the Globe or World icon at the top of your tree structure. In ConsoleOne, the [Root] object is represented by a tree icon.

The second special trustee object is called [Public]. Any right (NDS or file system) granted to [Public] is automatically granted to every single object within the NDS tree as well as any clients that are attached but not authenticated (that is, not logged in) to the network.

By default, [Public] is granted Browse object rights to the [Root] of the NDS tree; no attribute rights and no file system rights are given. As a result, a user can *browse* the tree before logging in to the network. If this is not acceptable to your organization's security policy, remove [Public]'s Browse right from [Root]. You can do this using either NetWare Administrator or ConsoleOne. The following steps outline how you can use NetWare Administrator to remove [Public]'s right from [Root]:

1. Select the [Root] object; change context as necessary.

2. From the Object pull-down menu, select Trustees of this Object. (You can use the right mouse button instead to bring up a similar selection list as the pull-down menu — make sure your mouse pointer is on the [Root] object before you click the right mouse button.)

3. You are presented with a screen similar to that of Figure 6.7.

4. Highlight the [Public] object, and then click the Delete Trustee action button on the upper right.

5. Select Yes in the confirmation dialog box to remove the object trustee.

WARNING

Be aware that if you remove the Browse right from [Public], certain applications, such as contextless login, where the user doesn't need to specify a context while logging in, may fail to function. This is a chance you may have to take to increase security.

The [Root] and [Public] objects are granted rights under certain events (such as installation of a server). These system default rights are discussed later in the "Default NDS Rights" section of this chapter.

Security Equivalence for NDS Security

NDS enhances the security equivalence capability of previous versions of NetWare. Now, three default security equivalences cannot be reassigned or revoked. These system-implied security equivalences include the following:

▶ All objects are security equivalent to the [Root] object.

▶ All objects are security equivalent to the [Public] object.

▶ All objects are security equivalent to each successive container object directly from the [Root] through the user's container object.

The first two assignments ensure that User objects have sufficient rights to access a server to log in. The third needs further explanation.

Because NDS is object-oriented and because containers are considered objects, NetWare 4 and higher enables file system and NDS rights to be assigned to container objects. When rights are granted to a specific container, all objects within that container and within its subcontainers receive the same rights.

Consider the example shown in Figure 6.10. By assigning a file system right to a high-level container, all users within that container and within its subcontainers receive the same file system right.

Rights granted to a container are automatically granted to objects and subcontainers within it.

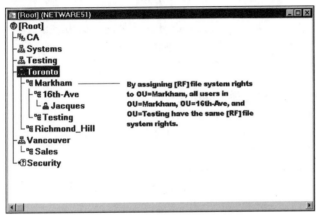

Think of container objects (used in this manner) as *super groups,* with no group membership list to maintain. They are simply there. This group membership assignment is actually done via the implied security equivalence of the object to the (parent) container.

In the past, this concept was (inaptly) called *ancestral inheritance.* In a sense, the rights are gained from the parent container, but they are not inherited in the way NetWare defines inherited rights. Further, according to NetWare's definition of the term, an inherited right can be blocked using an IRF. You cannot use an IRF to keep an object from receiving rights from the container to which it belongs. To say the rights are obtained via *implied security equivalence* is more accurate.

When you make a user a member of a group, the User object is thus security equivalent to the group object. This equivalent is not an implied security equivalent, however, because it is not automatic. You have to manually make the assignment. The same is true when you make a user the occupant of an Organizational Role.

TIP Although security equivalence provides a convenient means of assigning rights, *do not* use it when creating a backup Admin type user (an appropriate measure for previous versions of NetWare). In releases prior to NetWare 4, the Supervisor cannot be deleted. With NDS, however, any object can be removed from the tree, including Admin. If you create a backup Admin User object (say, Admin2) by making it security equivalent to Admin, and then inadvertently delete Admin, you are not able to manage your tree using Admin2. It has nothing to be equivalent to. You should instead create a backup Admin User object by giving it all object and attribute rights (including Supervisor and others) to the [Root] object.

Effective Rights for NDS Security

An object's NDS effective rights are determined in much the same way as file system effective rights. To determine the effective rights of a User object, the following list must be considered:

- Rights granted to the user explicitly.

- Rights gained via the user's security equivalents; for example, Groups, Organizational Roles, [Public], and any containers it belongs to, including [Root].

- Rights inherited from higher-level containers (not blocked by IRFs).

Figure 6.11 demonstrates a modified version of the flow diagram shown in Figure 6.4. This figure can assist you in determining your effective rights.

Some examples that follow in the "Special Security Examples" section of this chapter serve to illustrate the different NDS rights concepts presented so far in this chapter.

Looking up effective rights through the use of NetWare Administrator is much easier than using NETADMIN. NETADMIN only enables you to look up trustees of an object while NetWare Administrator enables you to check on both the trustees of an object as well as rights to other objects.

NDS and File System Rights

Generally, the NDS and file system rights are distinct and separate. Having the Browse object right to a Volume object, for example, is not the same as having File Scan file system rights to the volume. However, one instance exists in which NDS rights and file system rights "meet." When a user is granted Supervisor object rights to a Server object, the user is given Supervisor file system rights to the root of *all* the volumes on that server.

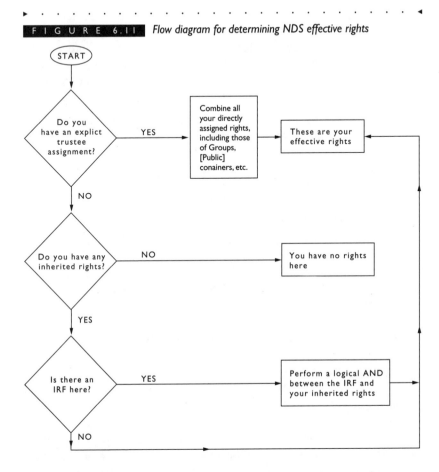

F I G U R E   6 . 1 1 *Flow diagram for determining NDS effective rights*

Remember that Supervisor file system rights cannot be filtered out using IRFs.

NOTE

If you want a user to be able to manage a Server object but not any of the file systems associated with it, do not grant that user Supervisor object rights. Rather, give the user [BCDR] object rights and [RCWA] attribute rights.

TIP

In the NDS environment, a trustee can be *any* object in the NDS; it does not necessarily need to be a user or a group, as is the case in earlier versions of NetWare. Granting file system rights to [Root], for example, automatically grants all users within the NDS tree the same file system rights (because all users have implied security equivalence to [Root]). The same concept applies to the [Public] and container objects.

NOTE

As previously mentioned, any clients that are attached but not authenticated (that is, not logged in) to the network get the rights assigned to [Public]. Therefore, it seems granting file system rights to [Public] may pose a security risk. However, in order for a workstation client to access files not in the SYS:LOGIN directory on a NetWare server, it must first authenticate to the server with the proper username/password set.

It is possible to assign file system rights to special-purpose NDS objects, such as Profiles and Directory Maps. You should avoid using these special objects for such purposes, however, because those that use them are not security equivalent to these objects; users will not inherit the file system rights as you might have intended. On the other hand, you can assign file system rights to Organizational Role objects because all occupants of an OR are security equivalent to the OR and, as a result, gain the file system rights.

Default NDS Rights

Knowing the available default NDS and file system rights is important. This knowledge helps to troubleshoot NDS rights problems and to minimize any potential security risks.

For every object creation, a set of default NDS rights assignments is made. The following sections describe four common events to serve as illustrations:

- ▶ NDS installation
- ▶ Server installation
- ▶ User creation
- ▶ Container creation

NDS Installation

Upon the initial installation of NDS (with your first NetWare 4 or NetWare 5 server), a User object Admin is created. Table 6.1 illustrates the rights granted.

TRUSTEE	OBJECT RIGHTS	ATTRIBUTE RIGHTS	FILE SYSTEM RIGHTS
TABLE 6.1	*Rights Assigned upon Installation of NDS*		
Admin	[S] to [Root]	N/A	N/A
[Public]	[B] to [Root]	N/A	N/A

TIP

To make sure that Supervisor object rights are not filtered out by IRFs at a lower level, grant Admin full [SBCDR] object rights and full [SCRWA] attribute rights to [Root].

To prevent unauthenticated clients from browsing your tree, remove [Public]'s Browse right to [Root]; assign the top-most container object(s) Browse right to [Root].

Server Installation

When a file server is installed into the NDS, the rights shown in Table 6.2 are assigned.

TRUSTEE	OBJECT RIGHTS	ATTRIBUTE RIGHTS	FILE SYSTEM RIGHTS
TABLE 6.2	*Rights Assigned upon Installation of a Server*		
Server	[S] to Server object	N/A	N/A
[Root]	N/A	[CR] to each Volume object's Host Resource Name and Host Server Name attribute	N/A
[Public]	N/A	[CR] to Message Server attribute	
Container	N/A	N/A	[RF] to SYS:PUBLIC

The Server object is given Supervisor object rights to itself so it can self-administrate some necessary attributes, such as Network Address. As mentioned previously, this Supervisor object right in turn gives full file system rights to the root of all the volumes on this server; therefore, the server has full file system rights to itself. The [Root] is given two trustee assignments to each Volume object associated with the server.

[Public] is given the Compare and Read attribute rights to the Messaging Server attribute. This is a hold-over from earlier versions of NetWare 4 where MHS (Message Handling System) Services were included as part of the operating system.

The container into which the server is installed is given file system rights, so users in that container (and its subcontainers) can log in, map drives, and access NetWare utilities.

User Creation

When a user is created in a container, the rights shown in Table 6.3 are assigned.

T A B L E 6.3	*Rights Assigned upon Creation of a User*		
TRUSTEE	**OBJECT RIGHTS**	**ATTRIBUTE RIGHTS**	**FILE SYSTEM RIGHTS**
[Root]	[B] to User object	[CR] to Network Address attribute [CR] to Group Membership attribute	N/A
User	N/A	[CR] to All Properties [CRW] to Login Script attribute [CRW] to Print Job Configuration attribute	[SRWCEFMA] to home directory
[Public]	N/A	[CR] to Default Server attribute	N/A

The User object is given enough NDS rights that it can read and modify its own login script and print job configurations. You can revoke the Write rights from these two attributes if you do not want your users to have the ability to modify their own login script and print job configurations.

Note that full file system rights (including Supervisor) are granted to the user's home directory. Administrators generally do not want their users to have the Access Control file system rights (or, needless to say, the Supervisor file system rights). You can change the home directory's file system rights assignment to suit your environment.

The assignment of the Supervisor rights to home directories is dependent on the NetWare utility used to create the directory.

NOTE

The Default Server attribute is used when a message (such as one from the SEND utility or a console broadcast) is to be delivered to a user. The message first goes to the user's default server, and then to the workstation where the user is logged in. If a user does not have the Default Server attribute set, he cannot receive any messages.

Container Creation

When a container is created, two trustee assignments are made, as shown in Table 6.4.

T A B L E 6.4		Rights Assigned upon Creation of a Container			
TRUSTEE	**OBJECT RIGHTS**	**ATTRIBUTE RIGHTS**	**FILE SYSTEM RIGHTS**
Container	N/A	[CR] to Login Script attribute [CR] to Print Job Configuration attribute	N/A

The two trustee assignments enable the users in this container to execute the container script upon login, as well as use the print job configurations in their CAPTURE commands.

Special Security Examples

Many of the default rights assignments are adequate for users to access network resources. Some situations, however, require additional or custom rights configurations. Three such scenarios are discussed in the following sections:

▶ Subtree administration

▶ Special function administrators

▶ Setting up special-purpose NDS objects such as Profiles, Directory Maps, and Aliases

Subtree Administration

Often, large networks assign different administrators to manage different portions of the NDS tree. Large internetworks — comprised of many departmental networks — in particular, utilize multiple administrators.

Two implementation approaches exist. For one, each tree branch is managed independently. No central administrator oversees the entire tree. This approach is typical of government-type installations. The other approach has a central administrator managing the whole tree, with subadministrators assisting in day-to-day operations.

NOTE

Subtree administrators (generally) do not have the necessary rights to add schema extensions. Supervisor rights to the [Root] object are required for such tasks.

To implement a purely distributed tree management strategy, you need to block any rights that might be inherited by the original Admin user (for each branch of the tree). The following steps make Sally the sole NDS administrator for O=Toronto and below (see Figure 6.12):

► . . . . ◄

F I G U R E 6.12 *A simple tree-branch administrator security setup*

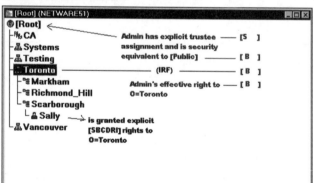

I. Grant Sally an explicit trustee assignment to O=Toronto with full [SBCDRI] object and [SRCWAI] attribute rights.

The granting of additional rights safeguards against the possibility of S being filtered by an IRF.

2. Place object IRF of [B] and attribute IRF of [CR] on O=Toronto to block any inherited management rights into this container. These IRFs effectively keep Admin from managing that portion of the tree.

You should, however, enable the Browse right to be inherited, so users can see this part of the tree — O=Toronto and below.

3. Remove any explicit trustee assignments Admin might have on O=Toronto or lower containers.

4. Grant Sally [SBCDR] object rights to herself. Remove any explicit trustee rights Admin might have on the object Sally.

This explicit rights assignment enables Sally to manage her own object rights, and keeps those rights from being affected by Admin.

If you need to set up an assistant administrator, it can be done but makes things a little more complex. The trick is giving the assistant administrator sufficient rights to manage the tree while, at the same time, ensuring that he or she cannot inadvertently cut off the central administrator. The following steps — using the setup in the previous example — illustrate one configuration that prevents administrative rights from being cut off from a tree branch:

1. Grant Sally an explicit trustee assignment to O=Toronto with [BCDRI] object rights, [RCWAI] All Properties attribute rights, and [RC] ACL attribute rights. It is not desirable to assign Supervisor rights here, nor to allow Sally the right to change any of the object trustee assignments. Thus, only Read and Compare attribute rights to the ACL should be granted.

NOTE

Remember, the ACL attribute is listed as Object Trustees (ACL) in the schema.

The setting up of assistant NDS administrators is one example where [RCWAI] attribute rights are used instead of granting the [S] attribute right.

2. Give Admin an explicit trustee assignment to both O=Toronto and CN= Sally, with full [SBCDRI] object rights and [SRCWAI] attribute rights.

3. Place an object IRF of [B] on the Sally object so that it cannot inherit any object rights to manage itself.

4. Verify that the Sally object has only the minimum amount of rights to manage itself — Browse object right to self; Read and Write attribute rights to Login Script and Print Job Configuration; and Read and Compare attribute rights to the ACL.

Make sure that the assistant administrators in this case do not have Write access to the ACL, where they could add/remove trustees, change IRFs, and so forth.

Special Function Administrators

The concept of setting up an administrator that can only manage a specific set of attributes, such as Telephone and Fax numbers, is straightforward. The actual implementation, however, is tedious and requires much manual labor. To facilitate the management of the Telephone attribute, for example, the administrator needs to have Compare, Read, and Write attribute rights to each user object's Telephone attribute.

Because the special function administrator is to be managing specific attributes of individual User objects, you must grant rights for each user. You cannot create a Group object and grant the administrator rights to this group, because it would be the attributes of this Group object that he would be managing, rather than those of the User objects.

Under NetWare 4, although the All Properties right works, you should not use it as a shortcut. This right applies to *all* attributes, *including ACL*. As mentioned previously, having Write access to the ACL is usually not a desirable option. A workaround is to write a simple application that will make global attribute trustee assignments. If you're familiar with the Visual Basic programming language, you can make use of the NDS-related ActiveX controls included in the Novell Developer Kit (NDK), which is available for download from http://developer.novell.com.

With NetWare 5 and higher, however, you can make use of the Inheritable container rights flag. You can simply assign the necessary attribute rights at the top-most container and let them flow down the tree structure.

Technical Information Documents (TIDs)

A number of Technical Information Documents (TIDs) are available in Novell's knowledgebase, which can be accessed at http://support.novell.com/servlet/Knowledgebase. These TIDs outline the various rights necessary for specific NDS administration tasks. Some examples are listed here:

▶ **TID# 2932404** — creating an organizational role object for the function of Print Administrator. The Print Administrator is defined as a user who creates and manages NDS Print Servers, Print Queues, and Printers.

▶ **TID# 2928483** — creating specific e-mail administrator roles for GroupWise 5.

- ▶ **TID# 2941025** — creating a User, Group, or Organizational Role to administer other users' list of NAL Applications and Launcher Configuration settings.
- ▶ **TID# 2941025** — creating a User, Group, or Organizational Role to administer the NetWare Registry Editor page of a user.
- ▶ **TID# 2934034** — creating a group administrator role (Organizational Role or User object) in NDS so that they will be able to add/remove members in groups.

Setting Up Special-Purpose NDS Objects

Chapter 4, "Special-Purpose NDS Objects" discusses the use of special-purpose NDS objects, such as Profiles, Directory Maps, and Aliases. All these objects help simplify NDS management and provide users with easier means of accessing resources. To use them effectively, however, proper NDS security rights need to be assigned. The following sections give the NDS rights required by users to access Profile, Directory Map, and Alias objects.

Profile Objects

The key purpose of a Profile object is to provide a common login script to a group of users. If the Profile object is in the same container as the users, no additional setup work is required. If the users accessing the Profile object are located in different containers, as is often the case, you need to grant those users the Browse object right to the Profile object, and the Read and Compare attribute rights to the Profile's Login Script attribute.

Directory Map Objects

For a user to make full use of Directory Map objects, you need to grant the user the proper file system rights for the directories to which the DM objects are pointing. Furthermore, the user needs to have Read attribute rights to a number of DM objects' attributes, such as Host Server and Path. It is more convenient for you to grant the user Read and Compare attribute rights to the All Properties attribute for the DM objects. This gives the user all the necessary rights (plus some extra rights, but it does not generally raise security issues) to access DM objects.

Alias Objects

Often when you have mobile users, User aliases are created to make logging in to the network easier. When you log in using an alias user name, the login script of the container holding the Primary object is the one executed. The Alias object, therefore, should be given Read attribute rights to the Login Script attribute of the container holding the Primary object.

## CHAPTER 7

Managing Partition and Replication

Chapter 1, "What is NDS and How Does It Work?" discussed the importance and need of partitioning and replicating your NDS database. In this chapter, you learn the procedures of performing partitioning and replication operations using NDS Manager.

In NetWare 4.11 and higher, NDS Manager replaces the Partition Manager utility that existed under the Tools menu in the NetWare Administrator utility in earlier versions of NetWare 4. NDS Manager provides the following features:

▸ Partitioning and replication services for NDS on a NetWare server.

▸ The ability to repair the NDS database from a client workstation, which reduces the network administrator's dependence on using RCONSOLE.

▸ NDS version update capability so that NetWare 4 and NetWare 5 servers in a network can be updated to a newer version of DS.NLM.

▸ The ability to print a list of partitions in the Directory tree, the partition replica list (the replica ring), and server data.

▸ Diagnostic features that enable the administrator to get a sense of the general condition of the NDS tree.

Furthermore, NDS Manager version 1.30 (and higher) has been updated for NetWare 5. Some of the enhancements include:

▸ **One executable.** The NDS Manager executable, NDSMGR32.EXE, works on both Windows 9x and Windows NT.

▸ **Transitive synchronization.** This new functionality greatly reduces synchronization traffic and allows for larger replica lists.

▸ **Cross platform checking.** Features that cannot be run on non-NetWare platforms are not attempted at all (rather than trying and failing). These include NDS version update and remote repair operations.

▸ **New APIs.** These include APIs for getting and setting NDS statistics, and an enhanced ping API for getting platform information.

▸ **Ability to partition any container class object.** This way, if a third party extends the schema with a container object (which is not a standard NDS container class object, such as Organizational Unit) that makes sense to partition, the operation works.

▸ **Schema Manager enhancements.** Updates to Schema Manager to support the newer object classes and attributes available in NetWare 5.

Before you use NDS Manager version 1.30, make sure you are using the latest version of the Novell Client software.

NOTE

Unless you're still running NetWare 4.10 or lower (which included Partition Manager), you should be using NDS Manager for all your partition management tasks.

NDS Health Check

Prior to performing any partitioning and replicating operation, you must ensure your NDS tree is in a healthy state. Three guidelines should be followed as part of your basic health check prior to any NDS partition management tasks:

▸ Always use up-to-date NDS software

▸ Ensure network time is synchronized

▸ Ensure all servers are communicating with each other

TIP

As a network administrator, you should establish a proactive health check of your NDS tree. If your tree is in a "dynamic state" you should consider performing weekly the health check procedures outlined in this section. This should be done if your NDS tree is in a state where new partitions are being created, new servers being added — or a combination of the two — on a frequent basis (perhaps two to three times a week). On the other hand, if your tree has a minimum number of changes — such as a new partition or server being added only a couple of times a month, or even less frequently, you may only need to perform the health check once a month.

The time frames given for scheduled checks are only recommendations and should be tailored for your individual organization's needs.

Keeping Your NDS Software Up to Date

Periodically, Novell releases updated version of DS.NLM (the NDS database program) and its management utilities (such as NDS Manager, NetWare Administrator, and ConsoleOne) on the Novell support Web site (http:// support.novell.com). These updates generally add features and contain bug fixes. You should try to keep your network updated with these new versions whenever possible.

When you obtain an updated version of DS.NLM, install it on all the NetWare servers in your network (or those non-NetWare servers that are running NDS, whatever the case may be). All servers, of the same version of operating system, should be running the same version of DS to take full advantage of any new features of DS.NLM.

You can verify, in a number of ways, which version of DS.NLM is running on a given server. One *quick* way is to issue the following command at the server's console:

```
MODULES DS.NLM
```

This reports the version of the DS.NLM module. Another way is to use the time synchronization check function in DSREPAIR.NLM, which is discussed in the next section.

Ensuring Network Time is Synchronized

Correct time synchronization is important because NDS partitions are replicated and need to be kept in synchronization with one another. Each event that occurs in NDS is marked with a timestamp. The timestamps are used to order the events or changes that occur on multiple servers. Timestamping of events keeps all NDS changes in proper order. A time synchronization check must be done regularly to ensure that NDS functions correctly. If time is out of synchronization when performing a Change Replica Type partition operation, for example, the operation does not complete.

Use DSREPAIR.NLM to see if your network time is synchronized:

1. Load DSREPAIR.NLM on a server holding a replica of the [ROOT] partition.

2. From the Available Options menu, select Time Synchronization.

3. The log file indicates if time is synchronized or not.

The following is a sample log file showing the network time *is* synchronized (Yes under the Time is in sync column):

```
/****************************************************/
NetWare 5.00 Directory Services Repair 7.16 , DS 8.38
Log file for server ".NETWARE_51.Systems" in tree "NETWARE51"
Time synchronization and server status information
Start:  Wednesday, May 10, 2000   4:11:23 pm Local Time


                              DS.NLM  Replica Time    Time is  Time
Server name                   Version Depth   Source  in sync  +/-
-----------------------------+-------+-------+--------+--------+---
```

```
.NETWARE5-TORONTO.Markha...7.30   1   Secondary Yes    +1
.NETWARE_51.Systems       8.38    0   Single    Yes     0


*** END ***
```

All Servers are Communicating with Each Other

As different servers may hold replicas of different partitions, it is important that all servers are correctly communicating with each other so that the replicas for any given partition are correctly and fully synchronized. It is especially important when you're about to perform any partitioning operations. Any server within the replica that that is not available (down or unable to communicate with due to down network links) causes the partition operation to be incomplete — the operation is not necessarily going to fail, but is not going to be capable of proceeding to the complete state, until all servers in the replica ring are up and communicating with each other.

You can easily check the partition synchronization status using NDS Manager. To view partition synchronization information in NDS Manager, do the following:

1. Locate and highlight the desired partition root object in NDS Manager.

2. In the Object pull-down menu, click Check Synchronization.

3. To read the partition status for the selected partition only, click OK.

4. To continue with the operation after preconditions have been met, click Yes.

A synchronization problem is indicated when the All processed = No line has a value greater than 0.

Partition Status

You should always check the synchronization and continuity status of a replica, and any child replicas, both before and after the partition operation. If you have synchronization errors, fix them before proceeding with the operation. Here are some general guidelines to follow when performing partition operations:

▶ Make sure your Directory tree is synchronizing correctly before you move a partition.

▶ If possible, always perform partition operations with the latest version of DS.NLM.

▶ After performing a partition operation, you need to wait for processes throughout the Directory to complete before you can perform an operation with that partition again.

TIP

The key to successful NDS partition management is patience. NDS is designed such that its traffic is not supposed to overwhelm your network. Therefore, allow time for NDS to complete its tasks. (This also means that you should avoid performing partitioning or replication operations during peak hours.)

Even though a partition operation may appear completed in NDS Manager, NDS requires time to synchronize any changes to a partition with the replicas of the partition. Many partition operations may take considerable time to fully synchronize across the network. While you can expect partition operations to complete within a few hours, the amount of time required for NDS to synchronize the changes in the tree depends on the following variables:

▶ The number of objects in the partition

▶ The number of replicas that must be synchronized

▶ The location of the replicas — they could be on a server across a (slow) WAN, for example

▶ Existing wire traffic

Overview of Working with NDS Manager

Using NDS Manager, you can manage partitions, replicas, servers, repair operations, DS.NLM version updates, printing, and preferences from a Windows workstation.

Most operations can be performed from either the hierarchical Tree View or the List of Partitions and Servers. They are represented on the button bar by the two icons that each have a magnifying glass on the lower-right corner. The other view from which you work in NDS Manager is the Partition Continuity View; from this view you can observe the condition of your tree and perform repair operations. Before using NDS Manager, you should take a few minutes to access these views and become familiar with their features and options.

The Tree View (see Figure 7.1) is the default view when you start NDS Manager. The Tree View has a hierarchical view that displays only container objects and NetWare Server objects in the current context. To view containers and servers below your current context, you must browse the tree by expanding containers. To view a list of all partitions and servers in and below your current context (without having to expand containers), select View ⇨ Partitions and Servers, or select from the button bar. To perform repair operations in Tree View, you must select a partition and then select Object ⇨ Partition Continuity or use the button bar.

F I G U R E 7 . I NDS Manager's Tree View is a hierarchical view that displays only container objects and NetWare Server objects in the current context.

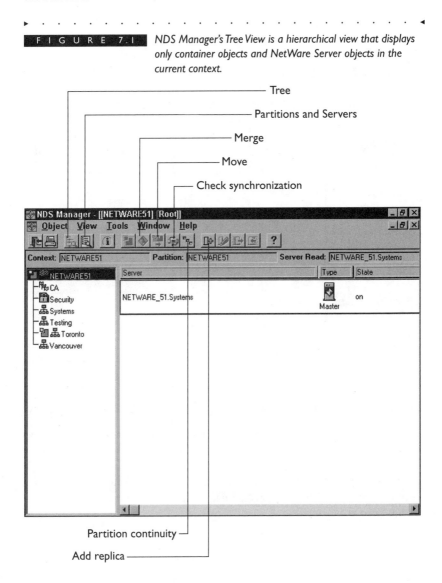

Tree

Partitions and Servers

Merge

Move

Check synchronization

Partition continuity

Add replica

The List of Partitions and Servers (see Figure 7.2) is one of the three views from which you can work in NDS Manager. This view displays all partitions and servers in and below your current context. If you want to see which partitions are parent and which are child partitions (the partition hierarchy), you must go to the Tree View. To perform repair operations, you must select a partition and then click Object ⇨ Partition Continuity from the pull-down menu, or use the button bar.

F I G U R E   7 . 2 The List of Partitions and Servers view displays all partitions and servers in and below your current context.

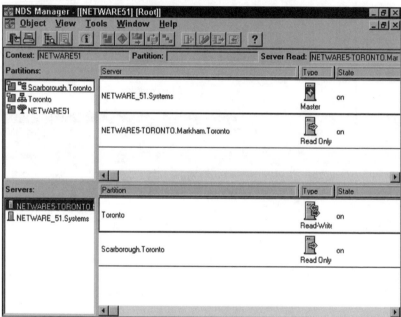

From the Partition Continuity view (see Figure 7.3), you can identify whether any of a partition's replicas are experiencing synchronization errors, and you can perform repair operations. To understand the partition grid, read it horizontally, one server at a time. Each row represents the replica list of that server. For more information about how partitions are named, and about partition root objects, see Chapter 1.

F I G U R E   7.3
Partition Continuity displays the replica list (columns) of each server (rows) that holds a replica of the chosen partition.

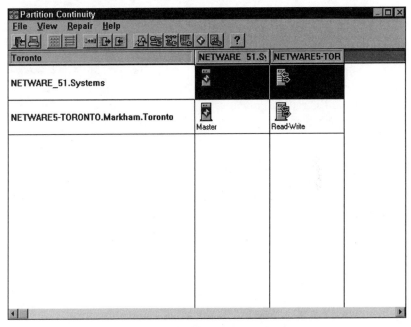

You can access the options to perform operations from the button bar, menu bar, or by right-clicking. A right-click of the mouse on a server, replica, or partition brings up a pop-up menu with most of the available operations for that object.

TIP

Sometime after a partitioning operation, the display is not updated right away. Press F5 to refresh the screen.

TIP

Creating Partitions

When you create partitions, you make logical divisions of your NDS tree. These divisions can be replicated and distributed among different NetWare servers in your network. When you create a new partition, you split the parent partition and end up with two partitions. The new partition becomes a child partition.

The process of creating a new partition is also known as a partition *split*.

To create a new partition using NDS Manager, use the following steps:

1. Ensure you're in the Tree View mode.

2. From the browser (in the left panel), select the container you want to be the partition root object.

3. Click the Create Partition button, or use the Object ➪ Create Partition pull-down menu, or simply hit the Insert key.

4. A Create Partition confirmation dialog box appears, displaying the following information:

   `Create a new partition from the following container?`

5. Select Yes to create the partition.

6. Another Create Partition dialog box is displayed showing if the preconditions for this operation have been met. If yes, it prompts you with:

   `Continue with this operation?`

7. Click Yes to continue.

8. A Creating a New Partition status dialog box is then displayed.

9. Click Close to continue. (The dialog box closes automatically after a few seconds if you don't click any buttons.)

In general, you should keep the number of objects in a given partition at less than 1,500, depending on your tree structure. However, this depends largely on your particular situation and configuration (the number of objects is a nonissue if you're running eDirectory). You need to strike a balance between the number of objects in a given partition and the amount of traffic generated and time delay due to tree walking.

Merging Partitions

At times you might want to combine smaller child partitions into a larger one for more efficient tree walking. When you merge a partition, the partition and its replicas combine with the parent partition, leaving only the parent partition.

You cannot actually remove a partition. Rather, you merge one partition into another. This operation is also known as a *join*.

To merge or join two partitions using NDS Manager, use the following steps:

1. You can merge a partition from either the Tree View or the List of Partitions and Servers, so choose one of the two views.

2. From the browser (in the left panel), select the child partition you want to merge with its parent partition. (The complete name of the partition's parent is automatically filled in. You can't change the information in this field. It always displays the parent partition of the partition you have selected.)

3. Click the Merge Partition button, or use the Object ⇨ Partition ⇨ Merge pull-down menu.

4. A Merge Partition confirmation dialog box appears, displaying the following information:

`Merge the following partition with its parent partition?`

5. Select Yes to merge the partition.

6. Another Merge Partition dialog box is displayed showing if the pre-conditions for this operation have been met. If yes, the prompt asks:

`Continue with this operation?`

7. Click Yes to continue.

8. A Merging Partition status dialog box is then displayed.

9. Click Close to continue. (The dialog box closes automatically after a few seconds if you don't click any buttons.)

Moving Containers/Partitions

NetWare 4.10 and higher enables you to move a partition root object (which is a container object) and its subordinates from one location on the NDS tree to another. Because you have to move the container and its contents, this task, essentially, is moving a partition.

Two conditions must be met before you can move a container or partition:

▶ The container object to be moved must be the partition root object. If the container is not already a partition, create a new partition with this container as the root object.

▶ The partition cannot have any child partitions. Merge any child partitions into the parent partition before performing the move.

TIP

Make sure your NDS tree is synchronizing correctly before you move a partition. If you have any errors in synchronization in either the partition you want to move or the destination partition, do not perform a move partition operation. First fix the synchronization errors.

To move a container using NDS Manager, use the following steps:

1. You can move a container from either the Tree View or the List of Partitions and Servers, so choose one of the two views.

2. Ensure that the two conditions mentioned previously are met. If not, create a new partition using the container as the partition root object, or merge any child partitions into the parent partition as necessary.

3. From the browser (in the left panel), select the partition you want to move.

4. Click the Move Partition button, or use the Object ⇨ Partition ⇨ Move pull-down menu.

5. A Move Partition confirmation dialog box appears, displaying the following information:

```
Merge the following partition (container) to a new context?
```

6. To move the partition to a context besides the root of the current tree (default), either type a new context in To Context *or* click the browse icon and select the destination partition from the browser (see Figure 7.4).

▶ · ◀

F I G U R E   7 . 4   *The Move Partition dialog box*

Move Partition   ☒

☐▤ Move the following container (partition) to a
        new context?

Container (Partition):
|Scarborough.Toronto |

To Context:
|[Root] | 🔢

☐ Create an alias for this container object

[Yes]   No   Help

NOTE

Keep in mind the object containment rules (refer to Chapter I if you need a reminder). If you're moving an OU, you can't use the default To Context setting (which is [Root]) as you cannot have an OU directly under the [Root] object.

7. If you wish to create an alias for the moved container, check the Create an alias for this container object checkbox.

TIP

When you move a partition, you should select the option to create an Alias object in place of the container you're moving. Doing so allows users to continue to log in to the network and find objects in their original container location — the Alias object created has the same common name as the moved container and references the new complete name of the moved container.

If you move a partition and do not create an Alias object in place of the moved partition, users who are unaware of the partition's new location may have trouble finding that partition's objects in the NDS tree, because they may look for them in their original location. This might also cause client workstations to fail at login if the workstation Context parameter (available under the NDS tab of the Advanced option in the login dialog box) is set to the original location of the container in the tree.

8. Select Yes to move the partition.

9. Another Move Partition dialog box is displayed showing whether the preconditions for this operation have been met. If yes, the prompt asks:

   Continue with this operation?

10. Click Yes to continue.

11. A Move Partition status dialog box is then displayed.

12. Click Close to continue. (The dialog box closes automatically after a few seconds if you don't click any buttons.)

After moving the partition, if you don't want the partition to remain a partition, merge it with its parent partition.

TIP

Depending on the number of objects within the container and the number of replicas that need updating, a move operation can take from seconds to hours. Schedule all partition management operations, such as splits and moves, for off-peak hours. You should allow one partition operation to fully complete and make sure all replicas involved are synchronized before starting a new partition management operation.

Aborting Partition Operations

To protect the integrity of the NDS database, only one partition operation can take place at a time. If a partition operation starts and one of the servers in the replica ring becomes unavailable — downed server or downed network link — the operation is suspended. If you try to start another partition operation, NDS Manager displays a -654 error, which is the "partition busy" NDS error code. You can either wait for the error condition to be rectified, or abort the operation.

TIP

A list of NDS error codes is available from the online help of NDS Manager.

You can abort a create or merge partition operation if the operation has not yet progressed past the stage at which the change is committed. You can use this feature to back out of an operation, or if your NDS network returns NDS errors or fails to synchronize following a partition operation. If you get an error that says a partition is busy, it doesn't mean that you should abort the operation. You can usually expect partition operations to complete within 24 hours (generally less). If a particular operation fails to complete within this time frame, you should then attempt to abort the operation in progress.

TIP

If replicas in your tree experience synchronization errors, an abort operation may not always solve the problem. However, you can use this feature as an initial troubleshooting option.

Before you can abort the operation, you must determine which partition is busy. NDS Manager displays this information in both the Tree View *and* List of Partitions and Servers view. The problematic partition shows a non-On state in the display (see Figure 7.5).

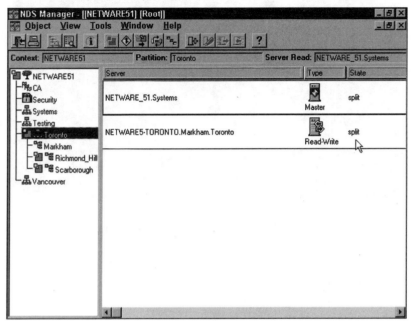

NDS Manager shows that a partition is suspended in a Split state.

If you are at a NetWare server, you can also use the DSREPAIR.NLM to determine which partition is causing you trouble. Load DSREPAIR on one of the NetWare servers that holds the partitions with which you're working. From its main menu, select the Advanced Options menu, and then select Replica and partition operations. This selection displays a list of all replicas stored on the server and their replica states (see Figure 7.6).

To abort a partition operation using NDS Manager, use the following steps:

I. You can abort a partition operation from either the Tree View or the List of Partitions and Servers, so choose one of the two views.

2. From the browser (in the left panel), select the partition where an operation has begun.

TIP

If you are attempting to abort a merge partition operation, select the partition (the child partition) that is merging with its parent. If you are attempting to abort a create partition operation, select the parent partition.

F I G U R E   7.6   *DSREPAIR shows that a partition is suspended in a Split state.*

3. Use the Object ⇨ Partition ⇨ Abort Operation pull-down menu, or right-click the partition and select Abort Operation.

4. An Abort Partition Operation confirmation dialog box appears, displaying the following information:

```
Attempt to abort the partition operation in process on
the following partition?
```

5. Select Yes to abort the operation.

6. Another Abort Partition Operation dialog box is displayed showing if the preconditions for this operation have been met. If yes, it prompts you with:

```
Continue with this operation?
```

7. Click Yes to continue.

8. An Abort Partition Operation status dialog box is then displayed with the message:

```
The selection operation has been submitted to NDS.
```

9. Click OK to continue.

You can also use DSREPAIR to abort a partition operation. Load DSREPAIR on one of the NetWare servers that holds the partitions with which you're working. From DSREPAIR's main menu, select the Advanced Options menu, and then select Replica and partition operations. A list of all partitions and their replica states appears. Select the problem partition to bring up the

Replica Options menu (see Figure 7.7). Select Cancel partition operation to abort the pending operation. You need to authenticate with a user name that has Supervisor object rights to [Root] before you can successfully cancel the operation.

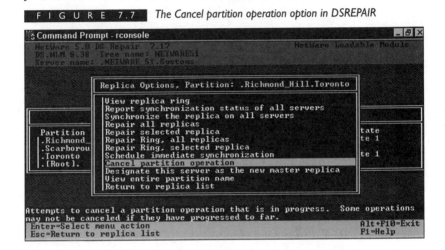

F I G U R E 7.7 *The Cancel partition operation option in DSREPAIR*

Creating Replicas

Creating multiple NDS partitions does not, by itself, increase fault tolerance or improve performance of NDS; however, strategically using multiple replicas does. Novell recommends that for fault tolerance, you should have at least three real replicas for each partition — if you have enough servers to support that number. "Real" replicas means Master, Read/Write (R/W), or Read-Only (RO) replicas; Subordinate Reference (SubRef) replicas are automatically created and managed by NDS, not the administrator.

NOTE

You can store only one replica per partition on a given server, while a single server can store replicas of multiple partitions.

To create a replica of a given partition using NDS Manager, use the following steps:

I. You can add a replica of a partition to a server from either the Tree View or the List of Partitions and Servers, so choose one of the two views.

2. From the browser (in the left panel), select the partition that you want to replicate on a server.

3. Click the Add Replica button, or use the Object ⇨ Add Replica pull-down menu, or right-click the partition and select Add Replica.

4. An Add Replica dialog box appears, as shown in Figure 7.8.

F I G U R E 7.8 *The Add Replica dialog box*

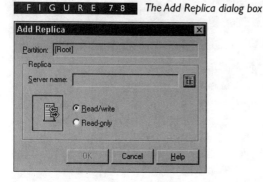

5. Click the browse button to select the server to place the replica on; you cannot type in the server name in the field.

6. Select the NetWare Server object from the browser and click OK.

7. Select either Read/Write or Read-Only.

8. Click OK.

9. Another Add Replica dialog box is displayed showing if the preconditions for this operation have been met. If yes, it prompts you with:

   Continue with this operation?

10. Click Yes to continue.

11. An Adding Replica status dialog box is then displayed.

12. Click Close to continue. (The dialog box closes automatically after a few seconds if you don't click any buttons.)

   DSREPAIR cannot be used to add a replica to a server.

NOTE

NDS Manager can perform add replica, delete replica, and change replica types operation on non-Intel NDS servers, such as Solaris.

Deleting Replicas

In certain instances you may need to remove one or more replicas for a given partition. For example, if you want to remove a server from the tree, you could delete replicas from the server before removing it. Removing the replicas reduces the chance of having problems removing the server. You can also reduce synchronization traffic on the network by removing replicas. Keep in mind that you generally don't want or need more than six replicas of any partition, unless they are across WAN links or are required for Bindery Services; for fault tolerance, you should maintain at least three replicas of each partition on different servers.

NOTE Deleting a replica only deletes a copy of part of the NDS database on the targeted server. The database can still be accessed on other servers in the network, and the server that the replica was on still functions in NDS.

To delete a replica of a given partition using NDS Manager, use the following steps:

1. You can delete a replica of a partition to a server from either the Tree View or the List of Partitions and Servers, so choose one of the two views.

2. From the browser (in the *right* panel), select the server holding the replica that you want to delete.

3. Right-click the replica and select Delete or simply hit the Delete key.

4. A Delete Replica confirmation dialog box appears, displaying the following information:

   ```
   Delete the replica of the following partition on the
   following server?
   ```

5. Click Yes to continue.

6. Another Delete Replica dialog box is displayed showing if the preconditions for this operation have been met. If yes, it prompts you with:

   ```
   Continue with this operation?
   ```

7. Click Yes to continue.

8. A Deleting Replica status dialog box is then displayed.

9. Click Close to continue. (The dialog box closes automatically after a few seconds if you don't click any buttons.)

Although DSREPAIR can be used to remove a replica from a server, it is best to use NDS Manager instead, as one can easily cause replica ring inconsistency and other NDS problems.

NOTE You cannot remove a Master replica. If you have to delete the Master for some reason (perhaps it is corrupted), you must first change its type to Read/Write or Read-Only, and then perform the delete operation.

Changing Replica Types

As mentioned previously the four replica types are Master, Read/Write (or Secondary), Read-Only, and Subordinate Reference. You can readily change the replica types between Master, Read/Write, and Read-Only.

Each partition *must* have a Master replica as all partition operations (such as a split or a join) are performed against that Master replica. If the server containing the Master replica is unavailable and you need to perform partition operations, you can promote a Read/Write or Read-Only replica to Master status.

You can change the type of an RW or an RO replica. However, you cannot use a change replica type operation to change the Master replica to a different type. Instead, if you change an RW or RO to a Master — and the original Master is automatically demoted to a RW replica.

NOTE You cannot change the replica type of a Subordinate Reference. If you need to "get rid" of a SubRef, you need to place a real replica of that partition on the server that currently has a SubRef; this is an Add Replica operation.

To change the type of replica of a given partition using NDS Manager, use the following steps:

1. You can change replica types from either the Tree View or the List of Partitions and Servers, so choose one of the two views.

2. From the browser (in the *right* panel), select the replica on which you want to change the type.

3. Click the Change Type button, or use the Object ⇨ Replica ⇨ Change Type pull-down menu, or right-click the replica and select Change Type.

4. A Change Replica Type dialog box appears, as shown in Figure 7.9.

F I G U R E   7 . 9 *The Change Replica Type dialog box*

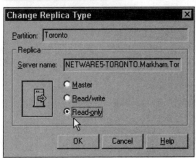

5. Select the new type and click OK.

6. A Change Replica Type dialog box is displayed showing if the preconditions for this operation have been met. If yes, it prompts you with:

`Continue with this operation?`

7. Click Yes to continue.

8. A Changing Replica Type status dialog box is then displayed.

9. Click Close to continue. (The dialog box closes automatically after a few seconds if you don't click any buttons.)

The Change Type operation should only take a few seconds to perform, unless the copy of Master you're trying to demote is located on a server across a (slow) WAN link.

You can also use the DSREPAIR.NLM to promote an RW or RO to Master; you cannot, however, change an RW to RO or vice versa. To change an RW or RO to Master, load DSREPAIR on one of the NetWare servers that holds the replica of interest. From its main menu, select the Advanced Options menu, and then select Replica and partition operations. This selection displays a list of all replicas stored on the server and their replica states. Select the replica to bring up the Replica Options menu (see Figure 7.10). Select Destinate this server as the new master replica.

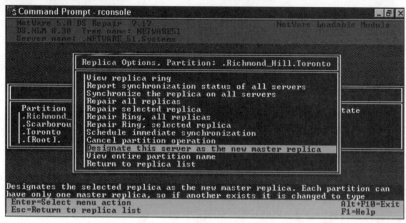

DSREPAIR shows that a partition is suspended in a Split state.

Rebuilding Replicas

When a replica is corrupted or incomplete, you can resynchronize it using the Master replica of the same partition. When you restore a server's SYS volume, for example, you should perform a replica resynchronization (using information from the Master) because the restored replica most likely contains outdated NDS information. You can wait for the normal NDS update process, or you can force a replica update manually.

When you choose to synchronize immediately, every server that holds a replica of the partition you choose attempts to synchronize its replica information with the replica information on the other servers. You can perform this operation to synchronize changes you recently made to Directory data. For example, if you modified container login scripts, you can synchronize those changes so users can be authenticated to the network immediately.

To force an immediate synchronization of a given partition using NDS Manager, use the following steps:

I. You can perform this operation from either the Tree View or the List of Partitions and Servers, so choose one of the two views.

2. From the browser (in the left panel), select the partition you want to synchronize.

3. Click the Partition Continuity button, or use the Object ⇨ Partition Continuity pull-down menu, or right-click the partition and select Partition Continuity.

4. From the Partition Continuity view (see Figure 7.11), click the Synchronize Immediately button (or use the Repair ⇨ Synchronize Immediately pull-down menu).

F I G U R E 7. 11   *The Partition Continuity view*

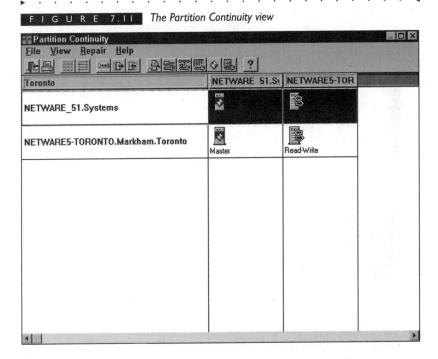

5. A Synchronize Immediately confirmation dialog box appears, displaying the following information:

```
This operation will generate network traffic. Do you
want to continue?
```

6. Click Yes to continue.

7. A Synchronize Immediately status dialog box is then displayed with the message:

```
The selection operation has been submitted to NDS.
```

8. Click OK to continue.

To manually force an NDS synchronization from a NetWare server console, enter **SET DSTRACE=*H** at the console prompt.

TIP

   If a non-Master replica becomes corrupted or has not received updated data for an extended period of time, you can force the replica on the chosen server to receive all NDS objects from the Master replica of the partition. While in process, this operation marks the replica on the chosen server as a new replica (the replica state can be seen in the replica list of the server from the Tree View or the List of Partitions and Servers). The replica's current data is *overwritten* with the data from the Master replica. Depending on the size of the replica, this operation may create a lot of network traffic, so it is best to run this operation during a period of light network traffic.

   You can receive updates from the Master replica from the Tree View, the List of Partitions and Servers, or the Partition Continuity view. First, select the server from the view (the row) whose replica you want to receive updates. Then click the Receive Updates button, or use the Repair ⇨ Receive Updates pull-down menu, or right-click the replica and select Receive Updates.

You cannot select this option from a master replica and you cannot perform this operation on a master replica. The master replica is assumed to be the most current and accurate copy of the partition, thus, a Master replica cannot receive updates from itself.

NOTE

   You can also send updates from a given replica to all other replicas, including the Master, of the partition. The other replicas of the partition then combine the new objects sent with the objects they already have. If the other replicas have data besides the data sent to them, they retain that data. This operation can create a lot of network traffic as it broadcasts the data to all other replicas, so it is best to run this operation during a period of light network traffic.

   You can send updates from the Tree View, the List of Partitions, and Servers, or the Partition Continuity view. First, select the server from the view (the row) whose replica you want to broadcast the data. Then click the Send Updates button, or use the Repair ⇨ Send Updates pull-down menu, or right-click the replica and select Send Updates.

WARNING

Do not be flippant about rebuilding replicas; using this process to fix minor NDS problems might create more problems than it fixes. Do not use this option when you experience the following errors: -602 (FDA6) — No such value; -632 (FD88) — System failure and unexpected results have occurred; and -635 (FD85) — Remote failure. For more information, refer to Novell's knowledgebase or the Novell's Guide to NDS Troubleshooting book.

Planning Replica Placement Using Replica Tables

Visualizing where all your replicas are located *or* visualizing their impact on the number of SubRefs being created, can often be very difficult. A replica table can help you plan and visualize replica placement; and can be especially helpful in finding where Subordinate References should be placed. A table also helps in NDS troubleshooting — compare the information listed in the replica table to what's actually out on your network, and you'll be able to spot any missing replicas quickly.

It is very easy to use a replica table by employing the following steps:

1. Create a table that has $n+1$ columns and $m+1$ rows, where n is the number of servers in your network and m is the number of partitions you have.

2. Fill out the server and partition names.

3. Place a Master replica of each partition.

4. Place Read/Write replicas to facilitate user access and fault tolerance.

5. Note where Subordinate References are automatically created.

Consider the sample NDS tree and partitions shown in Figure 7.12. The replica placement of the various partitions, including any SubRefs, is shown Table 7.1.

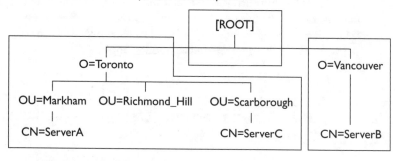

FIGURE 7.12 ServerA holds a replica for the **[Root]** and Toronto partition, ServerC holds a copy of **[Root]**, and ServerB holds a replica for the Vancouver partition.

| TABLE 7.1 | A Sample Replica Table |

SERVER NAMES	PARTITION [ROOT]	PARTITION TORONTO	PARTITION VANCOUVER
ServerA	M	M	RW
ServerB			M
ServerC	RW	SubRef	SubRef

By going through this simple exercise, you can quickly determine that none of the partitions have three replicas to meet the fault tolerance recommendation. In an NDS tree with many servers and partitions, you'll quickly find that a replica table is not only an excellent documentation tool, but also a good planning and troubleshooting aid.

CHAPTER 8

Managing Time
Synchronization

The Time Synchronization section in Chapter 1 helped you understand why time synchronization is important in a NDS environment, especially to NDS updates. This chapter discusses how you can design a fault-tolerant time-server configuration, yet at the same time reduce unnecessary network traffic as a result of time synchronization.

To start off, the following section quickly reviews the time synchronization server types.

Understanding Time Synchronization Servers

Time synchronization (TimeSync) servers are either time providers or time consumers; all workstations are time consumers. A NetWare 4 and NetWare 5 environment contains the following types of time synchronization servers:

▸ A **Secondary** time server is a time consumer. It takes time information from (at least) one time provider and synchronizes its time to that of the provider(s). It provides time information to workstations and clients.

NOTE

> Workstations running Novell Client software are also considered time consumers as they get their time from a NetWare server.

▸ A **Primary** time server is a time provider that synchronizes network time with at least one other Primary time server or a Reference time server. A Primary time server provides time to Secondary time servers and workstation clients.

▸ A **Single Reference** time server is the only time source (time provider) for the entire network. As a result, it determines the time for the entire network, without having to reference anyone else. Do not confuse Reference time servers with Single Reference time servers. They are two distinctly different types of time sources (see Figure 8.1).

▸ A **Reference** time server acts as a central point to set network time (see Figure 8.2). Primary time servers adjust their internal clocks to synchronize with the Reference time server. A Reference time server gets its time information from an external source, such as an atomic clock. It is a time provider.

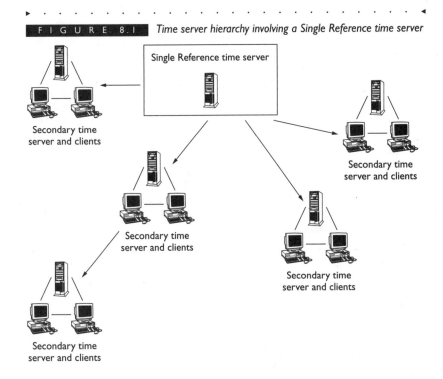

FIGURE 8.1 *Time server hierarchy involving a Single Reference time server*

Single Reference time server

Secondary time
server and clients

Secondary time
server and clients

Secondary time
server and clients

Secondary time
server and clients

Secondary time
server and clients

WARNING

No other time provider servers, such as Primary or Reference, can coexist with a Single Reference time server.

Table 8.1 shows a summary of the legal provider/client combinations. No matter what role the time server plays within the network time synchronization, all the following combinations provide time information to workstations (clients).

TABLE 8.1 *Legal Time Provider/Client Combinations*

TIME SOURCE	CLIENT
Secondary	Workstation
Primary	Primary, Secondary, Workstation
Reference	Primary, Secondary, Workstation (and Reference)
Single Reference	Secondary, Workstation

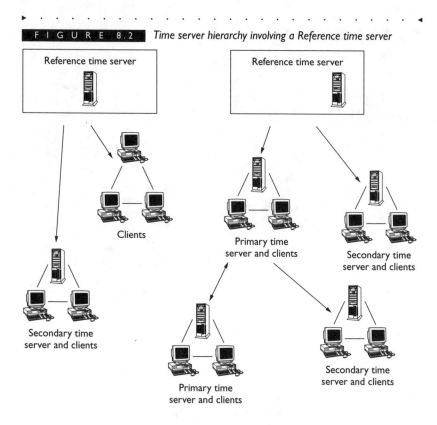

Time server hierarchy involving a Reference time server

NOTE   Because Reference servers do not adjust their internal clocks, multiple Reference servers never synchronize with each other, even though they poll each other for time information. If you have two or more Reference servers, a common external time source should be used to synchronize them.

TIP   A time synchronization solutions guide can be found at `www.connectotel.com/netware/timesg.html`.

Although neither normally done nor generally recommended, it *is* possible to configure a Secondary time server to obtain time information from another Secondary time server.

Understanding Time Source Configuration Methods

As discussed in Chapter 1, NetWare 5 provides two protocols that are used to synchronize time on a network — TimeSync (over IPX and IP) and Network Time Protocol (over IP). When using TimeSync, you can use two methods to keep your servers synchronized. These include:

- Default configuration
- Custom configuration

Because the functionality of NTP has been built into the newer TIMESYNC.NLM — as a matter of fact for NetWare 5.0 with Service Pack 2 or higher and NetWare 5.1, you do not need to, and cannot, load NTP.NLM separately from TIMESYNC.NLM — the following discussion centers around the TIMESYNC.NLM.

If you're using non-NetWare NDS servers, such as eDirectory for Solaris or eDirectory for Linux, you need to configure the UNIX servers to use NTP and obtain your time from the appropriate NTP time source(s).

TIMESYNC.NLM v5.08 or later can provide time to an NTP client through UDP port 123. For example, if you want your UNIX machines to take time from a NetWare server, set up NTP on your UNIX machines with the IP address or DNS name of the NetWare server. This is done by entering the following statement in the NTP configuration file (usually /etc/ntp.conf) for the UNIX system:

```
Server DNS name or IP address of the NetWare server
```

TIP

More information about using NTP with TIMESYNC.NLM can be found in the knowledgebase at the Novell Support Connection Web site; use TIMESYNC and NTP as the search keywords. A good TID on the topic is #10050215, "Timesync Frequently Asked Questions."

Default Configuration Method

Traditionally, NetWare servers use SAPs (*Service Advertising Protocol*) to detect and advertise the presence of services on the network. A server (of any service) sends out a SAP broadcast once every 60 seconds. By default, Primary, Reference, and Single Reference time servers use SAP broadcasts to let their clients or peers know of their presence on the network. At the same time, Secondary, Primary, and Reference time servers use SAPs to locate a time provider to contact.

To keep things simple, the (default) SAP configuration method assumes a two-layer design. The first NetWare 4 or NetWare 5 server on the network is configured as a Single Reference time server. All subsequent NetWare 4 or NetWare 5 servers are configured as Secondary time servers (refer to Figure 8.1).

Similarly, in an IP environment, the auto-discovery of time servers is done through Service Location Protocol (SLP), and no active advertisement traffic exists, as is the case of SAP—SLP traffic is only generated when TIMESYNC.NLM is loaded (at server startup by default) or when the SLP service or directory agent (DA) goes down.

NOTE

> For more information about SLP in NetWare environments, refer to a NetWare 5 book, such as Novell's Guide to NetWare 5. Also, you can check out Novell's knowledge base at http://support.novell.com.

The default configuration has the following advantages:

▸ It is easy to understand and requires no planning.

▸ By using SLP or SAP to auto-discover time sources, no configuration file is needed to provide this information to any additional time servers.

▸ The chance of synchronization error is reduced because a time receiver (Secondary server) only talks to a time provider (Single Reference, Reference, or Primary server) and never to another Secondary server for its time.

On the other hand, depending on the network configuration, the default configuration might not be the best method of implementing time synchronization on your network. The default configuration has the following disadvantages:

▸ If your organization is connected by WAN links and if each site has two or more Primary servers, using the default configuration might result in more network traffic than necessary.

▸ Test (time) servers can be disruptive in a large internetworking environment if they are brought up and down often. Due to the somewhat inefficient *Routing Information Protocol* (RIP) commonly used in IPX environments, propagation of SAP updates might take some time to reach all other time servers and clients. In the meantime, the time clients can possibly drift out of time while seeking a new time provider.

► In an IPX environment, because SAP packets are generated once every 60 seconds, a constant "background" level of network traffic is always present. If you have a large number of time providers, the traffic due to SAP on your slower network links could be significant.

► Using SLP in the IP environment means that a misconfigured server can possibly disrupt the network. For example, a Secondary server might synchronize to an unsynchronized server rather than to an authorized time provider.

► One time source means a single point of failure. Should the Single Reference time server fail or even the hardware clock in the Single Reference time server drift, the network is susceptible to time synchronization errors. Fortunately, a short-term loss of time synchronization (from minutes to a few hours) does not adversely affect the overall network time. A prolonged time drift, however, could cause problems in your Secondary time servers.

Should a time provider fail, you can quickly change a Secondary time server to a time provider by entering **SET TIME SERVER TYPE=***Time Provider Name* at the server console. The time server type can also be changed using MONITOR. This is discussed later in this chapter.

Custom Configuration Method

Instead of using SAP or SLP to auto-locate time servers and peers, you can manually list the specific time providers that a particular server should contact. The default file name for this configuration file is TIMESYNC.CFG, which is located in the SYS:SYSTEM directory of each server. Using the custom configuration method enables you to configure more than one time provider to ensure fault tolerance. The list of time providers on a network is referred to as a *configured list*.

By using a configured list to reference multiple time providers, when one time server goes down, the next configured time server becomes the time provider. Although the custom configuration method is not difficult, it does require some advanced planning. The following are some questions to keep in mind when designing a custom configuration:

► Which servers are your time sources and which are Secondary servers?

► Should you be using only Primary time servers or do you also need a Reference time server?

► If using a Reference time server, what is your external time source?

- Would your environment function properly with a Single Reference time server?
- Are you using SAPs/SLPs for your time servers?
- Are you using a configured sources list with no SAPs/SLPs? Or are you using a combination of both?
- If using a configured sources list, which time clients are going to be contacting which time sources?

You can use a combination of a configured sources list and SAP/SLP in custom configuration.

TIP

Secondary time servers contact the time sources in the order listed in TIMESYNC.CFG. They stop at the first reachable time source. Therefore, you should give the ordered list some thought during the planning and installation process. Enter the time sources in order of priority. For example, if you want a Secondary server to access the time source NETWARE51 whenever possible, NETWARE51 should be listed first in your configured list. A poorly ordered list might cause more network traffic and be prone to time synchronization errors.

The following is a typical TIMESYNC.CFG file for a Secondary time server; lines with two "#" symbols are manually added comment lines to help document the file:

```
## Configuration Parameters from server NETWARE5-TORONTO
# TimeSync.Cfg is now updated automatically,
# when changes are made on the System Console


# TIMESYNC Configuration Parameters


## Do not listen to time source SAPs/SLPs
Configured Sources = OFF


Directory Tree Mode = ON
Hardware Clock = OFF
Polling Count = 3
Polling Interval = 600
Service Advertising = OFF
```

```
Synchronization Radius = 2000
Type = SECONDARY


## Configured time source list from server NETWARE5-
TORONTO
# TIMESYNC Configured time source list
Time Source = NETWARE51
Time Source = MAINSERVER2
Time Source = BACKUP1
```

You should identify *at least* two time sources for each secondary server to ensure fault tolerance. In an IP environment, consider entering both the IP address and DNS name in your time sources field in case your DNS server goes down. Otherwise, if this were to happen, the Secondary server could not resolve the DNS name, and time would go unsynchronized.

NOTE Because the custom configuration does not use SAP/SLP to auto-discover time servers on your network, the custom configuration method helps prevent excess network traffic. However, because all time servers must be configured to obtain time from the appropriate time provider, this method requires additional administration.

Each TimeSync server that needs to get time from another server, or that provides time, needs to be explicitly configured as any of the following:

- Single Reference
- Reference
- Primary
- Secondary

NOTE You can specify a time "source" for a Single Reference time server but, because Single Reference time servers read time from their local hardware clocks and serve it to time clients, they do *not* change their time. In other words, even if you configure a Single Reference time server to obtain time from other time sources, those time sources are not used to change the time of the Single Reference server.

All configuration and administration of TIMESYNC.NLM (including the updating of the TIMESYNC.CFG file) can be done using SET commands at the server console or by using MONITOR—for NetWare 4, however, you must manually update the TIMESYNC.CFG file.

To configure TimeSync from the server console prompt, enter the following, in sequence:

```
SET TIMESYNC configured sources = ON
SET TIMESYNC time sources = Server name, IP address, or
DNS name of the source time server
SET TIMESYNC Restart Flag = ON
```

The restart is required for the new changes to take effect. On some rare occasions, you may need to unload and then reload TIMESYNC.NLM for the changes to take effect.

TIP

To enter two or more time sources, separate the time sources with a semicolon, as in SET TIMESYNC TIME SOURCES=10.0.0.6;10.0.0.7;. Note that you need to terminate the list with a semicolon.

To configure a time source for TimeSync in MONITOR NLM, do the following:

1. Load MONITOR.NLM.

2. Select Server Parameters from the menu.

3. Select the Time option.

4. Scroll down the list and change the field TIMESYNC Configured Sources to ON.

5. In the TIMESYNC Time Sources field, enter the Server name, IP address, or the DNS name of the source time server. To enter two or more time sources, separate the time sources with a semicolon, as in SET TIMESYNC TIME SOURCES=10.0.0.6;10.0.0.7;. Note that you need to terminate the list with a semicolon.

6. Scroll to the field TIMESYNC Restart Flag and set it to ON.

7. Exit out of MONITOR and issue the **SET TIMESYNC Restart Flag = ON** command at the server console prompt.

NOTE

If your time source is to be an NTP server, the same steps outlined previously are applicable. The only difference is when specifying the time source, append ":123" to the IP address or the DNS name (include domain suffix as necessary), as in SET TIMESYNC TIME SOURCES=10.0.0.6:123;10.0.0.7:123; where (UDP) port 123 is the standard NTP port.

Because Single Reference servers obtain time from their own internal hardware clock, you must change the time server type to Reference. This enables the Reference server to obtain time from an NTP time source and then deliver it to the network.

Using the custom configuration method for specifying time sources gives you complete control of the time synchronization environment. Also, you eliminate the network traffic due to SAPs/SLPs from time servers. By placing the time sources at strategic locations around your network, you can optimize the network traffic and provide redundant time sources in case of network link failures.

On the other hand, in order to have an effective custom configuration, advanced planning is required. Because each time provider and time client (a time consumer) must be manually configured, more installation time is required. If a new time provider is added to the network, or if the network undergoes a change, you might need to reconfigure a large number of other servers and clients.

NOTE

If you have a mixed NetWare 4 and NetWare 5 network or you have some NetWare servers running IPX and some IP, ensure at least one of your NetWare 5 servers have either IP and IPX bound, or the Compatibility Mode Driver (CMD) loaded. Meeting this requirement enables IPX-based servers to communicate with IP-based servers, thus permits TimeSync to function.

Choosing a Time Synchronization Configuration Method

As discussed in the preceding section, two configuration options are available (default or custom), each of which has pros and cons.

By default, NetWare 4 and NetWare 5 use the default method (via SAP or SLP) for configuring time synchronization sources. The simple case of a single NetWare server network explains why. With the time source being a Single Reference, it does not require another time source to achieve synchronization. If the server is a Primary time server, it needs another Primary (or Reference) time server to partner with. For a Reference time server, you need an external time source, which can be both a hassle and expensive for a single-server environment. A Reference time server also needs another time source with which to synchronize. Therefore, the default of a Single Reference time server is the only option that works universally.

For small networks, use the default time synchronization configuration. A small network here is defined as a network that has no more than one router hop between any two servers, and no *wide area network* (WAN) (slow) links between any of the servers. Up to 30 servers in such an environment can be considered a small network.

TIP Novell does not recommend using more than 30 servers with the default configuration method. If you have more than 30 servers or WAN links, use a Time Provider Group (discussed later in this section).

When using the default time synchronization configuration, take care in choosing which server is your Single Reference time server. It should be located in the center of your network topology (or as close to it as possible). The hardware clock should be trustworthy; otherwise, it causes time drift.

Time Provider Groups

Consider using the custom configuration option and create Time Provider Groups for large networks that have multiple router hops. Consider turning off time server SAPs to reduce overall network traffic.

A Time Provider Group generally consists of a Reference time server and a number of Primary time servers. You can use default configuration or configured source lists between these servers, depending on your need and network complexity. Two examples of Time Provider Groups are discussed next.

Time Provider Group in Smaller Networks

The Time Provider Groups can be implemented in two ways. In small to medium size networks, which have few WAN links, the Time Provider Group has a time provider in each remote location, as shown in Figure 8.3.

A Time Provider Group in a small network environment

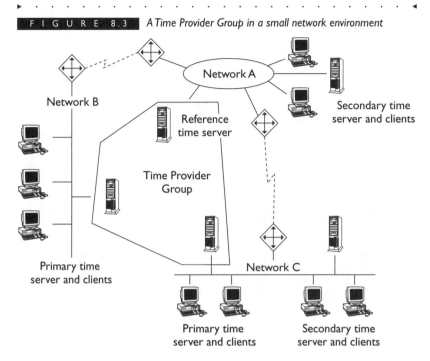

Each time provider (either a Reference time server or a Primary time server) provides time information to its local clients. They communicate with each other, either through SAP/SLP or configured lists, across the WAN links. Depending on your particular WAN topology, a configured list might work more efficiently than the SAP/SLP method.

This method works nicely for a small- to medium-sized WAN. If you have international sites, or sites in many provinces and states, a different Time Provider Group configuration might be worth considering.

Time Provider Group for Large Networks

In an extremely large WAN, you should consider using multiple Time Provider Groups. You can implement this configuration in two ways. Figure 8.4 shows a configuration in which all Time Provider Groups use the same external time source. To reduce WAN traffic due to time synchronization, place a Time Provider Group in each major remote site. These Time Provider Groups in turn support local clients or immediate WAN sites. In the example shown in Figure 8.4, the WAN spans four different U.S. states—Florida, California, Montana, and New York. Each regional WAN site has its own Time Provider Group supporting local clients and nearby WAN sites. The atomic clock at the U.S. Naval Observatory (USNO) in Washington, D.C., is used as the common external time reference.

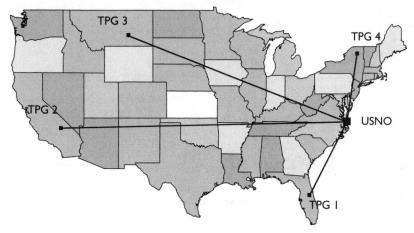

F I G U R E   8 . 4   *All Time Provider Groups (TPGs) use the U.S. Naval Observatory (USNO) as the common external time source.*

Earlier you learned that Reference time servers do not synchronize with each other. The definition of a Reference time server is that it does not adjust its own hardware clock. Therefore, for all Reference time servers (hence all time servers) to agree on a standard time, they all must use a common external time source. This is feasible and is highly desirable for a national WAN configuration. In the example shown in Figure 8.4, USNO's atomic clock is used for such a purpose.

What if the WAN is on a global scale? It might not be feasible to use a common external time reference. In such a configuration, you should use local external time references whenever possible.

Figure 8.5 shows a WAN that covers eastern Canada, the far western part of the United States, and Australia. At each major concentration, a Time Provider Group is installed. Each Time Provider Group uses its local external time source.

Many countries provide their national official time source through cesium atomic clock sources. Therefore, the cesium atomic clock at the *National Institute for Standards and Technology* (NIST) in the U.S. agrees with the clock located in at the *National Research Council of Canada* (NRCC) in Ottawa, Canada, which agrees with the one located in Geneva, Switzerland, and so on, to within a few nanoseconds (if not less) of each other. This is *more* than adequate for the purpose of time synchronization in a NetWare environment. In such a configuration example, one can say that the cesium atomic clocks form a "super" Time Provider Group.

F I G U R E   8.5 *TPGs using different external time sources*

National Research Council
Ottawa, Canada

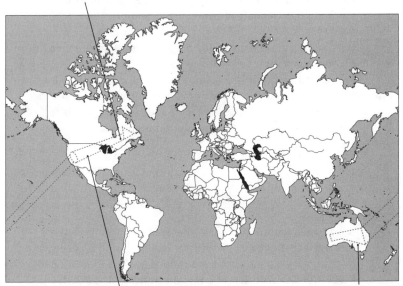

National Institute for Standards and Technology   Telecom Australia
Boulder, Colorado

General Time Synchronization Guidelines

The following guidelines (based on Novell recommendations) help you organize and plan your time synchronization environment:

▸ If you have 30 servers or fewer without a WAN, use the default configuration method. This method provides you with one Single Reference time server, with your remaining servers being Secondary time servers.

▶ If you have more than 30 servers or a WAN, set up some Time Provider Groups.

▶ Whenever possible, have Secondary time servers synchronize with a time provider, such as a Primary, Reference, or Single Reference time server.

▶ If you have to use a Secondary time server to synchronize another Secondary time server, keep the depth of this hierarchy as shallow as possible. The effect of the time synchronization radius is additive.

NOTE

The *time synchronization radius* is the minimum amount of time difference between time servers to still be considered time synchronized. The default time synchronization radius is 2,000 milliseconds or 2 seconds — for a time client directly contacting a time source, the client should be 2 seconds off, at most. However, if a Secondary time server follows another Secondary time server, the second Secondary time server could be off by as much as 4 seconds. The further away from a time source, the larger the potential error because the effect is additive. Your goal is to minimize the potential time synchronization error.

▶ Keep the number of time sources small to minimize time-related network traffic. Remember, time sources exchange time information with each other. By default, about 1 KB of data (resulted from three time exchanges) is exchanged between each time provider pair every 10 minutes.

TIP

The number of time exchanges per polling period is governed by the Polling Count setting (controlled by the SET TIMESYNC POLLING COUNT server console command or through MONITOR.NLM), which has a default of three. The default polling interval, as controlled by Polling Interval, is 600 seconds (10 minutes). As long as your server clock is not drifting and synchronization is maintained, the Polling Interval (which can be changed using the SET TIMESYNC POLLING INTERVAL server console command, or through MONITOR.NLM) can be extended to reduce network traffic.

▶ Place Secondary time servers at small remote sites. They can obtain time information across the WAN from a Time Provider Group or a (Single) Reference time server. The traffic due to Secondary servers requesting time information is minimal.

- Place one of the Primary time servers from a Time Provider Group at each of the large remote sites. It can synchronize time with the rest of the Time Provider Group members across the WAN, while providing time information locally to the Secondary time servers.

- If time drift is a concern to your network, use a Reference and connect it to an external time source, such as an atomic clock or a public domain NTP server on the Internet.

- If SAP/SLP traffic is an issue for your network (either locally or across the WAN), use the configured sources list method to eliminate SAPs/SLPs due to time servers.

How to Adjust Network Time

In some instances the time is in synchronization on the network but the actual network time is *not* correct because the time on the time provider has slowed or is incorrect. You can easily adjust the time using the SET TIME console command. However, be aware of possible implications to NDS before you change your network time.

WARNING

Changing time forward and then back on a NetWare tree can have serious repercussions. *Do not* set time forward and then back on a production tree for testing purposes. If time is set forward and timestamps are incremented (last login, and so on) you receive *synthetic time*. Synthetic time is NDS's way of protecting the objects in your tree from receiving future timestamps. For more information about synthetic time and how to fix it, refer to Novell knowledge-base TID# 10013670, "Synthetic Time – Summary / Fix."

Do not move time back on your network until after you are prepared to deal with synthetic time issues and thoroughly understand the issues involved with synthetic time.

If time needs to indeed be set, it should be done from the Single Reference or Reference time server. Setting time from a Primary or Secondary time server only results in unexpected effects, such as the time being changed again if a difference in time is found on the next polling interval.

To set time on a network the following parameters can be typed at the console prompt on the time provider:

```
SET TIME <MM/DD/YY> <HH:MM:SS> <AM or PM>
```

For example,

```
SET TIME April 1 2001 1:05:00 pm
```

The response that is generated from the server reads,

```
Time synchronization is active on the server. Are you sure
you want to change the time? n
```

Here, "n" (no) would be the default if you simply pressed return. To change the time, insert a "y" instead to respond yes — no return key is needed.

If time is moved forward on the network there should be no errors reported. If time is moved backward, Synthetic time is issued on the partition until the timestamp that is future in the partition(s) is reached.

In general, you should not use the server console SET TIME command to change time in a NetWare 4 or NetWare 5 environment. It is best to use the Time Adjustment console command instead:

```
SET TIMESYNC TIME ADJUSTMENT = [+/-]HH:MM:SS AT MONTH DAY,
YEAR HH:MM:SS [AM/PM]
```

Let's say you want to move your network time ahead by five minutes, for example, you enter the following:

```
SET TIMESYNC TIME ADJUSTMENT = +00:05:00
```

This command *schedules* the adjustment to occur one hour or six polling intervals (whichever is larger) from the time you enter the command. With the additional "at" (@) parameters, you can schedule it for a future time; for example,

```
SET TIMESYNC TIME ADJUSTMENT = +00:05:00 at April 1, 2002
08:30:00 am
```

advances the network time by five minutes at 8:30am on April 1, 2002 instead of the one hour or six polling intervals (whichever is larger) from the time you enter the command.

TIP

It is generally recommended that you schedule your time adjustment during a low usage period. Otherwise, there might be some out-of-order NDS update events.

The main advantage of the Time Adjustment command is that you can *cancel* the change should you change your mind later — the SET TIME command takes effect immediately. To cancel the adjustment, enter the following on the same time server:

```
SET TIMESYNC TIME ADJUSTMENT = CANCEL
```

The command must be issued before the scheduled time adjustment.

TIP

You should always verify the DOS time on a server before SERVER. EXE is executed because the initial time used by the operating system is read from the DOS clock, and not the CMOS clock.

In general, it is not necessary to adjust the local time on a given server. The local time is always synchronized to the network time. There might be rare occasions, however, when you need to reconfigure some time-related parameters, such as time zone or Daylight Savings Time information.

WARNING

You need to be patient when changing time information. Sufficient time should be allowed for the new time information to be propagated to all the other time servers and time clients, especially if you have WAN links.

Changing local time information, such as time zone, does not change the server's *Universal Time Coordinated* (UTC) time, but does affect the local time. It might take a few minutes, therefore, for the server's time to catch up to the proper time in the new time zone.

NOTE

Whenever you change something that affects time synchronization, the message TIMESYNC-5.9-62, *Time synchronization has been lost after xxx successful polling loops* is displayed on the server console. When time is again caught up, a TIMESYNC-5.9-63, *Time synchronization has been established* message is displayed. (The two numbers after the TIMESYNC message varies depending on the version of the TIMESYNC.NLM.)

You can use the TIME console command to monitor the progress of the server's time changing to match the network time.

Changing Time Server Types

In some instances you need to change the time server from one type to another. For example, when using the default configuration the Single Reference time server needs to be taken down for maintenance and you need to promote a Secondary time server to take its place.

To configure a server to be a certain type of time server, at the system console, enter the following command:

```
SET TIMESYNC TYPE = time server type
```

where time server type is one of Single (for Single Reference), Reference, Primary, or Secondary.

Don't forget to issue the SET TIMESYNC Restart Flag = ON command to affect the change.

Alternatively, you can use the MONITOR.NLM:

1. At the server console, load MONITOR.
2. Select Server parameters.
3. Select Time.
4. Select TIMESYNC Type and enter a time server type.
5. Select TIMESYNC Restart Flag and set it to ON.

## CHAPTER 9

Troubleshooting Common Problems

Despite the best possible planning, care taken during implementation, and user training, something may still go wrong with your NDS. Fortunately, because the majority of the common issues can be attributed to human error — such as misconfigured settings — they are easily rectified.

NetWare 4 and NetWare 5 have included functionality to observe NDS traffic on a server. The full scope of options for the DSTRACE console SET command falls outside the scope of this book, but this chapter does discuss the few of those options that are useful for troubleshooting NDS issues. The various DSTRACE options are introduced as needed.

NOTE

DSTRACE is also included with eDirectory for the various platforms, such as Windows NT and Solaris. Check the included documentation on how to activate this utility.

TIP

Detailed discussion on DSTRACE and other NDS troubleshooting techniques can be found in *Novell's Guide to Troubleshooting NDS* (from IDG Books Worldwide).

This chapter covers the following four NDS issues that are most common in managing an NDS network:

▶ Login issues

▶ Security issues, both file system and NDS

▶ Time synchronization problems

▶ NDS database inconsistency

Login Problems

Many of the initial problems users have with NDS are encountered when they attempt to connect to the network for the first time. Three of the most common causes of login problems are:

▶ NDS context specification

▶ Incorrect password

▶ Concurrent login limit

NDS Context Specification

One very common problem encountered by new administrators, and users who are familiar with bindery-based logins under NetWare 2 and NetWare 3 (or background from other operating systems, such as UNIX, in which no "tree structure" exists to worry about) occurs when they initially log in to the network after installation is completed. The newer versions of the GUI login interface don't show the context setting (which is only available after clicking the Advanced button; see Figure 9.1).

FIGURE 9.1 *More options become available after clicking the Advanced button.*

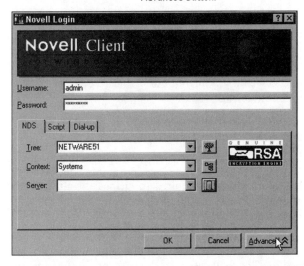

If you attempt to log in without either specifying the context or by specifying a distinguished name, the GUI interface returns an error similar to the following:

```
The system could not log you into the network.

Make sure your name and connection information are
correct, then type your password again.
```

Frequently, this is easily correctable by specifying the entire context when logging in. Figure 9.2 shows an example of specifying a complete login name during login.

F I G U R E   9 . 2
Using a leading period in the name enables you to log in
without having to click the Advanced button to set the context.

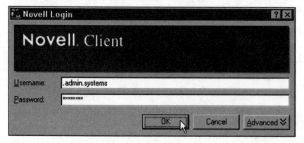

The leading period in the name forces the GUI interface to start from the
[Root] context, regardless what the current context setting may be, and build
the name from that point. If the leading period is not used, the name and any
additional context information that is part of the user name you entered is
prepended to the existing context. This might be desirable in some specific cir-
cumstances, but not necessarily in all situations.

User Password-Related Issues

Once a user figures out what their login context is, the next problem is generally password-related. Often times as part of the security requirement implemented by the administrator, users are required to change their passwords
periodically. Two situations exist in which a user cannot authenticate to a particular server after a password change.

One situation is when a user password expires and/or a user attempts to
change the user password (say, using NetWare Administrator) it confirms that
the password is changed, but the new password doesn't work — the user still
needs to use the old password. As discussed in Chapter 1, NDS relies on server
times being synchronized throughout the network. Otherwise, changes to
NDS may not be recorded. For example, if the server the user is attached to has
the wrong time (got ahead of the other servers in the tree), the user would
change his/her password locally, but because the timestamp on the change was
ahead of the rest of the network, it was invalidated and therefore not propagated throughout the rest of the NDS database (replicas). In such cases, the
problem can be easily fixed by changing the time on the server that has the
wrong time; Chapter 8 discusses how to adjust a server's time using the SET
TIME server console command.

X-REF

Later in this chapter, the "Time Synchronization Issues" section provides more information on how to determine if the network time is synchronized and, if not, which server is out of synchronization.

Similar problems can occur if the network time was once set in the future and then returned to the correct time — even on a single-tree network. If the network time was in the future and the password was changed, the timestamp for the private key property (part of the password key-pair) would be in the future. Then when the time is moved back and one tries to change the password, the password change does not take effect because the new private key has an "older" timestamp. In such a case, you need to use DSVIEW.NLM (for NetWare 4.1x or higher) or DSBROWSE.NLM (for NetWare 5.0 and higher) to look at the user's private key property to verify that this is the problem.

NOTE

You can find the details on how to use DSVIEW in the book *Novell's Guide to Troubleshooting NDS* and on the Novell Support Connection Web site at http://support.novell.com.

If a future timestamp is indeed the issue, and the date is not too far in the future, you can wait until after that date. If you can't wait, you have to call Novell Technical Support and arrange for a dial-in to change the timestamp.

If you're running NetWare 4.1x and it is using DS.NLM v6.09, you should be aware of the following issue. When a user changes a password, the public key for the user's object is updated. This is immediately replicated to all servers in the replica ring. Servers with external references also need to be updated, but this is not being done automatically at the time of password change; however, the problem fixes itself after about 12 hours.

NOTE

For more information about external references, refer back to Chapter 1.

The cause is that external references are not being updated when needed. Usually, when a user connects to a server holding an external reference of the user's object, the server returns a -669 ("Failed Authentication") error to a server holding a replica of the object. The server holding this object should then understand that the server with the external reference needs an updated public key, and should synchronize that information to that server. This then enables the user to login to that server with the new password.

Apparently with DS 6.09, in certain cases, the server with the external reference returns a -632 ("System Failure") error instead of a -669 error. This causes the server with the user's object to think that there was a system failure, and so it denies login and the user can't access the server. DS 6.09b or higher fixes this problem by forcing the server with the external reference to generate the -669 error instead of the -632 in this situation.

At the time of writing, DS 6.09 is the most currently released version and DS 6.09B is in field testing.

NOTE

Re-backlinking the external reference fixes the problem because it updates the public key — and by default, NDS' backlink process runs at 13-hour intervals or you can force the backlink process to run immediately by issuing the SET DSTRACE=*B then SET DSTRACE=*H console command. However, the problem is going to occur again the next time a password is changed.

This is one example of keeping your DS.NLM up-to-date to ensure a smooth running network.

NOTE

Concurrent Login Limit

One of the NetWare security features administrators implement is Concurrent Login Limit. It governs a single user who simultaneously logs in to the network from multiple workstations, and decides how many log ins from different workstations are permissible. Here's how it works.

When a user logs into the network, the server that authenticates the request, checks the Network Address attribute of the User object. The server compares the number of entries in this multi-values attribute against the value stored in the Concurrent Login Limit attribute. If the number of entries in the Network Address is less than what's specified in the Concurrent Login Limit attribute, the network address of the new workstation is added to the Network Address attribute and the user is allowed access to the network — no check is performed on whether the address of the current workstation is already recorded in the Network Address field. When a user properly logs out of the network — that is, not by simply turning off the workstation — the workstation's network address is removed from the Network Address attribute. If the number of entries in the Network Address is equals to or larger to what's specified in the Concurrent

Login Limit attribute, login is denied with an error message similar to the following:

```
Error: LOGIN-4.12-830: You are trying to log in to too
many stations simultaneously. The supervisor has limited
the number of connections you may have.
```

The problem lies in the "proper" logging out by a workstation. When a workstation is logged out (via the Window's Start ⇨ Shutdown procedure), the server(s) the workstation is connected to are notified of the event and the NDS is correctly updated. However, when the workstation is simply shut down (powered off) or restarted, NDS is not updated to remove the corresponding Network Address entry as the server is not notified of the "logout." In such an event, if the user tries to log in again (using the same or a different workstation), login may be denied because the Concurrent Login Limit may be reached. This problem is further complicated by the NetWare 5 Client software because the Workstation Manager (installed by default) requires two connections to the server.

NOTE For an indepth discussion about a NetWare 5 client needing two connections to the server and how that affects the Concurrent Login Limit, refer to Novell TID #10013518.

NOTE There's a known issue that if the servers have outdated LAN drivers, the event of a properly logged out workstation may not be recorded, thus NDS is not correctly updated. This also leads to future user logins being denied because the Concurrent Login Limit is reached.

Upgrading to DS 6.09 (or higher) for NetWare 4.11 and higher, and DS 7.39 (and higher) for NetWare 5.0 and higher, would address these concurrent login limit issues. However, if they do not, or for some reason you're unable to upgrade the DS.NLM right away, you can use DSREPAIR.NLM as a temporary fix. On a server holding a replica (doesn't have to be the Master) of the affect User object, perform the following steps:

1. Load DSREPAIR.NLM with the –N1 option, for example, the LOAD DSREPAIR –N1.

2. From the Available Options menu, select Unattended full repair.

3. If DSREPAIR reports several errors, run DSREPAIR again until no errors are returned.

The user should then be able to log in. The –N1 switch enables DSREPAIR to clear all the network addresses from all User objects that are more than one day old.

TIP

You can use the –N# switch to clear out User network addresses that are # of days old. If you experience constant problems due to Concurrent Login Limit (and yet you need to impose it), you can use a server automation tool, such as TaskMaster (www.avantitech.com) or CRON (included with NetWare 5 and can be downloaded from the Novell Support Connection Web site) to schedule the running of "DSREPAIR –N0 –U" on a nightly basis; the –U option runs DSREPAIR in the Unattended mode and then exits.

Security Problems

One main reason for installing file servers is to store data on them and make the data available to different users. However, some type of security measure must be implemented, or one user might be able to read another user's files when he's not suppose to, or a user can update a file when she's not authorized to. By default, NetWare implements a fairly tight file system security — in order for users to access the files and directories of network volumes, they must be given the appropriate file system security access. The default NetWare file system security — users have no access to any files and directories on NetWare volumes (except to their own home directories, if those were set up) — is opposite to that of the default NDS security.

As discussed in Chapter 6, it is very common to use Group and container objects as a means to grant file system rights. Very often, the administrator is comfortable using Group objects to assign file trustees but overlooks the possible implication of containers as "super groups" when used to assign file system rights. The following sections cover the situation in which a user gets insufficient rights or too many rights to the file system, as well as how to determine the NDS rights that one object has over another.

Too Few File System Rights

A number of conditions can result in a user having too few file system rights, so that the user isn't able to access or update the files on a NetWare volume. Some of these situations are:

- ▶ Administrator failed to assign the necessary rights to the user
- ▶ The User object was moved from one context to another within the tree
- ▶ A mismatch exists between information in a Group object's Members attribute and the User object's Group Membership attribute

It is possible for a network administrator to install on the NetWare server a tested and verified application that runs correctly, and then have the users find that they can't run the same application due to insufficient rights. Very often, this is because the administrator was logged in as Admin (or another user id that has Supervisor rights throughout the tree, thus also Supervisor rights to all NetWare volumes) during the software installation and testing; and, afterwards it is easy to forget to assign the necessary rights to the users so that they too can run the application. It is, therefore, suggested that network administrators have two login ids — one with Supervisor rights and the other without. The testing should be done using the "normal" id.

Another common cause is that the administrator has one of the users test the application by giving this user the proper rights, and then failed to assign the necessary rights to the Group object so that the rest of the users can have access.

As you get more comfortable with NDS, you are going to use containers to assign file system rights more and more, because containers act as "natural groups" — meaning any users in that container and below automatically inherit the file system rights assigned to a container higher up in the tree structure. Because the rights were assigned at the container level and if a user's object was moved from one branch of the tree to another (such as from OU=Sales.O=Toronto to OU=Sales.O=Vancouver), the user no longer inherits the rights from the original parent container. Sometimes this is desirable and sometimes not. Therefore, you need to check if the user's file system rights will be affected before you move the object in question.

The last situation is a little difficult to track down and only happens when a group's membership gets large or if a user belongs to many groups. In some *rare* instances, the Group object does not show a certain user in its member list, but the User object does show it as a member of the Group object (through the Group Membership tab in NetWare Administrator, for example). To determine if this is the case, that the User object is actually a member of the Group object, you need to look at the Group object's Members list as well as the User object's Group Membership list and Security Equal To list.

NOTE As discussed in Chapter 6, when a user is made a member of a group, it is also security equivalent to the Group object. This is why you should examine both the Group Membership and Security Equal To lists.

If you find a mismatch between the lists, an easy fix is to simply remove the group from the User object's Group Membership list (and it should automatically be removed from the Security Equal To list, but if not, remove it from that list too), and then make the user a member of the group again. If, however, you find there's a number of users with this type of mismatch, you should download the GroupFix utility from Novell's Support Connection Web site at http://support.novell.com (refer to TID# 2952770). GroupFix is a DOS application that synchronizes group members' Security Equal To attribute and the Group Membership attribute with the Member attribute of groups.

TIP

Not discussed here is the possibility of file rights at the lower portion of a file system tree being blocked by IRFs. You can use the RIGHTS.EXE /I to help troubleshoot such issues.

Too Many File System Rights

Because a user can obtain file system rights in many different ways (from direct trustee assignments, groups belonged to, and even from NDS containers), it is not always easy to determine or troubleshoot a scenario in which a user has full file system rights. The following procedure outlines the steps you can take in order to track the cause.

At the root of the volume type RIGHTS /T (RIGHTS.EXE is a DOS application shipped with all versions of NetWare 4 and NetWare 5) to see if there was an explicit rights assignment granted to the user or any group or container the user is a member of. If so then revoke that assignment and see if that resolves the problem.

If no explicit assignment exists, the user has most likely inherited the rights from NDS. That means somewhere the user, container, and so on was granted at least the Write (or perhaps even Supervisor) attribute right to the file server object's Object Trustees (ACL) property. They can get this by one or more of the following assignments:

► Having [S] object rights

► Having [S] or [W] right to All Properties

► Having [S] or [W] to the Object Trustees (ACL) property

One way to track this down is to select Trustees of this Object for the [Root] object, and then select Effective Rights and see what the user's effective rights are. Then if he has excessive rights, find the object in the Trustees of this Object list that was granted the excessive rights. Then do the same thing for each container between the [Root] and the server object, including the server object. At some point you see that the user's effective rights is more than the default (only Browse object rights and Read and Compare All property rights). It is then at this level in the tree that the assignment was made.

Consider the example NDS tree shown in Figure 9.3. The following steps illustrate how you can use NetWare Administrator to track down and fix the problem of Lisa having full rights to the SYS volume:

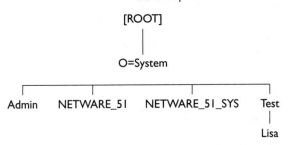

F I G U R E   9.3 *Lisa has full rights to the SYS volume even though she was given an explicit file system trustee assignment of* [RF] *to the root of SYS.*

[ROOT]
|
O=System
|
Admin   NETWARE_51   NETWARE_51_SYS   Test
|
Lisa

1. Launch NetWare Administrator and set the context to the [Root] by selecting View ➪ Set Context, and enter **[Root]**.

2. Right-click [Root] and select Trustees of this Object (By default the only trustees that are here should be [Public] and Admin).

3. Click the Effective Rights button.

4. Click the Search Tree icon that is to the right of the Object name field. Browse the tree and select the User object Lisa (located under OU=Test).

5. At this point you are returned to the Effective Rights dialog box. The user Lisa.Test.Systems are in the Object name text field. Normally a user only has Browse Object Rights and no All properties Property rights. That is what Lisa has (see Figure 9.4).

6. Now select the Selected Properties radio button in the Property Rights box. Search the properties list for the Object Trustees (ACL) property. Normally a user does not have any assignment to this field. Lisa has no rights for the Object Trustees (ACL) property.

7. Close the Effective Rights dialog box and the Trustees of [Root] dialog box.

► . . . . ◄

FIGURE 9.4   *Lisa has only Browse object rights to* [Root] *and no All properties Property rights, as per default.*

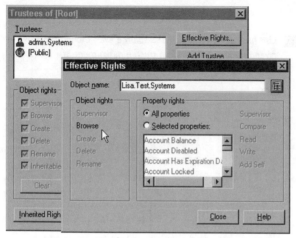

8. Repeat Steps 2–7 for O=Systems.

9. This time when you select Effective Rights for Lisa, she has all Object and Property rights (see Figure 9.5).

► . . . . ◄

FIGURE 9.5   *Lisa has full rights, not as per default.*

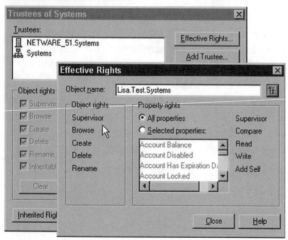

10. Close the Effective Rights dialog box and return to the Trustees of Systems dialog box. Normally the only trustee of a container is the container itself, but any object can be a trustee of any other object.

11. Highlight the Systems trustee. In the Object Rights box, one finds Supervisor is selected (see Figure 9.6). Normally the only rights a container has to itself is Read to the Login Script and Print Job Configuration properties. This is one place where excessive rights have been granted.

FIGURE 9.6 *Systems was granted* [S] *Object Rights to itself, not as per default.*

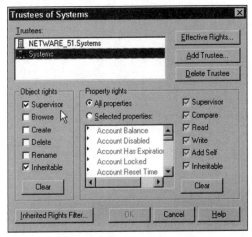

12. Select the Clear button in the Object Rights. This removes all previously assigned object rights.

13. Click OK to save the change.

14. Go back and check the Effective Rights again and verify that Lisa no longer has excessive rights.

15. Have Lisa login to the network and verify she does not have excessive rights to the file system any more.

For this example, you can stop at this point as Lisa no longer has full rights to the SYS volume. However, if O=Systems didn't have S rights to itself, you need to continue checking the server object, NETWARE_51 by repeating Steps 2–7, and noting that normally the Effective Rights for a user should only be Browse object rights on a Server object.

TIP

> When checking objects that have been granted rights, follow the rules for acquiring rights. Check all containers above the user, [Root], [Public], all groups the user is a member of, and any objects the user is security equivalent to (which includes any Organizational Roles).

The following are some questions you can ask to help determine the location in NDS of the source granting the user excessive rights:

- Is the user security equal to Admin?
- Is the user a trustee or a member of a group that is a trustee with supervisor rights or the Write property right to the Server object?
- Is the user a trustee or a member of a group that is a trustee of a container above the Server object with supervisor rights or the Write property right to the object?
- Is the user a trustee or a member of a group that is a trustee of [Root] with Supervisor rights to the Server object?
- Is the user in a container that is a trustee with Supervisor rights to a container above the Server object?
- Is the user under a container that is a trustee with Supervisor rights to the [Root] object?
- Is [Root] a trustee with Supervisor rights over a container that is over the Server object?
- Has [Public] been added as a trustee with Supervisor rights over a container that is over the Server object or to the Server object?

Rights Over Other Objects in the Tree

If you have a medium to large-size network, or if you have external consultants that come in and work on your network, it is a good idea to check, on a regular basis, what NDS rights other User objects (such as those of the consultants) may have over your own User object, Admin, and other User objects that are privileged. If its only a small number of objects you need to check, you can use NetWare Administrator and perform the Effective Rights check as outlined in the previous section. However, this is rather labor-intensive. Novell Technical Support has a DSRights utility that makes this easy.

DSRights is a DOS utility that can be used to list what trustee assignments one NDS object has to another NDS object, and how the rights were derived from the tree. The usage is simply:

```
DSRights <object A> <object B>
```

This displays a flow diagram of Object A and its equivalents with their rights to Object B. It also shows Object, All Property, and Selected Property rights. The following is sample DSRights output for trustee assignments Lisa.Test.Systems has to Systems:

```
D:\>cx .systems
D:\>dsrights lisa.test netware_51_sys


How Lisa.Test got rights to NETWARE_51_SYS
```

	Object	All Property
[Root]		
Inherited Rights Filter	[SBCDR]	[SCRWA]
Inherits from above	[ ]	[ ]
Equivalent to [Public]	[B]	
Effective Rights	[B]	[ ]
Systems.		
Inherited Rights Filter	[SBCDR]	[SCRWA]
Inherits from above	[B]	[ ]
Equivalent to Systems.	[Sbcdr]	[scrwa]

Effective Rights   [SBcdr][scrwa]

NETWARE_51_SYS

Inherited Rights Filter   [SBCDR][SCRWA]

Inherits from above   **[SB-dr][scrwa]**

Effective Rights   [SB-dr][scrwa]

Selected Property Rights

Host Resource Name
    Equivalent to [Root]   [cR]

    Effective Rights   [scRwa]

Host Server
    Equivalent to [Root]   [cR]

    Effective Rights   [scRwa]

You can see from the output (see the bolded line) that Lisa has full rights to
NETWARE_51_SYS through inheritance from above. This should direct you
to pay attention to her parent container(s). The fourth line above the bolded
line shows that Lisa gained her Supervisor rights through being security equivalent to Systems (as Lisa is a User object in that tree branch). Therefore, with a
little practice, you can easily determine, using the output from DSRights, how
an object received its rights in NDS.

NOTE

The rights listed in uppercase are explicitly given (as in [BCDR] to Object A). Rights listed in lowercase are implied, say, through security equivalence (as in [SBCDR]). Also, a dash means you can't create an object under a leaf object (as in [SB-DR]).

If you have a number of objects to check on a regular basis, you can create a batch file containing DSRIGHTS command and pipe the output to a file for later analysis. For example:

```
DSRIGHTS .LISA.TEST.SYSTEMS .ADMIN.SYSTEMS > DSRIGHTS.OUT
DSRIGHTS .TASHA.TESTING .ADMIN.SYSTEMS >> DSRIGHTS.OUT
DSRIGHTS .CHELSEA.TORONTO .ADMIN.SYSTEMS >> DSRIGHTS.OUT
```

DSRights can be downloaded from the Novell Support Connection Web site at http://support.novell.com/misc/patlst.htm#tools.

▶ . . . . ◀

Time Synchronization Issues

Because time synchronization is an essential part of a reliable NDS network, it is important to know strategies for resolving time synchronization problems quickly and effectively. Novell has supplied two tools to assist you in resolving time synchronization problems. They are:

- ▶ DSREPAIR.NLM
- ▶ The time synchronization debugging screens

Using DSREPAIR.NLM

One of the most common time synchronization problems is when a Single Reference time server is brought up with the wrong time. Because a Single Reference time server obtains time only from itself (its own hardware clock), it won't get synchronized with the correct time because it won't change its own time — and it doesn't synchronize with another time server anyway because you can't have another time provider coexisting with a Single Reference time server. The following steps outline how to resolve this problem using DSREPAIR:

1. Check whether the replica timestamps are ahead of actual time by doing the following:

   a. Load DSREPAIR on the server with replicas.

   b. Select Report synchronization status.

c. Review the timestamp value(s). The following is a sample output
from a NetWare 5.1 server and the timestamp entries of interest are
bolded:

```
/****************************************************/


NetWare 5.00 Directory Services Repair 7.16 , DS 8.38
Log file for server ".NETWARE_51.Systems" in tree
"NETWARE51"
Start:  Wednesday, May 24, 2000  12:26:58 am Local Time
Retrieve replica status


Partition: .[Root].
  Replica: .NETWARE_51.Systems
5-24-2000 00:26:33
All servers synchronized up to time:
5-24-2000 00:26:33


Partition: .Toronto
  Replica: .NETWARE5-TORONTO.Markham.Toronto
5-24-2000 00:26:38
  Replica: .NETWARE_51.Systems
5-24-2000 00:26:33
All servers synchronized up to time:
5-24-2000 00:26:33


Partition: .Scarborough.Toronto
  Replica: .NETWARE5-TORONTO.Markham.Toronto
5-23-2000 23:31:40
  Replica: .NETWARE_51.Systems
5-24-2000 00:23:21
All servers synchronized up to time:
5-23-2000 23:31:40


Partition: .Richmond_Hill.Toronto
```

```
   Replica: .NETWARE5-TORONTO.Markham.Toronto
5-24-2000 00:22:50
   Replica: .NETWARE_51.Systems
5-24-2000 00:23:21
All servers synchronized up to time:
5-24-2000 00:22:50


*** END ***
```

NOTE

Between NetWare 5 servers, because of the transitive sync vector, not all replicas of a given partition necessarily have the same time-stamp. The key point is that the timestamps are not far off from the actual current time.

2. At the server console, view the current server time by entering the **TIME** command.

3. If the time on a Single Reference time server is earlier than the actual time, set the time forward to the correct time (refer to Chapter 8 for the necessary steps).

4. If the time on a Single Reference time server is less than one week ahead of actual time, do one of the following:

   • Shut down the servers during off-business hours to allow actual time to catch up with the future timestamps.

   • Don't perform replica or partitioning operations until actual time catches up with the future timestamps.

5. If the timestamp is more than one week ahead, do not set the time backwards unless you have a good understanding of synthetic time.

As discussed in Chapter 8, synthetic time is a condition in which time-stamps are ahead of the actual time on a replica of a partition on a server. You can correct synthetic time using DSREPAIR, but you need to be aware of the possible consequences that can be caused by the repair process. Refer to TID #10013670 for details before you attempt a repair of synthetic time errors.

Using Time Synchronization Debug Screens

When using NTP, you need to ensure that UPD port 123 is not blocked anywhere on your network. Because NTP uses UDP port 123, it is necessary for traffic on that port to be allowed to freely cross your network. If you have firewalls or filtering routers in place between your network and the Internet and you are using NTP, UDP port 123 must be permitted to cross the boundary to the Internet. In determining whether NTP is operating correctly, two debugging commands are very useful:

▶ **SET TIMESYNC DEBUG = 7.** This command enables a time synchronization debugging screen showing the interaction between NetWare time servers on the internal network, as well as communication with external NTP time sources.

▶ **SET TIMESYNC DEBUG = 0.** This command disables the time synchronization debugging screen.

The SET TIMESYNC DEBUG commands can be used even if you're not using NTP.

TIP

Upon entering the SET TIMESYNC DEBUG = 7 command at the server console, you should see the following messages:

```
TIMESYNC: Press ALT-ESC to switch to Timesync Debug
Screen.

TIMESYNC Debug set to 7
```

When you toggled to the Timesync Debug Screen, you should see something similar to the following (the exact wording varies a little depending on the version of TIMESYNC.NLM)—the server this message was displayed on is a Secondary time server:

```
TIMESYNC: Polled server NETWARE_51 (Reference/Single
Reference)

          offset.h = FE640370  offset.l = 83CC36E1


Uniform Adjustment Requested: -0.08E0FE3E

This server is configured as a SECONDARY

  *** Time is synchronized ***Adjustment exceeded Maximum
Offset and was limited to 600
```

You may find the debug screen to be blank on a Single Reference time server because it is not communicating with other time servers. Therefore, the debug screen is most useful on non-Single Reference time servers, such as Reference, Primary, and Secondary time servers.

NOTE

The following two message groups are of interest here:

- The Polled server message group
- The Uniform Adjustment message group

The polled server message group:

```
TIMESYNC: Polled server NETWARE_51 (Reference/Single
Reference)
        offset.h = FE640370  offset.l = 83CC36E1
```

shows the target time server that the current server is polling. In this example, the server is NETWARE_51 and it is a Reference or Single Reference time server. OFFSET.H and OFFSET.L reflect the calculated time difference between this server's time and that of the target time server. These are 64-bit signed real numbers with an implied hexadecimal point separating the whole and fractional parts (10 years is the maximum value for the current 64-bit number to handle).

NOTE If you don't see this Polled server message displayed on the trace screen at all, the server does not know of any time sources. This could mean one of two things. If you are using auto-discovery, this server did not detect any time server SAPs/SLPs. If you have disabled auto-discovery and are using a configured time source list, the list is probably empty. You can check the state of the list by using the SET TIMESYNC TIME SOURCE = console command, as discussed in the SET TIMESYNC TIME SOURCE section.

The Uniform Adjustment Requested shows how much time adjustment (in hex) is applied to this server. The plus or minus sign indicates whether the adjustment speeds up or slows down the time. A plus sign suggests this server's time is behind the polled server's; a minus means this server's time is ahead.

NOTE An adjustment value of 0.0E0F98DD (or 0.235903197 decimal) corresponds to one clock tick (1/18th of a second).

To correlate the adjustment value to a clock time, first convert the hex value into decimal (ignoring the decimal point), divide by 235903197, and then multiply by 0.056. This equation gives you the adjustment value in seconds. From the sample message displayed above,

```
Uniform Adjustment Requested:  -0.08E0FE3E
```

the adjustment requested indicates that the current server is a fraction of a tick (0.63 tick or 35 milliseconds) ahead of the polled server:

```
8E0FE3E (hex) = 148962878 (dec)
148962878 / 235903197 = 0.63 ticks
0.63 x 0.056 = 0.035 seconds = 35 ms.
```

A Uniform Adjustment Requested value of +0.00000000 means the two servers are in exact time synchronization. It is common (and expected), however, to see small adjustment values (within a tick or two) due to the randomness between servers.

Also included with the newer TCP/IP protocol stack on NetWare servers, you can enable the TCP/IP debugging screen that allows every TCP/IP packet passing in and out of the server to be shown at the system console for troubleshooting purposes. To use the TCP/IP debugging screens,

► **SET TCP IP DEBUG = 1.** Enables TCP/IP debugging. With TCP/IP debugging enabled you see packets shown on port 123 whenever an NTP request or reply is transmitted or received.

► **SET TCP IP DEBUG = 0.** Disables TCP/IP debugging.

The discussion about TCP/IP packets is beyond the scope of this book. Refer to Novell's Guide to Troubleshooting TCP/IP and Novell's knowledgebase at http://support.novell.com for more details.

TIP

The SET TCP IP DEBUG = I option dumps all incoming and outgoing packets processed by the TCPIP.NLM. It is very useful in troubleshooting and debugging problems with packet translation, filtering, or connection issues. However, the displayed information scrolls down very quickly on the system console in this mode and you may not be able to get all the information they require. The best way to capture the information is to first load the CONLOG. NLM, SET the debug parameter to I, capture the IP information, and finally unload CONLOG.NLM. The resulting CONSOLE.LOG file in SYS:\ETC contains all information written to the system console.

NDS Database Inconsistency

The NDS database becomes inconsistent when replicas of a partition cannot be synchronized and the distributed information becomes dissimilar or corrupted. Keep in mind that the NDS database is a loosely consistent database and it needs time to replicate and synchronize changes. However, persistent problems might indicate that replicas are out of synchronization.

To troubleshoot NDS database inconsistencies, follow these steps:

- ▶ Identify the inconsistency using tools such as NDS Manager.
- ▶ Use documented help (such as online help in NDS Manager, Novell's Technical Information Documents, TIDs, *and so on.*) to create a strategy for resolving the inconsistency.
- ▶ Perform corrective actions.

NDS database inconsistencies can manifest themselves in the following forms:

- ▶ Client symptoms
- ▶ Unknown objects in NDS
- ▶ NDS error messages

Client Symptoms

The following client problems might indicate that replicas are out of synchronization:

- ▶ The client prompts for a password when none exists for the user account.
- ▶ Client login takes dramatically more time than usual.
- ▶ Modifications made to NDS seem to have disappeared (i.e. keeps reverting back to the old settings).
- ▶ NDS rights assigned previously seem to have disappeared.
- ▶ Client performance is inconsistent; errors cannot always be duplicated.

If these symptoms occur, use one of the methods described later to check for synchronization errors.

Unknown Objects

The presence of unknown objects (yellow question mark icons) within the NDS tree can indicate a problem with synchronization — but not always. Sometimes objects become unknown during Merge Partition and Create Partition operations. This is normal because a partition root is changing. You may even see some unknown objects during an NDS restore. These unknown objects should return to a known state when the operation is completed.

However, if these symptoms occur and persist, check for synchronization errors as described in the following list.

NOTE

Volume objects become unknown objects when the Server object associated with the volume has been removed. These unknown objects can and should be deleted.

NDS Error Messages

The NetWare server produces NDS synchronization error messages whenever the server is unable to complete the synchronization process with another server. To view these messages, you can:

► **Check for Synchronization Errors with SET.** You can use a SET parameter to watch the synchronization of the Directory database. Enter **SET DSTRACE = ON** at the server console. This command brings up another screen (accessed via Alt+Esc key sequence) on which you can watch the replicas synchronize with each other. The following message indicates an inability between two servers to synchronize replicas:

```
SYNC: failed to communicate with server
<CN=NETWARE_51B> ERROR -625
SYNC: End sync of partition <name>. All processed = NO
```

NOTE

On NetWare 5 servers, follow the SET DSTRACE=ON command with SET DSTRACE=+S. Otherwise, you see a blank DSTrace screen.

TIP

For more information about the SET DSTRACE commands and error codes, refer to *Novell's Guide to Troubleshooting NDS*. You can also look up the meaning of the various error codes using the online help in NDS Manager.

► **Check Partition Synchronization using NDS Manager.** To view partition synchronization information in NDS Manager, do the following:

1. Locate and highlight the desired partition root object in NDS Manager.

2. In the Object pull-down menu, click Check Synchronization.

3. To read the partition status for the selected partition only, click OK.

4. To continue with the operation after preconditions have been met, click Yes.

A synchronization problem is indicated when the All processed = No line has a value greater than 0.

Bare in mind that simply performing a partition synchronization check might provide incomplete information because it only checks for synchronization errors on the first server in the replica list that responds to the request. Synchronization errors might be occurring on other servers in the replica list. To check for synchronization errors among all servers in a replica list, perform the partition continuity check.

Refer to Chapter 7 for more information about NDS Manager.

NOTE

▶ **Check Partition Continuity using NDS Manager.** To check for synchronization errors on all servers in a replica list, do the following:

1. Locate and select the partition root object in NDS Manager.

2. In the Object menu, click Partition Continuity.

A replica icon with an exclamation point indicates a server with synchronization errors.

Additionally, the Partition Continuity window identifies replica list inconsistencies. Each row in the Partition Continuity window is a server *and* its replica list. Each column should contain the same replica type icons, indicating that the replica lists of all servers (row heading) agree on the replica type (icon in cell) stored on a specific server (column heading).

A replica list problem is identified whenever the replica types in a column are not all the same, or whenever a row or column does not contain a replica type icon in each cell.

Finding Help for Resolving Inconsistencies

Once an error has been detected and the error code identified, you can consult the NDS Manager online help, a NetWare 5 product documentation, Novell knowledgebase, or the *Novell's Guide to Troubleshooting NDS* book for a description of the error and the actions you can take to resolve the problem.

The NDS Manager error code documentation provides a brief description of the problem and presents a series of actions to help you resolve the specific problem. To view error code information in NDS Manager, do the following:

1. Using Partition Continuity, identify a server generating an error.

2. Double-click the server error code icon. The error code is displayed in the "Current sync error" field.

3. To view help information on the error code, click the ? (Help) button to the right of the "Current sync error" field.

WARNING

NDS inconsistency errors can be caused by a wide range of problems. Many of the actions that attempt to repair the database can cause problems if executed improperly or at the wrong time. For these reasons, you should follow the recommended troubleshooting actions described in the online help, or consult an expert before attempting the repair.

In NDS Manager, you can also find help information about an NDS error code by doing the following:

1. In the Help menu, click Contents.

2. Under Reference, click NDS and Server Codes.

3. Under NetWare Directory Services Error Codes, click List of Codes.

4. Click the specific error code you want information on.

Correcting Database Inconsistencies

The action you take to resolve NDS database inconsistencies depends on the specific error being reported. When repairing NDS database inconsistencies, follow these guidelines:

► Let the system run for a few hours. It might synchronize and correct itself. Sometimes the inability to synchronize is simply due to communication errors (-625s) and it may be beyond your control should the failure be the service provider of your WAN infrastructure.

► Do not bring down the server; this prevents self-correction.

► Perform repair actions only when they are called for in the error code help *or* documentation.

► Do not attempt partition operations on a partition that is already experiencing problems. You might cause more synchronization problems.

TIP

The key to repairing NDS problems is patience. NDS has a lot of self-healing algorithms built-in but you need to give it time to do its task.

Most NDS inconsistency corrective actions are to be performed from the Partition Continuity window in NDS Manager.

WARNING

Some actions should not be taken lightly. For example, you should not receive updates for a given replica unless you have exhausted all other possibilities. Receiving updates can cause excessive traffic on a network because the entire replica is sent to the server receiving the updates.

If you performed either the Remove Server or Delete Server action on an active server, you've caused major headaches — an active server whose Server object is deleted must have NDS reinstalled and all replicas readded.

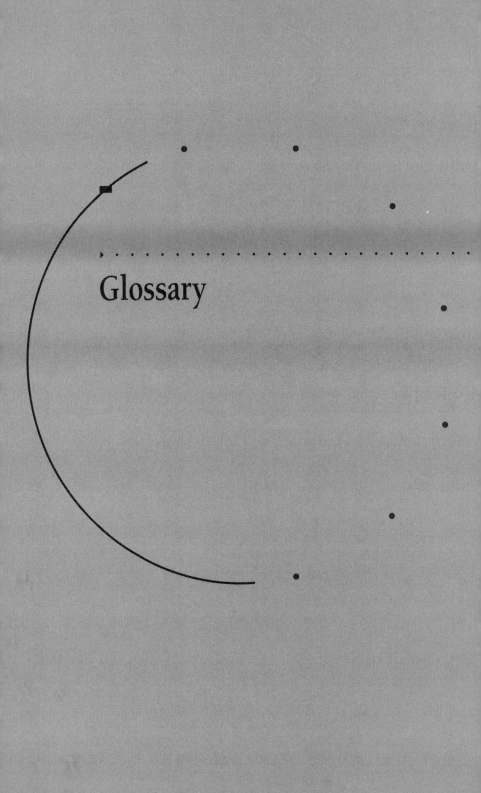

Glossary

Access control list: Each object in Novell Directory Services contain an attribute called ACL that lists the other objects that have been assigned trustee rights to it.

Access rights, file and directory: Each file and directory has access rights assigned to it that control how each user is permitted to manipulate it. For example, a user may create (C) a file but not delete (D) it. Each right is called a flag. *See* Attribute, file and directory.

Account restrictions: Properties of a User object that control when the user logs in, how often the user must change passwords, and so on.

ACL: *See* Access control list.

Admin: A "super user" account initially assigned to the person installing NDS. Admin has all rights to all objects in the NDS by default, but it can be limited by an Inherited Rights Filter.

Alias object: An alias is a pointer to another object in the NDS tree, which may reside in another container. Each object in the directory tree, with the exception of [Root], may have an alias associated with it.

Attribute, file and directory: A property of a file or directory that controls what can happen to that file or directory. Attributes, which are also called flags, can be used to restrict users from deleting files, renaming files, changing files, or the like. Attributes can also be used to identify files and directories that have been changed since their last backup, that should be purged immediately if deleted, and so on.

Attribute, NDS object: A piece of information associated with an NDS object, that helps to define that object. For example, a User object's attributes could include the user's last name, trustee assignments, login script, and e-mail address. Attributes are sometimes called properties.

Attribute rights: Each object has attribute rights that apply to it and that tell it what it may do with an attribute. Attribute rights are Add or Delete Self, Compare, Inheritable, Read, Supervisor, and Write.

Bindery: The database of network information that was used in previous versions of NetWare (version 3.12 and earlier). The bindery is a flat database, which means it cannot recognize container objects that help organize other network entities. In addition, the bindery is specific to a server. Each server has its own unique bindery, and cannot recognize objects in another server's bindery. The bindery was replaced by the NDS database in NetWare 4.*x*, intraNetWare, and NetWare 5.

Bindery context: A portion of the NDS database assigned to look like a flat bindery database to specific applications that require network objects to be in a bindery format. This feature is provided so that older bindery-based applications can still function in an NDS environment.

Bindery services: A service of NetWare 4 and NetWare 5 that allows management of objects in NetWare 2.*x* and 3.*x* networks under NDS. Also referred to as *Bindery Emulation*.

Browser, NetWare Administrator: The view of the NDS tree and its objects, as displayed by the NetWare Administrator utility. You can see information about NDS objects by opening objects from within the Browser.

Classes: *See* NDS object class.

CN: Short for Common Name.

Common Name: Every NDS object has a name that is unique within its context in the tree structure. This is called Common Name when it refers to a resource within the NDS tree.

Container login script: *See* Login script.

Container object: An NDS object that contains other NDS objects. Organization objects and Organizational Unit objects are both container objects. *See also* Leaf object.

Context: *See* Name context.

Country object: An NDS object used in trees that cross country boundaries. For example, in a multinational company, the country objects may be CA, US, and GB. Country object names are defined by the International Standards Organization and follow a standard naming convention defined by the organization.

Directory context: *See* Name context.

Directory Map object: A pointer to a server drive path normally used to map drives in login scripts or batch files. This is done so that login scripts need not be changed when a drive path changes — it is sufficient just to change the Directory Map object.

Directory Services: *See* NDS.

Directory schema: *See* NDS schema.

Directory tree: *See* NDS tree.

Distinguished name: *See* Full Distinguished Name.

DN: *See* Full Distinguished Name.

DS.NLM: This is the Directory Services NetWare Loadable Module. This NLM creates and manages the NDS database on a NetWare server.

DSMERGE.NLM: This NLM is used to merge two NDS trees or to rename a tree.

DSREPAIR.NLM: This NLM repairs the NDS database and replaces BINDFIX in NetWare 2.*x* and NetWare 3.*x*. It can also give status on replication and can be used for troubleshooting and problem determination.

Effective rights: The combination of trustee rights that the user can ultimately execute. A user can have effective rights to NDS objects, as well as effective rights to files and directories. A user's effective rights to an object, directory, or file are determined in one of two ways: the user's inherited rights minus any rights blocked by the IRF, or the sum of all the user's direct trustee assignments and security equivalences to other objects. *See also* Trustee rights *and* Inherited Rights Filter (IRF).

Full distinguished name: An object's full name, which also indicates its position in the tree. An object's full distinguished name (or full name) consists of the object's name, followed by the names of each of the container objects above it in the tree. Each name is separated by a period, such as Tasha.Sales. Company.

Group object: An NDS object that contains a list of users who belong to the Group object. Groups enable you to manage security, printer assignments, and other issues that may affect many or all of the users in the same way.

Home directory: A directory (folder) on the network created especially for a specific user. All users can have their own home directories, in which they can store their applications, work files, or personal files. Users generally have full trustee rights to their own home directories.

Inheritance: The gaining of trustee rights at a lower level of the NDS tree or file system, because you were granted those rights at a higher level. NDS trustee rights can be inherited, as well as file system trustee rights. If you are granted a new trustee assignment at a lower level, you no longer inherit rights from a higher level.

Inherited Rights Filter (IRF): A way to restrict the rights that a user can inherit from a higher level in the NDS tree or file system. If you remove a right from an object's or directory's IRF, users can no longer inherit and use that right at this level.

IRF: *See* Inherited Rights Filter (IRF).

Leaf object: An NDS object that can't have any other objects beneath it in the NDS tree. Users, groups, printers, and print queues are all examples of leaf objects. *See also* Container object.

Login script: A set of commands that execute when the user logs in. Login scripts automatically set up the users' workstation environments with necessary drive mappings and other types of useful environmental settings. Container login scripts execute for all objects within a container. User login scripts execute for specific users. Profile login scripts can be created to execute for a group of users.

Master replica: A replica type that may be used to change the makeup of a tree and controls partitioning operations.

Name context: An NDS object's location in the NDS tree. For example, if user Tasha is located in an Organizational Unit object called Sales, under the Organization object called Company, Tasha's name context is Sales.Company. The names of the container objects in a name context are separated by periods.

NDS: *See* Novell Directory Services.

NDS object: An entity defined in the NDS database that represents a physical network resource (such as a server, workstation, or printer), a software network resource (such as a printer server, print queue, or volume), or a human or organizational resource (such as a user, group, or department). An NDS object contains properties that define the object, specifying such characteristics as the object's name, security rights, and so on.

NDS object class: A particular type of object that has been defined, such as Server object, User object, Print Queue object, or Volume object.

NDS schema: The overall plan that defines and describes the allowable NDS object classes, their properties, and the rules that govern their creation and existence. The schema determines how objects can inherit properties and trustee rights of other container objects above it. In addition, the schema defines how the Directory tree is structured and how objects in it are named.

NDS tree: The figurative representation of the NDS database's hierarchical structure, showing the Root object at the top, and container objects forming branches beneath the root.

NetWare Administrator: A NetWare 5 utility that enables you to work with NDS objects on the network. This is one of the primary utilities used in NetWare 5 for management tasks, and can be run on workstations using Windows 3.1, Windows 95, or Windows NT.

Novell Directory Services: A database that contains information about every object in the NetWare 5 network. Using this database, NetWare 5 can identify each object, know where it's supposed to be in the network, know who's allowed to use it, know what it's supposed to be connected to, and so on.

NWAdmin: *See* NetWare Administrator.

O: The abbreviation and notation for Organization. *See* Organization object.

Object: *See* NDS object.

Object rights: Each NDS object has rights associated with it that control what that object can do. These rights are Browse, Create, Delete, Inheritable, Rename, and Supervisor.

Organization object: An NDS container object, located immediately beneath the [Root] object in the NDS tree, which generally represents the company or organization to which the network belongs. The Organization object contains all other container objects, as well as all the leaf objects (such as servers, users, and printers) that reside within that organization.

Organizational Unit object: An NDS container object that is located beneath an Organization object or another Organizational Unit object. The Organizational Unit object often represents a department, division, or project team within a larger organization. The Organizational Unit object can contain leaf objects (such as users or printers), as well as other Organizational Unit objects.

OU: The abbreviation and notation for Organizational Unit. *See* Organizational Unit object.

Partial name: *See* Relative Distinguished Name.

Partition, directory: Portions of the NDS database that can be replicated on different servers. A Directory partition is a branch of the Directory tree, beginning with any container object you choose. Partitions can also hold subpartitions beneath them (called child partitions). If you have a smaller NDS database, the whole database can reside in a single partition. Using partitions can improve network performance, especially if the network spans across a WAN (wide area network). Partitions also can make it easier to manage portions of the tree separately.

Primary time servers: In NDS environments, NetWare servers are classified as primary time servers, single reference time servers, reference time servers, or secondary time servers. The primary time server helps other servers determine the network time.

Profile login script: *See* Login script.

Property: *See* Attributes, NDS Object.

Property rights: *See* Attributes rights.

RDN: *See* Relative distinguished name.

Read-Only replica: A replica type that is updated by other servers in the replica ring, but does not update those other servers.

Read/Write replica: A copy of the Master replica that may be used to change the makeup of a tree.

Reference time servers: Used to help determine the network time, but they differ from primary time servers in that they use an external time source to determine it. While reference time servers participate in time synchronization, they do not adjust their time except in response to the external time source.

Relative distinguished name: A shortened version of an NDS object's full name, showing the name context only partway up the NDS tree. Also called partial name.

Replica: A copy of the NDS database stored on a server. You can have several replicas of the NDS database so that if one server goes down, all the other servers can still access the NDS database from another replica on another server. There are four replica types: Master, Read/Write, Read-Only, and Subordinate Reference.

Replica ring: A list of all the servers holding a copy of a given replica.

Rights: *See* Trustee rights *and* Effective rights.

[Root] **object:** The highest-level object in the NDS tree.

Schema: *See* NDS schema.

Secondary time servers: A type of time server that does not help determine the network time. They receive it from a primary, reference, or a single reference time server.

Security, file system: A set of NetWare security features that control how users work with files and directories. File system security includes trustee rights (which grant users rights to work with files) and file and directory attributes (which restrict any users from performing specified activities on files). *See also* Trustee rights.

Security, login: A set of NetWare security features that control whether or not users can log in to the network (and, optionally, when they can log in, what kind of passwords they use, and so on).

Security, NDS: NetWare 4 and NetWare 5 access rights that regulate how NDS objects can use other objects (for example, whether or not one user can change another user's allowable login times, or whether one user can delete or change a print server). *See also* Trustee rights.

Security equivalence: An assignment that grants you the same trustee rights as another user. Your trustee rights become "equivalent" to the other user's rights.

SET parameter: A server option you can change to optimize your server's performance. SET parameters control things such as how buffers are allocated and used, how memory is used, and so on. You can change these parameters by loading MONITOR.NLM and selecting the SET parameters you want from menus. SET parameters are also called server parameters.

Single reference time servers: The sole server on the network to determine the network time. Small networks ordinarily use a single reference time server. Single reference time servers are not compatible with reference or primary time server types.

Subordinate reference replica: A replica type that contains a copy of a partition root object but no information about objects of the rest of the partition. Subordinate references are used only for NDS treewalking.

Synchronization: The process of maintaining the integrity of the data in the partition across multiple servers.

System login script: A type of login script used in previous versions of NetWare. This was replaced in NDS by container login scripts. *See also* Login script.

Tree: *See* NDS tree.

Treewalking: The process of resolving the location of an object within the tree.

Trustee: A user (or other object) who has been given trustee rights to an object, file, or directory.

Trustee rights: Permissions that allow users or objects to perform specified tasks. NDS trustee rights control whether users can work with other NDS objects and their properties, such as viewing other objects, changing their properties, deleting them, and so on. File system trustee rights control how users can work with files and directories, specifying whether a user can delete a file, change it, open it, and so on. *See also* Effective rights.

Typeless names: A method of naming which does not include the object type. For example, Tasha.Sales.Company is a typeless name. If the object type is included, it is called a typeful name. CN=Tasha.OU=Sales.O=Company is a *typeful name.*

User account: The information about a user that enables the user to log in to the network. When a User object is created in the NDS tree, the user's account is automatically created.

User login script: *See* Login script.

Index

D

E

F

Continued

my2cents.idgbooks.com